MONGOL RALLY

THREE WEEKS INTO THE UNKNOWN

JA Irving

It was a gruelling adventure and an epic challenge. On the face of it, all we had to do was get from London to Mongolia, overland. But looking deeper it was going to be a lot less simple than it had first appeared. We had minimal planning, bought a horribly underpowered car that was fit for scrap, had no external support, no prior expedition experience or survival knowledge and decided to do it all in the name of charity. And as if we needed to make it a bit more challenging, we only allowed ourselves three weeks to complete the adventure. I hadn't even heard of half of the countries we were intending to cross and certainly didn't speak the languages. But anyway, we had a spare summer, a desire to try something different and had also agreed that prep and training are much over-hyped – we'd go for it anyway and see how things turned out. It couldn't be that hard after all…

Here's my account of how it happened, what we came across, the scrapes we got into and how we got out of them, along with a selection of the numerous photos I took on the way.

Contents

Country Codes

AT	–	Austria
BE	–	Belgium
CN	–	China
CZ	–	Czech Republic
GB	–	Great Britain
KG	–	Kyrgyzstan
KZ	–	Kazakhstan
MN	–	Mongolia
RO	–	Romania
RU	–	Russia
UA	–	Ukraine
UZ	–	Uzbekistan

Preface

I never intended to write this and I don't believe I have any particular literary skill to justify having done so. However, throughout the journey I kept a detailed diary of the events that occurred on this epic adventure and transcribed them purely to serve as a legible record to look back on in the years to come.

The intention had been that the transcribed diary be for myself, based on the facts as they happened and without exaggeration or embellishment, as I felt this was the only way to write it. This remained the case, yet as I wrote it and it grew in length various people showed an interest in reading the completed account so it seemed only fair to get it published.

This account isn't intended to be perfect; it is based on my personal views of the places, cultures and people I saw and nothing else, but it gives a good snapshot of my experiences on the 9,592 miles to Mongolia. Some of the experiences defied belief, some were mildly terrifying but there are none that I will ever forget.

That's pretty much it really; the political and geographical facts have been checked by myself, but that is far from a guarantee that they're correct. Various people have asked for a copy once it was finished and, well, here it is – in future think about what you're asking for!

MONGOL RALLY

Starting Out

It was a simple but completely insane idea and it all came about over an idle conversation with a friend Paul Fox (Foxy) in a bar in London's Covent Garden, December 2005 – to drive from London to Mongolia in an underpowered car in just three weeks. Ten years ago such a journey would have been impossible and we weren't even sure if it would be possible now. I was due to graduate from university in the summer and had just come out of another job interview; Foxy was about to head out to Val d'Isere for a ski season, leaving both of us with a free summer. We needed something to do and from the tiny bit of info we had about the rally it sounded ideal. And that was it. We said we'd do it, chatted about it over a few more beers and from that point forward the momentum of the whole concept took hold and there would be no going back. More and more people were asking us about it and the more it was talked about the more it *had* to happen.

By 6th January my brother had set up a website for us, we had started collecting for Cancer Research UK and Mercy Corps; funding the adventure ourselves and doing something worthwhile at the same time. That meant all we needed was a car, some kit and a vague idea of where we were heading so we wouldn't get too lost on the way to Mongolia. It all seemed too easy.

The rally itself was part of an 'organised' event. Organised in so much as there was an official start and official end point. Nothing in between, no route to follow, nothing laid on and absolutely no support. It sounded perfect and appealed massively. We held-off chasing any corporate sponsors until we'd secured a place on the rally, which was a close thing, as all the entries had sold out in less than an hour. Places were limited to 200 to reduce the number of cars breaking down, with the potential of being dumped, littering the countryside between London and

Mongolia and also to ensure that we were a rare enough sight at the borders to make it entertaining for both the ralliers and the border guards. Too many cars and the process would become routine and very expensive as the guards would demand ever increasing bribes. Neither would be a good thing.

Now that we had a website, with some info on it to make us look like we had a vague idea what we were doing and an entry, it was time to start chasing for sponsorship. I wrote to a few local newspapers and they lapped it up (as they should considering I'd effectively given them a pre-written feature!) and this publicity in turn gave us credibility with the companies we contacted.

The most exciting part at this point was picking a route and the type of car we'd take. As there was no fixed route we had a completely blank canvas to work from. We had four options; north through Scandinavia, across the middle of Russia, through central Asia or south through Turkey and Afghanistan. It not being a race meant the route was all about travelling to the most interesting and exciting sounding places. The north sounded cold and not that special, the middle sounded very flat and uninspiring and the south was not the wisest choice given the relentless bombing of the Taliban that appeared to be flavour of the month with the Americans. That left central Asia which looked pretty amazing and varied and had the potential for a lot of off-road driving.

With Foxy's return and my exams completed, late May was spent looking at cars. The rules of the rally permitted a car with an engine of one litre or less and preferably fit for scrap. After some brief research we picked the Suzuki SJ as the perfect vehicle for the adventure. I'd have loved to have taken an old mini but they seemed pretty expensive, generally in terrible condition and, given their ground clearance, probably wouldn't make it, so the Suzuki made sense. Suzukis were also exceptionally cheap. On 30th May, after trawling eBay® and the internet free-ads, we lined up a number of SJ's and went hunting. We started out from Bristol, heading to the south coast somewhere near Southampton to see the first one. It was in good condition but at over £1,000 would only serve as a reference point for us to aim for. It was a revelation actually getting to drive one and realising just how basic, slow and uncomfortable they were. We paused at a country pub for lunch then drove up to Leicester to see another. It was a shed. We got to the third, late in the day, near Kings Lynn. It was the Santana variant with a five speed gearbox, but it drove OK and the guy selling it seemed quite honest. The only doubt in our minds was the mention of a new clutch in the eBay advert, but no mention of it ever having been fitted. We suspected the car was a little bit dodgy and looked at everything for issues. We needn't have. When we said that we intended to drive it the 230 miles back to Bristol, the seller looked shocked that we'd drive it so far and asked why we wanted it. With the story told, he showed us around the back of his lock-up where he had another six SJ's. In his spare time he took them around the UK (even around the world in his younger days) to race them and he loved our story so much that he agreed to give the car a full going over and gather together a set of useful spares. All for the £500 asking price. We couldn't have asked for a better deal. So, after one day and a 380 mile journey we had the 'buggy' to which we would become so attached.

We eventually got our hands on the buggy the next week and I had the dubious pleasure of driving it the 40 miles to Foxy's Dad's factory in Bourne, Lincolnshire. This would become the base for our preparations. It was still worrying just how uncomfortable and slow the buggy was, considering how long we'd be driving it for. We spent the next week tidying it up, cleaning the grain and lead-shot out of the back and playing with the mechanics to gain an understanding of how it all worked. It was going to be in for a shock given that it looked like it had spent all its life on a farm and we were going to add two years' of its average mileage to it in less than four weeks. We cannibalised Foxy's old Ford Sierra for comfy seats, speakers, an engine cooling fan and anything else we could use to make life better. From what we had read about the climate of the countries we were heading to, and the fragile nature of the buggy's engine, the second fan could prove to be a necessity rather than a luxury.

Hours before the transformation began

We re-carpeted it, filled and painted the rustiest bits of the bodywork and painted the wheels. Extra spotlights, a mains power transformer and a second battery were fitted. The buggy was unrecognisable. From an uncomfortable shed-of-a-car it became reasonably comfortable and looked a lot smarter.

With camping equipment, oils, a clutch and other spare parts arriving from our sponsors, we enlisted a graphics company to produce some stickers to advertise them on the buggy. This really finished it off.

Bourne & Galletley Practice kindly agreed to provide us with the cocktail of injections and immunisations we needed for our adventure and various bits of medical kit. When our team t-shirts arrived we even began to look as if we knew what we were doing. We took the buggy from Lincolnshire where it had been reborn to Bristol, then to see my parents in Yorkshire and finally down to London. It never faltered and we learnt to recognise which sounds were normal and which weren't. We also got used to travelling everywhere at 50mph, which actually became quite relaxing and meant we always had a clear road ahead of us!

After our work was finished

By 13th July we only had three of the visas we needed and none of the maps, so headed to London to speed things up. With some careful planning we hoped to be able to get four visas in two days. We were at the Kazak embassy by 08:45 and joined the long queue, consisting mostly of couriers from tour companies. When we finally made it inside the building we spent the next three hours queuing, with no seats, in a room no more than ten feet square. Then the computer failed and it looked like we'd get nothing that day as they were due to shut up shop at lunchtime for the rest of the day. Fortunately, with fifteen minutes to closing time, we lodged our applications, hoping that there'd be no more issues so we could collect our passports the following morning.

The next day, to make the most of our time, and on a tip-off from one of the couriers we'd met at the Kazak embassy, I went straight to the Chinese embassy for 07:30 to join the applications queue whilst Foxy went to the Kazak embassy to collect our passports. The queue for China was massive even though it wasn't due to open until 09:00; it was then only open until 11:00 for those wanting same day processing. Against expectations, the queue moved quite quickly and soon I was inside the embassy, subtly letting people pass me such that I stayed near the front of the queue until Foxy and the passports arrived. Security didn't like this one bit but after some persuasion they agreed to let me remain in the queue on the condition that whenever I got to the front I moved back ten places. A strange idea but it kept them happy. Until I crossed the green line and they went mad. Don't ever cross the green line unless instructed to do so. When Foxy called to say he was outside, I made the unforgivable mistake of answering the call. The guards went mad again and I was nearly thrown out there and then. Somehow I got away with it; we applied just in time and went for a fry-up while we waited.

On the way to the café, we saw the Kyrgyz embassy which was next on our list and decided to pop in to see if there was anything we could do to get the process started. What we found was a room in a basement, no bigger than a bedroom, with two of the most work-shy guys I've ever met and, surprisingly, no queue. There was nothing we could do without our passports and they were due to close at 12:30. After eating, we rushed back to China and joined the huge queue for collections, getting our passports just after 12:00. A quick run around the corner and I was back at Kyrgyzstan, though Foxy had had to leave to catch a train. The officer wanted me to fill the forms in from an internet café but, as I could see them on his desk, I suggested it would be easier to do it in the office. Reluctantly, he agreed, though when it came to Foxy's application it required Foxy's signature. The officer simply pointed and told me to sign it. This was surely a sign of things to come! And with that we were done. We decided to get Moldovan visas en-route as they were supposed to be easy enough to get and didn't need an advance application.

And that was pretty much all of the preparation. We bought some maps, not enough to cover the entire route but hopefully enough to get by. We didn't plot a route, instead choosing to pick a few countries that sounded fun and decided to worry about the nuances of the detail as and when we got there. We didn't want to overdo the prep as it would be more exciting to find difficulties and overcome problems as and when they arose.

22nd July – London, GB to Heerlen, BE

The epic adventure began sadly, though expectedly, with a hangover. The previous afternoon we had travelled from Foxy's in Lincolnshire to a friend's house in Kent. The intention was to be nearer Hyde Park ready for the off so we could be one of the first cars there, and so one of the first to leave. This would all have been fine had we not spent too much time enjoying the heat wave we were having by cashing in on one last barbeque, cold beers, gin & tonics, oh, and a touch of whisky – cheers Nick and family! This left us being late for the start and also short of petrol which was proving to be difficult to find. We were struggling and hadn't even got to the start yet. We should have just given in at this point and spent a relaxing summer island hopping in the Med or diving in Thailand.

Waiting for the off in Hyde Park, London

The whole 'event' in Hyde Park turned out to be a bit of a non-event. There seemed to be far too many cars and not enough people to deal with them. As such, we never got to see many other teams and only really chatted to the teams of cars parked beside us while we waited to sign various semi-official documents. These would allow us to leave the buggy in Mongolia without having to pay thousands of dollars in import taxes. We'd have to wait until Prague to meet the 157 other teams. Assuming everyone made it that far... which they didn't. The cars started to leave at 14:00 though we didn't leave until 15:00 as we were that far back in the queue.

Leaving Hyde Park, London

It was good to be finally moving after so long planning and thinking about the rally, and great to be driving out of Hyde Park with a small hardcore group of spectators cheering us on and who were now braving the heavy rain that had also arrived to see us off. Rain which highlighted our buggy's first defect. Just after crossing the start line, the driver's wiper blade flew off and now we couldn't see out. Fortunately, the London traffic was moving so slowly that Foxy had time to jump out of the buggy and tie-wrap it back on without us even having to pull off the road. The rain was a definite sign that it was time to leave the UK and get going but at this point we encountered yet another problem.

Israel and the Lebanon were having a bit of a war and some do-gooders with nothing better to do had decided to protest along the roads we were intending to take from Hyde Park. This created massive amounts of traffic chaos (and as it turned out did nothing to stop Israel either) so the next couple of hours were spent trying to escape the traffic – without a map. We had maps of Moldova, Uzbekistan, Kazakhstan... but not London. At least there were loads of other rally cars scooting about with the same problem, all hooting at each other. Luckily this issue didn't last too long as we found the perfect solution to the traffic.

While driving though the weekend traffic along Brompton Road, through Knightsbridge and past Harrods, it dawned on us that while we had paid a huge £500 for our buggy (to which, admittedly, we were becoming quite attached), that was significantly less than the tens of thousands paid by the owners of the Aston Martins, Ferraris and Porsches surrounding us. They had a lot more to lose than us and, strangely, we started to make good progress weaving in and out of the traffic as they obligingly opted to make room for us. Then the buggy broke. Again. With the rain now starting to blow through the open passenger window, Foxy tried to wind it up, only for the rusty mechanism to give way and the glass fall into the bottom of the door and out of reach. Quickly pulling the door panel off we were able to botch it back well enough to keep the rain out but the window was now inoperable.

We finally hit the A2 leaving London behind and heading for Dover. At this point, we realised that we hadn't eaten since our hungover breakfast, and were forced to stop at a well-know burger restaurant as it was the fastest food we could find and we were already late. This was to prove a big mistake, but the effects of last night had meant that not stopping was out of the question. Whilst cruising along at 90km/h is very calming it really does take a long time to get anywhere. Especially to the 18:00 ferry. Soon, the delays around Hyde Park, the stop for food and the slowness of the buggy all became too much and we were looking close to missing our ferry. Mindful of how far we had to go and how much we had to look after the buggy we did the only sensible thing - we ramped up the speed to a bit over 100km/h. So much for the idea of taking this marathon journey steadily. The buggy still seemed happy but it was worrying to be passing a few rally cars already broken-down on the hard-shoulder.

We reached Dover at 17:50. For some reason the check-in man said this wasn't enough time to drive the 50 metres to join the queue of cars already boarding our ferry and as such we had to wait an hour and a half for the next one. I blame the burger. Hardly a good start considering how far away Prague was. That said, the wait was a laugh as we got to meet more people there than we'd met in a whole afternoon in Hyde Park. There were also a few puzzled holiday makers (the kind going for a week on the beach rather than driving to Mongolia) who seemed to place us into one of two categories – mad or adventurous. It also gave us time to fix the window mechanism. Almost by design, we had a suitable product, QuikSteel liquid metal, from Kalimex, one of our sponsors, and quickly mixed some to bond the window mechanism back together. A very simple fix that cured a niggling problem. Top stuff.

We also used the time to take a look over the engine bay – pretending to know what we were looking for. It was lucky we did, as nestling on the bottom of the buggy's industrial looking chassis was the radiator coolant reservoir, which had decided to drop off, allowing the coolant to escape. A couple of tie-wraps soon fixed this and saved us

Repairs at Dover

from cooking the engine after less than 320kms of driving. Feeling quite lucky at this point, we repacked the tools into the buggy ready to board the ferry, only to discover that we had now lost one of the sets of keys into the boxes of tools. This really wasn't the start we were looking for.

The ferry itself was ok and we met a few more people and compared cars, routes and (lack of) preparation. Everyone was in high spirits and there was lots of banter about who had the best cars, those who seemed over confident and those who appeared to be absolutely clueless. We certainly hadn't done too much prep. We also learnt that a

Suzuki Santana (the Spanish variant of the Suzuki SJ, which was the one we had bought) had never made the finish in the history of the rally and that they have notoriously weak gearboxes. We had a whole selection of spares donated by AVR (the garage we bought the buggy from), but oddly enough hadn't brought a spare gearbox. Instead, we tried to find some Pro-plus caffeine tablets to help us through the nights but ferry shops being what they are we failed miserably.

Hitting France was good; this really was the beginning now that we had left our first country behind. We also soon left the people we had just met behind. Having discovered that our buggy was good for 100km/h there would be no hanging around with those still trying to conserve their cars – not that this was a race of course, more that there was a party to get to in Prague. Rumour was that the beer was cheap. Very cheap.

We drove on through the night, crossing France and into Belgium by midnight where for the first time I realised just what it was we were undertaking. We weren't just on a long journey, driving for a couple of days to get somewhere, like Italy, having a holiday then heading back. We were literally driving as far as we could, continually heading east, for days on end, through places I'd previously never heard of, or thought possible to get to by road, then leaving the buggy and flying back. We might not ever make Mongolia; it didn't bother us. There were so many unknowns making it a strange and extremely exciting prospect. Oddly, the potential dangers never even entered our minds – or we chose to ignore them.

23rd July – Heerlen, BE to Prague, CZ

By 00:20 we were passing Brussels and the weather was damp, foggy and gloomy. We stopped at another filling station for fuel. The buggy was only good for a maximum of 290km on a tank and this would only get worse now that we were travelling at 100km/h. We got some snacks and strong, sugar-filled, black coffees. Here we bumped into some ralliers, including one guy doing it on a motorbike. We agreed to meet somewhere near the Nürburgring in Germany in the early morning so we could do a lap before carrying on to Prague. The circuit is open to the public and we fancied a crack at the lap record in our buggy. Given the 'Ring' is probably the most famous car racing circuit in the world, it would be quite an evocative place to take our thoroughbred buggy for a thrashing to mark the start of the second day of its marathon adventure.

Leaving the filling station we aimed for the Brussels ring-road, only to miss the junction we needed. This gave Foxy his first ever taste of driving on the 'wrong side of the road' as we had to leave the motorway to take to the local roads to get back on course. Foxy took this quite literally and soon we were actually on the wrong side of quite a major road! Luckily, at this time of night there were no other cars about and we safely got back on the right side without incident.

Now, before we left London we had taken a look on AutoRoute to see how far this part of the journey was (775 miles should you care). This didn't sound too bad if you consider that we were due to leave Hyde Park at about 14:00 and arrive in Prague late on the Sunday afternoon, some twenty-four hours later, making an average of 32mph – if we drove for the full twenty-four hours. However, things never work out as planned and already we'd been delayed by more than two hours, lost another hour due to the time difference, and hadn't really considered time for stopping for fuel, food or to chat to other ralliers, let alone sleep.

Excluding stops and considering the delays, the time difference and the ferry, we were already needing to average over 40mph if we didn't stop at all – with stops we'd be lucky to make the party at all. We decided at this point that we would drive for ninety minutes then take a break to swap drivers. We'd continue doing this for as long as we could to make progress and then stop for a while, but only if we really had to. It was clear that the Nürburgring wasn't a realistic option as we'd then have too far to travel in the afternoon. It was looking seriously doubtful if we'd even be in Prague in time for the start of the party.

So we went to Holland instead.

I'm still not too sure why we went to Holland. It was the middle of the night, we were tired though still very excited and before we left we had loosely said that the route 'might' go through Holland – or rather AutoRoute had said this. In reality, Holland was going to be a detour of an hour or so. But we went for it anyway. It would be another country on our list and neither of us had been before. In the end, all we saw of Holland was about 80kms of motorway, a filling station and a lot of darkness. If, and when, I do go back I'll make sure it's in the daytime and try to visit somewhere while I'm there. On this occasion I doubt it was worth the detour.

We were now into Germany and so far had had no issues at any of the borders. This had been the main issue we were expecting to encounter on the journey but we were now four countries down and hadn't been stopped once. Yet. Hardly a surprise for this area, but still a good feeling considering that the buggy was covered in stickers and suspiciously full of equipment.

Tiredness was starting to take its toll, but we'd now realised that our original aim of pitching the tents for a few hours of sleep was completely unrealistic In fact, stopping to sleep in the buggy was out of the question, given just how slowly Prague was arriving. Coffees became more frequent, as did driver changes, but the adrenaline from the excitement of the start of our adventure kept us going.

By 06:00 in the morning, we were still in Germany and the mist was burning off. We were driving into the sun rise (this was the first of many on the journey, and they were hard to miss given that we were always driving east, so was still a novelty) and everything was perfect. Until the road ended.

Early morning mist, Germany

Considering that we were following one road all the way from France to Prague, we hadn't paid much attention to the map, as it's generally hard to get lost on one straight road – unless of course someone completely removes it. At this point we met some other ralliers who had had the same problem but seemed to have an idea where they were heading. How wrong can you be? We soon discovered that they were as lost as us. We attempted to navigate using the free compass we'd been given at the rally's start, only to find that the needle was sticking and it was practically useless. After not too long, we found the road again and we were heading east again, but it was all wasting time that we'd rather be spending in Prague. We left the other guys behind; they had opted to drive at 80km/h while we were still optimistically sticking to our 100km/h – after all, those beers were still a long way off! We were back on the right road and making good progress but that almost came to a sudden end…

It was in Germany, on the autobahn, just after dawn at about 07:40. I was having a kip in the passenger's seat when the buggy reached a new record of 85mph. Now that's not bad for a rusty 15 year old, 1 litre, 4x4 buggy, laden with spares and camping kit, designed with the aerodynamic efficiency of a brick, for use on farms and small holdings the world over. We were going downhill with a good run up and thankfully no-one was looking, so all was good. Well, it would have been good but literally *no-one* was looking! I was asleep and so was Foxy! It was probably the wailing screams of the buggy's engine that woke us and thankfully not the sound of us impacting the German forest.

Ironically, this gave us enough of a wake up call that we decided to stop for a power-nap. Twenty minutes later, we'd had enough of that and hit the road again, slightly refreshed and keen to get moving again. I was still absolutely ruined, power-naps clearly do nothing for me, but Foxy was on it and back at the wheel.

Soon after, we stopped at a service station for fuel, had a wash and cleaned our teeth. A great way to wake up and something we would continue to do throughout the entire journey. On leaving the services, the adventure playground caught our eye and that was that. The buggy was dumped and we were off on the slides. Proper German slides, not the tiny, no-chance-of-hurting-yourself-in-case-you-sue-us ones we've now got in the UK. There were some very bemused looking Germans, but we were having fun – probably fuelled by the onset of delirium induced by our lack of sleep and excess caffeine.

At about 12:00, just before Dresden where we were due to turn south into the Czech Republic to Prague, we had our second worrying moment. I completely missed the junction (and the one after that), for which there can be no other reason than I was semi-sleeping while driving. I was acknowledging directions from Foxy and simply ignoring him as I focussed on the horizon while listening to the Arctic Monkeys on the iPod through the buggy's radio.

iPods are incredible. This must have been one of the most important things we took; forget the spares, the medical kit and the money. The iPod meant we were able to take one almost indestructible item with all our music on it and so avoid having to listen to dodgy, local Euro-pop on the radio. A small, but essential, item which probably went a long way towards keeping us sane along the way. It also helped out in other ways, specifically for pacifying guards at border posts.

Anyway, we were almost on the last leg of this part of the adventure when we hit our first traffic jam since London. And it was a big one. It was the Czech Republic. Czech border control is more like what we had been expecting – a long and drawn out process with no apparent reason for the delay. We spent a couple of hours queuing, then finally got through with no issues. As is always the case with queues, it was other people creating the delay. Later, we discovered that most of the other ralliers had taken a different route, crossing the border further to the south, and had not queued at all.

Just having entered the Czech Republic

The first thing that struck me on entering the Czech Republic was the amount of prostitutes on the side of the road blatantly touting for business (at least they were wearing very, very short skirts and provocatively thumbing cars, so I assumed they were prostitutes –

though to be fair, they may just have been overly-friendly, under-dressed locals?!), and the market stalls lining the side of the road, selling everything you could ever need from food, to clothes, to car spares.

It was now a short run down to Prague. The only map of the city we had was the tiny one in the back of our European atlas (it looked like it had been designed for walkers). Not the most useful map. After a few wrong turns, seeing the same street a couple of times, we found the square where there was a car park, where we were due to meet the others.

Negotiating Prague, Czech Republic

The problem was that between us and the car park, the Czechs were part way through making a nice new metro station and there was no way across. We were literally metres from the entrance but couldn't reach it. Back the way we had come, round most of the one way system of Prague again and we were there, having picked up another lost rallier who decided to trust our sense of direction. Checkpoint One, 15:06, meaning we'd been on the road solidly for twenty-three hours and six minutes (thanks to the time difference on the continent). We dumped the buggy in the underground car park, where there were a couple of other rally cars and a few people milling about. We found two other guys who seemed as bored with the procrastinating as us and we all headed to the bar where we were supposed to meet. Annoyingly, there was no-one there and it was almost empty. Strange, considering how late we thought we were and that we'd been one of the last cars to leave London.

We went back to the street and found a more 'local looking' bar serving pizzas, with old fashioned trams running past its street-side tables. The four of us tucked into some beers (at less than £0.50 a pint) and pizza, and watched the world go by. Again, the toilets proved to be a great place for a 'shower'. We spent a couple of hours chatting about the problems of the Suzuki SJ's – which they were also driving – and what lay ahead, while enjoying more cheap beer. It turned out that one of the guys was only there for the trip to Prague, and the other guy, a keen sailor and yacht broker, was meeting his girlfriend the next night and she would be making the rest of the journey with him. Sadly I can't remember their names, but it was strange to meet them as I had originally expected everyone on the rally to be a student.

It was early evening so we moved on to the official rally party, where there were now a few more people, and spent the rest of the night drinking beers – which were strangely almost a £1.00 a pint here. It became apparent as to why it had been so quiet earlier on; when we got to Prague we had only been the 8th car in. As more and more teams arrived, the service got worse and worse, but it was great to meet so many of the teams and chat about the problems they had had already and the routes they were planning to take.

We arranged to set off in the morning to visit the Church of Bones with some guys we'd been drinking with who knew how to find it. This was a place we had seen on 'The Long Way Round', a film by Ewan McGregor who rode a motorbike all the way around the world; albeit with a full support crew. We hadn't realised that it was going to be on our route too. For most of Europe the only map we had was a road atlas; we hadn't envisaged spending much time here, preferring to get to the less accessible countries on the route which we were less likely to get back to in the near future.

It was now getting late – very late considering we hadn't slept since after the barbeque on Friday night, excluding that twenty minute power-nap. At the bar we had received various offers to crash on people's hotel floors (we hadn't had felt the need / got around to booking one in advance) but in the end the majority of people simply headed back to the car park and slept by the cars. We took this option too. So, it was out with the ThermaRests and sleeping bags – thanks here to another two of our sponsors for great pieces of kit – and some tinned fish. We really were living the high life!

Oddly enough, it turned out to be one of the best night's sleep I've had in a long time; on an oily concrete floor in an underground car park.

24th July – Prague, CZ to Lake Neusiedler, AT

After such a great sleep the wake up call wasn't so good. It was the fumes from the exhaust of the rally car next to us. Nice.

We put the ThermaRests in the buggy we wandered out into Prague in search of breakfast. It was at this point that we realised that we didn't speak a word of Czech and, not being in the tourist-heart of Prague, there was very little understanding of English. Not a major problem, but it did occur to us that for the rest of the journey this was a problem that wouldn't go away. We managed to get some breakfast in a little café and again used the toilets to get washed. At this café, however, the toilets were 50 metres down the street, across a courtyard, in a dingy room in the far corner with no light. This was much more like what we had been expecting from Eastern Europe.

Back at the car park we realised that we had no money left, after the beer monkey had stolen it all the night before, and we still had a car park to pay for; which didn't take credit cards. Apparently, the department store above the car park had a cash machine so I headed off to find it. Again, not simple considering that I can't speak or read Czech. However, it was a bit of a give-away when I saw the queue of other ralliers all trying to get money out of a machine. In the meantime, Foxy was trying to find the guys from the night before so that we could follow them to the Church of Bones. They were nowhere to be seen. In the end we found someone who actually had a copy of the 'The Long Way Round' with them and we copied down the name of the town. But it was so small it didn't feature on our map. After asking a few more ralliers, we found one who had a detailed map and copied that down too. Now all that was left was to exit the car park. The machine wouldn't take our money, but in the spirit of Eastern Europe, though not wanting to sound like I'm generalising on this too soon, the attendant opened the gate and pocked the money! He then proceeded to do the same with all the English cars following – a good profit for him that morning!

Driving through Prague was beautiful with the historic buildings and trams. Trams which seemed intent on making our life difficult; at one point we founds ourselves parked at a tram stop, surrounded by trams, in what turned out to be a car-free zone, but we were in high spirits in a buggy covered in stickers so didn't really care; we'd just blag our way out of trouble if we needed to.

Stuck in the tram system!

Leaving Prague we stopped for fuel. The best quality available was 91RON (normal fuel in the UK being 95RON/98RON) for about £0.55 per litre and from here on it would only get worse.

We arrived in Kutná Hora, a World Heritage site to the south east of Prague, where the Church of Bones is situated, hoping to be able to find it without much trouble. The problem was that the town, even though it only has a population of about 20,000, was much bigger than the village we had anticipated. We had no idea which direction to head in, or any translation for 'the Church of Bones, please'. We headed to the police station for some advice. Inside, behind the counter, we found a policeman, and in front of him, a man wielding two very large shotguns. For a moment I thought we had walked in on a heist but fortunately it was nothing that exciting. As soon as the initial worry passed it was clear that he was simply showing them off to the policeman and proudly chatting about them. When he left we spoke to the policeman and soon discovered he didn't understand any English. We didn't understand any Czech. We politely left.

We drove around the town for a while making educated guesses and soon found a huge church that had just been renovated. By now the sun was getting pretty hot. We went inside and asked, not being too sure if they would approve of the place we were looking for. Fortunately, the girl spoke English and directed us to the Church of Bones which was, as is always the case when you ask for directions, just across the road. She looked disappointed that we didn't want to look at her church but to be honest that's not what we had gone to see and it was much like any other church, just cleaner.

The Church of Bones is actually a very, very small Roman Catholic chapel called Sedlec Ossuary, and from the outside you would have no idea what it hides within. Inside, however, there are the bones of between forty and seventy thousand humans, arranged into towers, patterns on the walls and built into ornate chandeliers – one of which contains at least one of every bone in the body.

The Church of Bones

There were neat pyramids of leg bones six feet high and skulls in piles up to the ceiling. Thousands of them all neatly arranged, as if that was the normal thing to do with skeletons. It was quite eerie and morbid but very interesting and well worth a visit. Apparently, the bones are from the cemetery next door that couldn't cope with the sheer number of deaths due to the Black Death plague in the fourteenth century, and the Bohemian wars some years later, and were arranged by a woodcarver.

Back in the sunshine we bumped into the guys who we'd met the night before who had suggested travelling to the church together. They had had fewer problems finding the church but had been delayed by drinking too much the night before. Taking a look at our map we estimated that we could make it to a huge lake, Lake Neusiedler, to the south of Vienna, Austria in time to set up the tents and get a good nights sleep. Vienna wasn't directly on our route, but was somewhere neither of us had been and had to be worth a visit, and also the lake looked like a good place camp.

All the roads through the Czech Republic were deeply rutted where the wheels of the trucks had forced the tarmac deeper into the road, causing our buggy to sway side-to-side as the wheels rode up and down the sides of these ruts. The best way to describe it is like a farm track with the two ruts where the wheels go – except these were tarmaced and supposed to be main roads. It was causing all kinds of problems for our little buggy which had wheels much closer together than the trucks, leaving us lopsided with two wheels in the rut and two wheels out.

As we neared the border with Austria, we stopped to buy some food and beers ready to cook later in the evening. We assumed the food would be cheaper in the Czech Republic; considering that the 500ml bottles of beer were only £0.20 I doubt they could have been much cheaper anywhere else. It was strange, but already we were comparing the cost of countries in terms of the price of beer and petrol. Simple things.

As we got closer to the border, there were again the prostitutes trying to attract the visitors as they came from across the border and the market stalls selling practically everything for virtually nothing.

There were no issues exiting the Czech Republic and we were soon into Vienna as the sun started to set. Not a huge distance from Prague but we hadn't started the day until quite late and had made several stops on the way.

Posing for photos, Vienna

As with Prague, the only map we had of Vienna was a small city map. We hit the ring road and did almost a lap to get a feel for the city the aimed inwards heading for the biggest church we could see – on the assumption that churches tend to be in the centre. The plan worked and soon we were in the historic heart of Vienna. With it being late in the evening the palaces and museums were fairly quiet, so we took the opportunity to take the buggy right up to the front doors of all the ones we could so that we could take photos; after all, we didn't have the time to walk to them all, there were no bollards to stop us and obviously we couldn't read the 'no access' signs!

More 'danger photos', Vienna

At the fourth palace, we managed to get right to the base of the grand steps leading to the front door. I was parked up waiting for Foxy to take the photo from the street below when I was approached by a man speaking with a very dry, monotone German-sounding accent:

"Are you allowed to drive here?"

"Possibly not, I'm just sightseeing."

"Are you lost?"

"Err, yeah, probably"

"Where are you trying to get to?"

"Mongolia."

Then, as if it had all become clear to him and all made perfect sense as to why I was parked right on the palace steps in a car-free zone:

"Ah I see, you probably are lost...I'm afraid I can't help you."

Making a swift exit from the final location, Vienna

And with the photo in the bag we left. Within an hour we must have seen most of the sights of Vienna and I have to say it is absolutely gorgeous. Having been to many European cities, I have seen none as beautiful as Vienna and will definitely be going back when I get the chance. There is so much to see and do, without having to do anything at all.

Happy that we had seen the main sights, we headed south to find the lake. At which point the weather changed and a gigantic thunderstorm broke. Just what we needed. To make matters worse, the buggy had now developed a considerable misfire. As we were almost at the lake we decided to ignore it; there was nothing we could do at this time of night. We decided that it could be the wet conditions interfering with the sparkplugs and leads and hopefully nothing more serious with the engine.

We opted to head down the east side of the lake to give us the best route out in the morning and about halfway down we found a huge campsite on the waters edge. Sadly, the campsite was already closed for the night. This really wasn't what we needed, although the rain had now passed. Fortunately, at this point an official looking person walked past and after twenty minutes of persuasion in his midge-ridden office he agreed to lift the barrier and let us in; he liked our buggy and seemed happy that we weren't there to cause chaos on his tranquil campsite.

We pitched our Mountain Equipment tents in a few moments (another sponsor to thank) and got out the cooking kit. This consisted of two top of the range, multi-fuel stoves. One supplied by Primus and one by Go-System (more sponsors, thanks!). These worked a treat and cooked some lovely pork steaks for us, which went down well with the Czech beers. With the midges eating us as fast as we were eating the pork, we grabbed another beer and headed to the waters edge, where there was a slight breeze keeping the midges at bay, and lay on the wooden jetty. The silence was perfect with the stars now reappearing after the thunderstorm, but we soon gave up, wandered back to the tents shattered, and had another great sleep.

25th July – Lake Neusiedler, AT to Transylvania, RO

As is always the case with camping, we were woken early. 06:30 to be precise. At which point we met our neighbour. It turned out that we had woken her up late the night before, but luckily it was the smell of our cooking (which apparently she thought was lovely) that had woken her and not our talking, and anyway she had soon gone back to sleep – hungry. She seemed nice enough and we explained what were doing. After cooking a proper English breakfast on the stoves, we had our first real showers since Saturday morning and headed off, the misfire having mysteriously resolved itself.

We had, loosely, planned to go to Slovakia but ended up missing it out and going straight to Hungary. This straightened our route out slightly; after all, Slovakia was only on our route so that we could drive through Bratislava. We decided that with the likes of easyJet and Ryanair, Slovakia could wait until another trip as we would only have spent a couple of hours there anyway.

Entering Hungary was no problem at all and we were now back on the same deeply rutted tarmac roads as we had seen in the Czech Republic. Hungary was also the beginning of our journey though the more 'interesting' countries, with an increasing reputation for lawlessness, corruption, bribery, kidnap and police and military intervention starting to becoming evermore prevalent the further east we travelled. I'd heard a lot about it, but now it was time to see if my suspicions and preconceptions would be confirmed, or if they were just ill-informed, malicious and sensationalised rumours from a time gone by. To a certain extent I actually hoped they were more than just rumours.

A new problem we found in Hungary was that our mobile phone had stopped working. For the journey we had taken a 'OneRoam' mobile sim card. This supposedly allowed us to piggyback off local phone

44

networks and so text home with our news updates for a low, fixed-price all over the world. As the sim card had only arrived in the mail a couple of days before we left, we hadn't had the chance to test it properly. Up until now, the text service had been fine, although outgoing calls had never worked. Now nothing worked. Not a major issue but another problem none the less.

We also realised while driving through Hungary that we had no local road-tax. This occurred to us as we were talking about how we hadn't remembered to buy a vignette for the motorways in Austria (or the Czech Republic for that matter) and became more apparent when we came to a queue for a roadside road-tax checkpoint. Luckily, we managed to dip out of the queue, onto the wide area of dirt at the side of the road, and sneak around the back of the policeman into a filling station and avoided getting stopped. I say 'sneak around' but we were hardly inconspicuous and I think we only got away with it as the policeman couldn't be bothered to follow us. A close call. By 12:30 we were passing Budapest but decided not to stop, as we wanted to make the border and be into Romania before dark so as to find somewhere to camp. We hadn't found a lot to stop for in Hungary either so were happy to punch on through to Romania; aiming towards the second 'checkpoint', the city of Odessa in Ukraine. Checkpoint in so much as it was one of the larger towns we had used in plotting our general route.

There were three options for the route in Romania. Keep north and skirt round Moldova and into Ukraine; head south and along the shores of the Black Sea, staying in Romania all the way to Ukraine; or cross central Romania and Moldova to Ukraine.

Option one looked dull. We had been told that option two could be impossible, as the thin stretch of Romania between the Black Sea and Moldova is notorious for bandits and smuggling, and as such, the border is very tightly controlled. The guards have been known to simply turn people away with no explanation leaving them with no other option but to back-track for hundreds of miles. We went for option three. Far from the sensible option in hindsight, but none the less an exciting and challenging prospect.

Entry to Romania was relatively painless and hassle free and the first thing we noticed was the amount of police along the roadside. They were everywhere. They all had lovely new cars, in stark contrast to the clapped out cars the locals all had, and more importantly to us, radar speed guns. It was almost as if it was the first day the police had been issued with them and they were all on the roads trying them out. In the buggy this shouldn't have been a problem, as it wasn't the raciest number, but the problem was we had no idea what the speed limits were and there weren't any signs. Every police car we passed, (and there were a lot) had at least one motorist pulled over in the process of being fined; often with a second or third queued up waiting to be processed. Added to this was the way that the speedo needle jumped about erratically when travelling at about 30mph (which we guessed to be about the limit) so it was never clear just how fast we were actually going. Though I did wonder where the money came from for all the new police cars when everyone else looked so poor. Probably from all the speeding fines. Fortunately, we didn't get pulled and carried on our way to the first big city, Arad, just inside Romania.

The moment we stopped at the first set of traffic lights we were pounced on by a group of smiley window washers. We tried to wind-up the side windows as quickly as possible in anticipation of the begging that would inevitably begin the moment they'd finished, but it was too late. They saw us starting to wind up the windows and dispatched one of their team to start the begging by shoving his arm through the rapidly closing window. This wouldn't have been much of an issue, but we genuinely had no money to give them. The smiles soon disappeared and so did we when the lights changed – with a lovely, clean windscreen!

As we left the built up area around the city and headed towards the mountains of Transylvania paranoia set in. We noticed a brand new silver Mercedes following us from a distance. It stuck out like a sore thumb compared to the other clapped-out cars, which were mostly held together with rust and body-filler. This continued for some time before it passed us and disappeared. With it gone, we had a moment of relief, until we passed him again. The driver had stopped and was casually chatting to the traffic police. He then followed us before overtaking and again, he waited up the road with the next group of police cars. This happened several times and was actually starting to bother us, until we had a new preoccupation. We realised that we still had no local money, nowhere to get any and no petrol. Never a good situation but one we would find ourselves in time and time again.

We pulled in at a very small local filling station and tried to talk to the attendant and some other guys who were milling around. They didn't speak English, we didn't speak Romanian, but somehow my GSCE German was enough for us to get by with, so we conversed in broken German. And then tried to explain that we only had euros or dollars to pay with! This, eventually, seemed to be acceptable and so we got 40 litres; filling the buggy and one of the jerry cans. It seemed cheap enough and everyone was happy. We even got some change in local Romanian money. We had no idea what the Romanian money was worth so took a guess based on how much they were charging for a litre of petrol and what we expected it would cost – assuming we hadn't been ripped-off.

This was another job we should have done before we left. We should have noted down rough exchange rates for each of the countries we were going through so we at least had a general idea what we were getting or paying. More importantly, we should have tried to get hold of some currency for each of the countries we were travelling through, although this is not physically possible for some. Hindsight's an incredible thing.

The difficulties begin, Romania

We were happy again now that we thought we had enough petrol to get through the wilds of Transylvania to the far side of Romania, where we assumed they would take credit cards or we'd find a bank. We also seemed to have lost the Mercedes that had been tailing us for so long as we turned off the main road to cross the mountains in search of an ice cave. The ice cave was to be found somewhere in the heart of the Transylvanian mountains, on a tip-off from the 'Lonely Planet Guide to Romania' that we had been reading throughout the day.

At this point the road became like no other I've ever seen. Previously, I've driven over the French Alps to Italy, along the Pacific Coast Highway of western America, and along some very narrow cliff top roads in various other countries, but this was in a different league. The road was incredibly narrow with switchbacks every hundred metres or so and was unbelievably steep. On the corners, the tarmac was either deeply rutted through wear and tear or worn right though to the gravel beneath. It was painfully slow going, but we had engaged four-wheel drive and the buggy was coping well. It was a fine balance to keep the momentum up around the corners so as to avoid having to use first gear, yet without cornering too fast for our unstable buggy. It was also drinking petrol. There was no alternative now as we were too far along to turn back, but with no money and limited petrol to get out of the mountains it could prove disastrous for us. We pushed on, making very slow progress as the road rose into the clouds and deeper into the thickly forested mountains.

As we got deeper into Transylvania, the road continued to get worse and worse, like it hadn't been maintained once in the many years since it was first laid. It probably hadn't and probably never would be. The upside of this is that there was virtually no traffic and certainly no foreign tourists. The deeper we got, the more of a time warp it became. We were the only vehicle on the road; all the locals had horses and carts. The houses had wells by the roadside instead of running water and there were haystacks in all the fields. These had been made by the locals using scythes and pitchforks. Every local we passed was carrying a scythe or pitchfork, and they all looked like peasants; much like the extras you see working in the village scenes of a medieval film. And yet we were still only 1,100 miles in a straight line from London. Transylvania was starting to get especially eerie and a little unnerving.

Every person we passed would stop walking, working or doing whatever they were doing, to watch us from the moment we entered the periphery of their range of vision until we had left it. They would stare with an impassive, almost expressionless look that seemed to have a tinge of bewilderment and disgust – as if we were intruding on their private world that time had forgotten. I felt as if they were weighing us up, although they gave no open sign of any reaction to us. It really did feel as if the place was full of hillbillies and country-hicks and that we would be accused of being in league with the devil and imprisoned because of our motorised cart.

It was at this point that we read the Lonely Planet in a bit more detail and discovered that the entrance to the ice cave was only accessible by foot, along an eight mile track. We would therefore have a sixteen mile walk, plus time in the cave, and it was already late afternoon due to the time we had spent snaking our way up and into the mountains. We decided that we couldn't really spare the best part of a day sightseeing at this stage of the adventure and would instead find somewhere to camp and get some food. A much better idea.

We soon came across a small, very small, village and before we knew it, had passed through. However, we had spotted some tents in a field. But before we got to turn the buggy around, we found ourselves driving though a very strange scene. On the edge of this tiny village, miles and miles from anywhere, the Romanians were building and developing an entire ski village from scratch. Everything from individual luxury chalets to hotels, shops and ski lifts. In a few years it will be incredible – although I have no idea what the locals will make of it. We turned back and headed for the field where the tents were, passing all the staring locals we had passed minutes before, staring at us once again. At the place we turned around there was one person, no more than a few feet away, and I couldn't lose his gaze once I'd caught his eye. He clearly had no intention of looking away and neither did the others. I really didn't feel welcome.

At the campsite, we managed to communicate that we wanted to pitch the tents for the night and got them up just before dark while Foxy worried about the risk of tic-borne encephalitis. We had had a whole load of vaccinations before we arrived, but Foxy had missed this one because at the time, some doctors were still awaiting its full approval. I'd chosen to get it elsewhere. The tics are rife in areas of long grass in Eastern Europe and certain parts of Russia, in fact in areas just like this field and much of the rest of our adventure. Luckily for us, the locals must have scared them all away, as Foxy was fine. Adjacent to the field was a small, local bar serving food so we went across with the maps and grabbed a beer and the menu. As expected, we had no idea what we were looking at or ordering so had a stab in the dark and hoped for the best.

We took time to take a proper look at the maps for the first time since leaving London.

The intention had always been to plan the route whilst we were travelling, to avoid feeling that we were forcing ourselves to go along a defined route, and so always have the freedom to divert at any point we wanted. The spirit of the journey was to have an adventure and we felt that too much planning would take this element away; at least that's the excuse we had for our (lack of) route planning. The downside was that we were never quite sure how far we'd be travelling or what the terrain would be like next. This meant that we never knew quite how long we would need to travel to get to the next border crossing. At this stage of the journey this was not a problem, but we were mindful that for certain countries, such as Kyrgyzstan, we had very limited time to cross the country due to the limitations imposed by our visas. Because the visas had to be obtained from the embassies in the UK, they were already printed in our passports. This dictated the earliest we could enter a country and when we had to leave by. They were not flexible in any way, generally had a narrow timeframe, and over-stayed visas commonly result in deportation or imprisonment – either would spell the end of the adventure.

For the moment we could travel as we wanted because we were confident we would arrive ahead of schedule at Uzbekistan, where our first time-critical visa began, but the plan was to push though Europe to get to the less accessible places nearer to Russia and beyond. These would be places that we would be less likely to make it back to on future trips and so we decided to aim to spend more time there. While sitting in the bar, however, we estimated that simply to get out of the mountains and off the tiny road we were on would take at least five hours and that was in addition to the majority of the day we had already spent on it. Maybe we wouldn't have that much spare time to get to Uzbekistan?! More importantly, there would be nowhere to get petrol, or Romanian Leu to buy it with, until we were out of the mountains. We were using far more fuel than we'd anticipated as the buggy strained itself over the twisty mountain roads and estimated that we would run out somewhere in the mountains the next morning, before the first town.

The food arrived and worries about fuel were quickly forgotten. Two bowls of soup, which was verging on a stew, with chips to start, followed by chicken and bread. Perfect, if a bit random – we'd have to improve our menu skills later. We paid with the change we'd got from the filling station, and were now left with just a few pounds worth of Romanian money and at least twenty-four hours to survive in the country.

We got an early night in the peace of the mountains, ready for an early start, in the hope of getting near to the Moldovan border. This would mean that we should be able to enter, cross and exit Moldova in one go on Thursday. We had been advised against spending more time than we had to in Moldova – particularly at night and especially if we were camping. The country is renowned for mild banditry and we had been advised that travelling at night should be avoided unless we wanted to make ourselves an obvious and prominent target. The same was said to be true of most of the countries we had to cross for the rest of the trip, so we hoped to be able to limit most of our travel to the daylight hours – although the reality of this would prove to be an impossibility.

26th July – Transylvania, RO to Husi, RO

We awoke very early in the morning. It was freezing, with a thick, wet mist hanging in the calm mountain air. The tents and sleeping bags had done a top job, but the outside of the tents were soaking as we packed them away into the buggy.

We headed out of the mountains, passing growing crowds of local workers with their scythes and pitchforks, waiting for old vans to pick them up and take them to work. They were all still staring at us. As we were now leaving, I decided to go for a reaction and started waving at one of them through the open window. Unbelievably, he smiled and waved back! Perhaps the locals were friendly after all and we had just misread them. Either way, they clearly didn't see many outsiders.

Often there was no real road at all

We were now getting towards the valley bottom, the mist was clearing and the road was improving. Well, it was getting less twisty, but there were still stretches without tarmac, and several areas where landslides had wiped out half the width of the road. There was no opportunity to relax while driving as there were no warning signs or traffic cones; just gaping holes in the road.

By the time we hit the valley bottom, it was mid-morning; the mist had fully cleared and the views were fantastic. The air was so clean, crisp, fresh and clear making all the colours incredibly vivid. We passed forests, waterfalls and alpine rivers until we joined a main road, where the land flattened off and we started to pass through villages and small towns again, leaving Transylvania behind.

Early morning, Transylvania

We used the last of our money to buy some food at a roadside café and took the chance to dry the tents in the warm sun. We were amazed to get thousands and thousands of Romanian Leu in change – much more than we'd even paid. Later in the day we discovered that the currency has experienced such hyper-inflation that 10,000 of the old bank notes were worth just one of the new, and we were being given the unwanted old notes in our change. It didn't worry us as they were worth less than a pound, but it was strange all the same.

It wasn't long before we had completely left the seclusion and time-warp of Transylvania behind and at 14:45 we entered the outskirts of Brasov; halfway across Romania and the first big town we had seen since early the previous day when we had passed Arad. We found a petrol station and managed to get fuel with euros and minimal hassle.

Tired and caught off guard at the traffic lights, we were soon targeted by the windscreen cleaners and again the buggy was surrounded. The lights went green and there was no way we could move and even with the other cars stuck behind us honking their horns the cleaners wouldn't move. Again, we had no money to give them so eventually pushed a couple of Marlborough cigarettes out of the part open window into the hands of one of the cleaners. It seemed to do the trick and we were off, and back on our guard.

We must have taken about two hundred Marlborough Lights with us. Neither of us smoke but we were very aware that almost everyone along our route would, and that American cigarettes would be very welcome and a good ice-breaker. We even had an open box on the dashboard with a lighter to look as if we were giving people our 'personal' cigarettes. A nice touch we thought, and it proved very useful later in the journey at the border crossings.

We were still struggling to come to terms with just how primitive the country was. Even in the towns people were using horses and carts. All the villagers got water from wells; many people in the towns did too. Cars seemed to be mostly owned by the police and those that weren't looked to be on their last legs. Locals would be walking down the road with scythes, pitchforks or two cows. We never did find out why, but people always had two cows, never one or three or more; just two. Every mile or two, there were people at the side of the road selling cherries, apples and peaches from wooden buckets. The children would try the hard-sell, thrusting their buckets up at arms length towards the buggy, giving us puppy-dog eyes as we drove past. Added to this, at most junctions there would be several people thumbing for lifts. I assume many of the street sellers were Romanys selling the fruit they had collected in the countryside.

As the day went on, the road remained quite good – tarmaced without too many major potholes, and we were on target to get near the Moldovan border by nightfall. We were both looking at the hillside ahead of us at the exact moment a lightning bolt struck a tree just a few hundred metres away. The weather was hot and humid and a gigantic thunderstorm had unexpectedly broken out around us. The road was instantly rushing with water, getting deeper and deeper, when suddenly the buggy went into a torrent that crossed the road, coming up over the bonnet, covering the windscreen and momentarily blinding us. I flicked the feeble window wipers on and held the wheel straight hoping that there was nothing ahead of us. Fortunately, the road was straight and we had stayed on our side, avoiding the oncoming traffic. A scare we could have done without. I pulled over and we took a break while a few cars crawled past at a walking pace in the pouring rain. Most had pulled over, like us, waiting for some respite. Soon enough it stopped, the sun was back, misty-steam filled the air and we were on our way.

Again, the buggy was misfiring badly at low revs and would cut out whenever we came to a standstill. It was also running very hot. We hoped it was to do with the rain, or perhaps the heat due to the long and hard day the buggy had had. Taking the optimistic view, we again hoped it would resolve itself again by the morning.

It was now 20:45, we were nearing the Romanian/Moldovan border near Bacau and Vaslui and were looking for somewhere to stop and camp when, in the middle of nowhere, we were pulled over by the police. It turned out that they had stopped us at the junction of the road that leads to the border, just after the last village before Moldova. They checked our documents and asked us where we were going. 'Moldova' we said, they glanced at each other, gave a wry smile and wished us luck. They clearly knew more of the place than we did!

Our first real warning of things to come – from the police

A couple of miles later, completely in the middle of nowhere, we took a track off the road to try to find somewhere out of sight to camp. Sadly, the terrain was too flat to be inconspicuous, so we just stopped a few minutes drive from the road and cooked some food as darkness fell. Before we left London we had stocked up on tins of ready made curry, sweet and sour chicken, minced beef and similar easy to cook foods. We had tins of vegetables and packs of rice and pasta so we were able to knock up quick and reasonable meals at times like this. The mosquitoes were, as usual, enjoying us more than we were enjoying them, so we started to tidy away ready for bed.

Camping in bandit country, Romania

As we were packing up the cooking equipment we could hear cars in the distance, back along the track we had come along. This began to worry us. We knew Moldova was hardly the most friendly or safe place (and Romania is not a great deal better) and here we were, alone, camping near the border in possibly the most lawless area of the whole country. In my mind this was prime bandit country; scrubland between the last village and the border, at night, with no sign of life – perfect for smuggling, kidnap and for us to be robbed. We turned off our head-torches and waited. Soon enough, two cars came over the crest into sight, their headlights shining just to the side of us. They had almost passed when they stopped no more than a hundred metres away. We could hear their voices and they must have seen us. Then they drove off into the distance along the track. Where they were heading, I have no idea, as the nearest villages were all in a completely different direction. The mosquitoes were getting the better of us again so we had to get into the tents and go uneasily to bed, wondering if the men in the cars would return.

27th July – Husi, RO to Odessa, UA

We awoke early in the grasslands, which were still fresh, wet and quite cold with the morning dew, grabbed a biscuit bar out of the buggy for breakfast and packed the tents away, hitting the road by 06:15. The plan of camping near the border had worked; we would be at the crossing in less than an hour and therefore get into and, more importantly out of, Moldova within the day.

This was important for us because of what we had learnt before the trip and from the odd person we had been able to talk to en route. We'd learnt that parts of Moldova were notorious for bandits, kidnap, robberies and extortion and so was not somewhere we wanted to hang around, especially if we had to travel after nightfall. More worrying was the region of Transnistria.

This is a breakaway region, a renegade Soviet state, which we understood to be to the northeast of the country. In March 1992, two years after demanding independence, the inhabitants of the region decided that they wanted to be fully independent of Moldova and more aligned with Russia. They had a few quiet words with the Russians who were very understanding and, through the Russian 14th Army stationed in Moldova, delivered an epic amount of armaments by the train load (around 42,000 tons). On the night of 2nd March, the Transnistrians, with their kindly supplied Russian military hardware, rolled over the bridge on the river Dniester and started a war with the Moldovan army. After several weeks of erratic and intense fighting, the vastly outnumbered Moldovan army agreed to unofficially recognise the area of Transnistria, giving de-facto control to the Transnistrians. At least it ended the war, although by now hundreds of lives had been lost. As you'd expect, this wasn't the end of it, both sides believing that they came off worst from a casualty point of view, and so sporadic reprisal attacks still take place to this day, with no side getting any nearer to a final compromise. The significant economic wealth that Transnistria won has long since been squandered, with just a few military officials benefiting, and the region is seriously struggling. A further worrying point we were able to ascertain before we left was from the Foreign Office website.

In Iraq, Somalia and one other equally dangerous area, South Ossetia if I remember rightly, the Foreign Office advises against all but absolutely essential travel, but gives a contact number to call should everything go wrong and you need urgent assistance. In Transnistria they advise against all travel and state that should you need help, there is nothing, absolutely nothing, they can or will do to help. You would be entirely on your own. Transnistria also appeared to have an unsavoury record of arms smuggling, human trafficking, human rights abuse, arbitrary arrest and torture.

As such, and as you would imagine, we had carefully planned to cross the centre of Moldova, thereby avoiding the smugglers and bandits to the south and Transnistria to the north. We were still worried enough about the general reputation of Moldova; it would be bad enough crossing it, without the added dangers of these other areas to contend with.

Anyway, even without these added concerns, it was only about five minutes into the drive towards the border that we realised this was not going to be a simple day. The misfire that had been dogging our progress of late was now permanently with us. The buggy had no power and we found that we had to change down as low as second gear just to keep the buggy going, even on the flat roads. We changed the spark plugs. The old ones where thick with a crystalline build-up on the electrodes and we were much happier, thinking we'd fixed it. But no such luck. We changed all the plug leads and the HT lead. No change. We drove for another six miles, which got us to the Moldovan border, but by now it was clear that we'd have to get help to get the problem fixed. And we didn't want to be trying to do this in Moldova.

At the border we optimistically tried changing the plug leads again. It was pointless, but we felt it was worth a go. Soon a guard walked over demanding we move the buggy. Apparently, we were parked in a heavily restricted area, but with wires strewn across the innards of the engine bay, the buggy was going nowhere fast. We tried to ignore the guard's threatening demands while we reconnected the wires. We had no choice but to turn back. For some reason this particularly irritated me; perhaps it was the tiredness, the small feeling of defeat or the not knowing what the problem was, but I really didn't want to have to turn back along the road we'd just driven. I even briefly thought our rally could be over.

There was a real sinking feeling between us as we had to back-track and admit that we were beaten. The buggy was seriously sick and we couldn't place our finger on the problem. We guessed at damaged piston rings, the carburettor or dirty fuel. All things that we couldn't fix and could require major work to repair.

We managed to limp back to the last town we'd passed and soon found a garage. There was a small feeling of relief, until it dawned on us that we had no way of speaking to the mechanics. I went in and managed to coax one of the mechanics out to look at the buggy. I tried to show him, with actions and sounds what the problem was, but we were getting nowhere. He walked off inside and I began to think he had lost interest, when he returned with a man in a shirt who must have been the manager, so I tried to explain the problem over again. Again it was fruitless, so I hopped in the buggy, started it up and drove it forward. With the engine under load the problem was self-evident. The manager disappeared inside and urgently pulled a mechanic off another job. By now several mechanics were crowding around the buggy, looking it over with interest. They seemed never to have seen a right-hand drive car before and were fascinated that we had two batteries (we had installed a second to power the spotlights, extra cooling fan and to provide a 240 volt supply so we could charge camera batteries). They also loved all the sponsors stickers and to be working on a 'proper' rally car. We didn't have the heart to try to explain how rubbish the buggy really was.

The head mechanic was soon deep under the bonnet, having spanners passed to him as he called for them, much like in an operating theatre. He clearly was the top guy they had. Within only a few moments, he had done a couple of checks and isolated the problem. His head popped up and we understood that he was asking where we had bought our benzene (petrol) from. 'LucOil', we told him. Everyone groaned and laughed! Apparently, LucOil are, apparently, less than honest and often sell very low octane fuel while advertising it as a much higher octane. The problem was that the timing was now incorrect for the engine to burn this low octane fuel properly; this also explained why it was running so hot. The mechanic reached down and centred the crankshaft. Then, with the engine running, loosened and gradually turned the distributor while revving the engine with his other hand which he had on the throttle linkage. He then adjusted the points in the alternator by bending them with a screwdriver until they looked about right to him. It all looked very dodgy but within a few moments the engine sounded sweet and everyone was smiling; not least us. Not content with that, he insisted that I take him for a test drive to ensure that it really was working fine whilst in use.

There was a huge joke between the mechanics as I drove off, due to the head-mechanic, in the passenger seat, pulling scared-looking faces and pretending to hold onto an imaginary steering wheel that they all thought should have been on his side of the buggy. The buggy was perfect. Better than it had ever been, even the occasional backfiring had gone away (we later matched these symptoms perfectly with our Haynes manual. Interestingly, the manual states that the points cannot be adjusted and that the unit must be replaced; in Romania however, a screwdriver fixes it just fine).

Back at the garage, everyone was still smiling. But we now had the issue of how to pay. They asked us for 200,000Leu (£3.70). We had none. They suggested €5 (£3.30). Again, we had none. We offered dollars, the only currency we had, and again they asked for five (which, at £2.70, was a good amount less than we had started at!). It was an absolute bargain and they were delighted with the five dollars. We were just delighted that they would accept dollars, though it was hardly surprising given their average wage was something like £20 a month. Before we left they warned that as we headed east the fuel would get worse and worse. This seemed strangely ironic if you consider that petrol gets worse the closer you get to its source. In anticipation we got the mechanic to show us what he had just done. It looked simple enough and we hoped that we'd remember should we need to do it again.

More importantly, we were back on our way with the engine running cool, and far smoother than ever before. Our spirits were high as we headed for the border again.

As soon as we got to the border to exit Romania we were turned straight around. We weren't too sure why but had been directed back to the nearby filling station. Apparently, on entering the country we should have bought a 'Ro-vignette' – some form of temporary road tax. The same road tax we had so far avoided buying in the other countries. We went back half a mile to the nearest filling station and bought one for a dollar. We also filled the buggy up with petrol as the garage took Visa, and by now we were very, very low on fuel.

Back at the border we joined a queue of three cars which didn't seem to be moving anywhere. We discovered that we had to go into the large, imposing, concrete, communist-looking buildings with huge symbolic, concrete statues on top, visit several offices and sign a few forms, both for us and the buggy. We got our transit visas and paid a few fees, in dollars, of $3 to $4 (£1.60 to £2.10) for nothing in particular. It all appeared to be above board and we got receipts so we were happy enough. We were even able to get some dollars exchanged for Moldovan Leu in a small office in the customs hall.

The officials didn't seem too concerned with the masses of kit we had in the back of the buggy, and painlessly enough we were into Moldova, keen to see what lay ahead. In all honesty, it wasn't much different to the other countries we had seen in the rest of Eastern Europe, with huge field of crops – mostly wheat and bright yellow sunflowers as far as the eye could see – and small, rolling hills on the horizon. It was even beginning to be a bit of a let down that there weren't bandits on the roadside waiting to pounce on us – and we did look! We started to relax that there would be nothing to worry about after all.

Then, almost halfway across Moldova, a few miles past the capital, Chisinau, we came to a military checkpoint where armed guards checked our documents and stamped our passports. It was bizarre and almost as if we were leaving the country, yet we were still about sixty miles from Ukraine. We thanked them and carried on regardless, assuming it was just another check, then double checked the map and had a quick read of the Lonely Planet. We soon lost our new found confidence as we realised that ahead lay a river called the Dniester and on the other side had to be Transnistria. It all made perfect sense but it had been a massive oversight on our part. We had just checked out of the official part of Moldova and were now heading straight into the heart of rebel-held Transnistria. We had thought it was much further to the north. There was no way we could go back as our Moldovan visas were only single entry and we had just received the exit stamps. We had to take our chances in Transnistria, and anyway, it was only a couple of hours drive to get to Ukraine on the other side so we still had plenty of time to be out before nightfall. We knew that most of the areas in these regions become much more risky with nightfall, so had to be off the road by then – and ideally into Ukraine.

Driving along the road from the checkpoint, we assumed that we could now just drive straight on into Ukraine. We were just settling into the idea of Transnistria and its dubious reputation being nothing more than rumours when we rounded a corner and came to a sudden and ominous stop.

Across the whole of the road was a moveable wooden blockade, heavily wrapped in barbed wire. Directly in front of it was a military guard, facing us, dressed in a full chemical warfare suit – including the hood, even in the summer sun – with a machine gun levelled directly at us. At this point I vividly remember thinking back to the Foreign Office warning that there was nothing they could, or would do to assist us should things turn nasty; and here we were, right in the middle of it.

I stopped the buggy right there in the road, unsure whether to drive closer to the guard, get out of the buggy or wait where we were. Driving away didn't seem like a sensible option. Doing the wrong thing would no doubt anger him, and it could be quite dangerous if we drove too close when we shouldn't. We decided to wait and let him make the first move. While waiting we also spotted several militia, a heavily armoured vehicle with a large artillery gun next to it, pointing along the road we had just come, shielded from sight at the side of the road and covered by camo-netting. This was really not somewhere we wanted to be; but it was all strangely captivating at the same time and I almost felt detached from the reality and gravity of the situation.

A few seconds later, but after what seemed like an eternity, a small number of soldiers appeared from the sides of the road in full military uniform, with machine guns and gigantic communist-era hats. They stood around the buggy and then one approached me on the driver's side. He stood, with his machine gun levelled through the door at my stomach and started barking at me in what sounded to me like Russian. I looked blank without trying to stare too much. He realised that we had no idea what he was saying so, while going red in the face from shouting, he tried in English with a heavy Russian accent:

"Dis is no longer Moldova! Dis is our country! Dis is Transnistria! We control dis area! Why you come here!?"

Good question! I didn't want to say that we were lost and have to ask for directions, so tried to explain that we were trying to get to Odessa in Ukraine. He wasn't impressed and probably didn't understand, or care to understand. He demanded our passports and documents, which were taken from us into a concrete hut by another uniformed man. We were ordered out of the buggy, and they indicated that we should get our bags and follow them into one of the other concrete huts beside the road. Reluctantly, we had to leave the buggy unattended so we hurriedly locked it and followed one guard into the hut while another ushered us in from behind.

Inside was a tatty counter and behind it was sitting a hugely built official in military uniform. He looked angry and annoyed at having been disturbed. In turn, we each had to empty every item from our rucksacks and try to explain what every item was. He was very confused by the iPod, sun cream (he though this was for homosexuals and questioned me briefly on this – apparently it's illegal to be so in Transnistria; luckily he believed me that I'm not) and various other bits of our kit, so we had to carefully show him what each was for and how they worked. He then wanted to see our cameras and proceeded to look through every single one of the photos. Suddenly, he became very excited about something on the camera and started talking to his colleague.

Immediately, it dawned on me what had happened. Before we had left we had got $1,000 (£535) in small bills (mostly one and five dollar) so that we could use these to pay for work on the buggy along the way, exchange them for local money where there were no banks and, if necessary, to use as bribes. At the barbeque the night before we left, we'd decided to spread the money around on a table and take some comedy photos of us posing with it. Equally bad were the photos of us acting out a scene from the film Casino using rolls of dollars and about half a kilo of sugar neatly lined up across a glass coffee table – you get the picture. We had then put the dollars into sealed packets hidden in the doors and deeply under the carpets of the buggy, to reduce the risk of having them all stolen should we get robbed. Except now in Transnistria no-one was laughing. In that moment, we had changed from a curiosity to a potentially huge pay day – if they could find the money and bags of supposed-narcotics they thought we had. They really did seem to think we were multi-millionaire coke-addicts. Not the kind of reputation you need in this kind of lawless place.

Having exhaustively searched our bags, we were taken back to the buggy, all the time the guards were saying the word 'dollars' and gesturing that we should pay them. Some would walk alongside us and whisper it, while others were more blatant and would openly ask, and even demand. We denied having any, though our credibility was definitely in ruins now that they had seen the photos. We unlocked the buggy thinking, albeit optimistically, that we might be ready to get on our way. However, predictably, the guards started poking around our kit in the back of the buggy, in the foot wells – in fact, anywhere they could. This was going to be a long job.

As the driver I was targeted, and got the most irritated looking guard. He marched me back into one of the empty concrete huts, with no windows, and the metal door was shut solidly behind me. Foxy and I were now separated, and again I found myself thinking of the warnings on the Foreign Office website. He gestured that I should sit on a short-legged, hard, wooden bench, while he continued to bark rapidly at me in Russian, before taking a seat himself on the other side of the desk. He leaned threateningly across towards me, all the time with his machine gun in his hands, resting on the desk, pointing at me. Strangely, before we had set off on the trip we had talked and joked excitedly about situations like this, but the reality was somewhat different to talking about it over a few pints in a clean, relaxing bar in London.

I was genuinely scared for possibly the first time in my life. I was practically in a cell, in a militia-run, unrecognised country with a man opposite me, his machine gun levelled at me, and he answered to no-one. It was time to think of a plan, quickly, and to be careful what I said.

From somewhere, he had got my passport back, and was leafing through the pages looking at the visas we had got before we left – his interest was focussed on the Moldovan one. They had an absolute hatred of the Moldovans. The visa clearly stated we had paid $30 (£16) each for them, and he was going to be wanting far more than this to get through his 'superior' country. Especially with the photos. With the occasional word of English and lots of angry sounding Russian words, he questioned me as to where my Transnistrian visa was. This was interesting, considering that no such thing can be officially purchased; after all, there is no such country. He gestured, scribbled on a tatter of paper and shouted at me that the only place to purchase the necessary visa was a town 125 miles away, back in Moldova; at least that's what I assumed he was saying. Obviously, this was not the truth and also impossible, as we no longer had a visa to get back into Moldova and there was nowhere to buy them at the control point we had left just a few miles ago. I protested that it was impossible and that he should just let us through. He seemed to understand this and became even angrier than before. He didn't like the idea of someone else trying to tell him how things should be. He was trying to make it appear that he would be doing us a huge favour by letting us travel directly through his country and so was determined to get more money out of us for the favour.

At this point he set his price. $400 (£215) each. This was ridiculous. The average monthly salary in this area was about £16.

I protested my ignorance at what he was demanding and calmly asked if it would be ok for us to leave now. He scribbled $400 again on his scrap of paper and banged his first on the table as he leaned closer towards me. I continued talking at him in English – he didn't understand a word – but even though he was becoming increasingly agitated, the more I spoke to him I noticed him showing the slightest tinge of being open to negotiation. This was going to be a long and drawn out game. I suspect at this point I could have simply offered him $100 (£54) and we'd probably have been on our way, but doing so would only have led to problems down the road as word spread and more bribe-hungry militia decided to try it on. It would also mean I was admitting to having money, and if I was prepared to give away $100 easily he'd probably just take it, then demand more. Gaining my confidence, or rather forgetting the severity of the situation, I decided that we would pay nothing – or at the most, match the $30 of the Moldovan visa. It was a matter of principal. I'd forgotten the Foreign Office warnings; I hadn't been shot, robbed or thrown in a cell yet and was now interested to see how long the guard would keep up his shouting before he considered compromising or backing down. I wondered how Foxy was doing.

I continued to deny that we had any money at all, claiming that all we had were credit cards. Credit cards are useless at border posts as they have no way of using them, but give travellers a credible way of having access to money once through the border. The demands and questioning continued for what seemed like forever. It was going round in circles and going nowhere. I hadn't seen a single person, except for the guard, since I entered the room. Then a soldier came in. The guard's tone changed and for a split second all his anger and threatening behaviour was gone. This was very interesting as it could be an opportunity to make some progress now that he appeared calmer. I tried to speak to this soldier, hoping he could help me out, but didn't get a chance. He clearly wasn't important, was aggressively shouted at for interrupting my interrogation and dismissed. We were alone again and the anger was back.

I was starting to lose track of time and the guard was losing his patience. To be honest so was I, but it was now the principal of the matter that was important to me. I expect he had been hoping for some easy money and was becoming frustrated at the time he had to spend on me. He finally cracked, the mood turned and he suddenly stood up, crashing his machine gun down on the desk between us, grabbed my right shoulder with one hand while swinging his right fist towards my face – after all the warnings we had heard about Transnistria I can't pretend I wasn't worried but strangely, deep in my mind, I didn't think he would hit me. Thankfully, he didn't. Following this he seemed very keen to wind up our 'negotiations' and within thirty minutes or so, eventually settled for giving him $20 (£11) each and two packs of cigarettes. Foxy had said the Marlborough's were going to be useful!

He allowed me to leave the concrete room and go back outside, into the seemingly blinding sunshine, to the buggy where Foxy had been waiting all this time. I returned to the room with the money and cigarettes. Momentarily he demanded more money, but saying 'no' once more was enough for him to give up and let me go. Then, almost as I was out of the room he shouted at me again – one of the packs of cigarettes had two missing, as we had given them away to the window cleaners in Romania. I couldn't be bothered arguing anymore, shrugged and continued walking to the buggy. The deal had been done and we were free to leave.

It transpired that Foxy had been having quite an amicable chat to the guards in the sunshine, eating their sunflower seeds and discussing our journey. I really had got the short straw in this one! Either way, it had been an experience for both of us. I was still very agitated and on edge and neither of us was a great deal happier about the next few hours ahead. These were supposedly the officials, the organised part of the militia we were dealing with. We just hoped that we wouldn't meet any of the true militia that run the interior of Transnistria.

The guards outside appeared reasonably friendly, considering, and moved the barricade to let us pass – although the man who had held me for so long still looked angry and dissatisfied and separated himself from the others.

Foxy told me how the guards had said they have a bet where they take it in turns to see who can extort the most from people passing through the border; my guard had clearly failed miserably. In all fairness, being a border guard is one of the worst military jobs in any part of the world and I suppose they have to do something to entertain themselves – we just didn't know to what lengths they would go to achieve their aims.

In silence we moved forward in the buggy, wondering what lay ahead. We had scarcely moved twenty metres and we were stopped again. This was a beyond a joke. This time we were both taken into a room with several guards. They asked to see our visas. Unbelievable. We had supposedly just bought these from the previous building but, as you would expect from a bribe, I had no proof of this. Losing my patience and keen to be out of this concrete room, I tried to explain that I had just arranged this with the other guard and that I would go back to get him to verify this. I knew this would never happen but it was a chance to waste their time and gave me something to do. It was satisfying to be doing as I wanted, rather than doing as they said, and also got me back in the sunshine. They didn't seem used to having people question them and do anything but exactly what they said.

As I walked back to the first interrogation room I could see my guard watching me. I pointed to my passport and told him to come with me to the other room, to tell the new guards that I had just paid for the visa. The guard was having none of it, gesticulating that he had no idea what I was talking about. As I asked again, his mood clearly changed and he moved towards me, threatening to take me back into his room. I backed off and walked back towards the room where Foxy was, unsure what to do next. I had no intention of spending hours stuck in another room going over the same ground again; equally, I had no desire to pay them off. Then we had the most amazing stroke of luck.

In the queue of cars waiting to come though the border was an English registered Land Rover Discovery. I walked over and knocked on the window to ask if they knew how we could get through the border. They clearly knew something we didn't, as they were actually in the queue and not at the side getting the special treatment. The driver wound down his window and seemed surprised to find an Englishman standing outside. I briefly explained what had happened, and before I could finish, his wife, in the passenger seat, had jumped out of the car and was walking towards me. It transpired that she was from Transnistria and married to Scott, the driver of the Land Rover, and were on their way to Odessa for a holiday together. My story had really angered her and she hurriedly walked me to the room where Foxy was. Inside, she started to reprimand the guards, shouting and pointing at them. She grabbed our passports from them, and dragged us out of the room to the much more official looking counter, where the other cars were queuing. The guards lamely protested at the five foot tall lady who had just embarrassed the group of seven or more guards, all of whom were huge and well in excess of six feet tall. They were clearly going to be getting nothing from us today!

The lady was hugely apologetic about what had happened, explaining that it happened all too often to foreigners and naïve locals alike, and that she hated the way they acted. She presented our passports at the desk, exchanged a few heated words with the officials, and had us entered in the book and registered to enter Transnistria. She even paid the one dollar needed on our behalf, insisting that we not pay her back. She walked us back to our buggy where her husband was now waiting. As we did, we passed the guards again, all looking very hacked-off, but now not willing to come near us. This was the best luck we could ever have hoped for.

We had a chat to Scott and his wife about what we were doing. They wished us the best of luck and we exchanged phone numbers. Before we left they also gave us a warning. Whatever happened we were not to stop. If we had an accident, if the buggy was breaking down or if anyone, official-looking or not, tried to stop us, we were to continue driving. Stopping would, at the least, result in us losing most of our money and possessions, or worse, much worse. They kindly offered to wait until we were a couple of minutes down the road before leaving themselves, should the guards have decided to follow us. We thanked them and after almost seven hours at the border, began our crossing of Transnistria.

Upon returning home, I have since read stories that suggest pushing the guards was not the best idea, as a few people who have angered the Transnistria militia too much have been thrown in 'prison'. Odd, considering prison is something they don't have in Transnistria, and the people have never been seen again. Perhaps deep down they liked us…

At every junction there were heavily armed men waiting and loitering around; occasional armoured vehicles with artillery guns readied beside them. Some wore uniforms; some were dressed in everyday clothes. It really did look like a war-zone; only with traffic and pedestrians milling about on the streets. As we crossed the river Dniester we passed our first militia-run checkpoint – fortunately, they didn't try to stop us, they were busy with other cars, and we continued in silence, leaving the men, their guns, grenades and RPGs behind. For the first time, neither of us had much to say; instead watching the road and the ditches to the side to see what lay in wait.

Throughout the entire journey we had been quite chatty and in good spirits, even in the morning of no sleep heading for Prague, but here we must have barely said a handful of words to each other in the two hours or so it took us to reach the Ukraine border. I would love to describe the region to you but I can't remember myself. I was too preoccupied with the driving and watching the people and traffic for any signs of danger. I have never felt as unsafe and uneasy anywhere in my life – and doubt I ever will again. We hoped this wasn't a sign of the countries to come. This truly was somewhere we neither should have been, nor somewhere we were welcome. That is a bit of a sweeping statement as we only spent two hours inside the border and the only people we met were the rebel guards at the checkpoint, but that's how it felt, and with the militia's presence at every turn, I feel it's justified.

At the exit border, the Transnistrian guards took our passports, while the people who looked like customs guards took our vehicle documents. We tried hard to keep an eye on who had which documents and where they were being taken so that we didn't lose anything. Customs were demanding money for some form of road tax but after twenty minutes of saying we had no money they gave up. The military guard now wanted money for himself but Foxy got the customs man to tell him that we had no money. It eventually worked, and we were out of the region and in the queue for Ukraine. We sent one last text to the couple we had met entering Transnistria – without fail they had been texting us every five or ten minutes to check if we were ok; if we had difficulties they had promised to come to help us straight away – thanking them for their kind support.

All we had to do now was get to the relative safety of Ukraine. It's funny really, considering how our perceptions were changing. Before leaving we had considered Ukraine to be one of the more risky countries, renowned for bandits, corruption and kidnap. Now we considered it the safe option for the night!

The queue was long, but we were happier now and glad to have got through Moldova with no problems. The Ukrainians tried to make us pay a pollution tax – we assumed it to be fictitious – so decided not to pay. We were on a roll from Transnistria and weren't going to cave in here. We took the usual stance of having no money and would be using credit cards for cash, confident our plan would work.

Customs seemed happy with our claims and allowed us to move on to the military check. They, however, weren't so easily convinced and now had our passports. I followed one of the guards as he walked off with our passports while Foxy talked to the guards by the buggy – again insisting we had no money. After a few minutes doing nothing in particular my guard walked back to the buggy as he was failing to get money from me. At this point everything went wrong.

The guards were instructed to start searching the whole buggy in detail. They asked if we had any illegal substances. No. Did we have any drugs? No. Did we have any guns? No. The questions kept coming and coming. This really was starting to get very irritating. We had spent all day stuck at border posts, arguing with guards and travelling nowhere, all because the guards were corrupt and wanted to pocket our money. And I was tired. I idly raised my hands to my shoulder as if I was holding an RPG and jokingly told the guard that all we had was a rocket launcher and to stop wasting our time. For a split second he gave me a very serious look and I really thought I was heading for the cells. Either way, his mood was now very much against us. He really had no sense of humour. Or perhaps he could smell the dollar bills in the door panels of the buggy. It seemed so, as he then asked one of his subordinates who was poking around the inside of the buggy to remove the door linings and there, in full view, was a fat wedge of dollar bills. In all fairness, there wasn't that much there as most were one dollar bills, but it looked a lot, and more importantly we had been caught lying. This could turn very nasty. We had just denied having any money and he had found a couple of hundred dollars in the very first place he looked. By rights I expect he could have taken the lot, stripped the vehicle, found the rest, taken that and arrested us.

We tried explaining that the money wasn't ours and that we were delivering it to sick kids in Mongolia and that was why we were driving through all these countries. We did impressions of sick kids and pointed to the sticker on the buggy trying to make our point understood. There was some truth in it, but it didn't quite wash that we needed to carry the money in person, stuffed in the door linings. He could see the money and he wanted it; still we both got play charades for a while as we tried to get the message across as to who the money was for!

So far at the border crossings we had noticed one thing in common. There seemed to be some kind of code of conduct whereby officials wouldn't actually take money unless we physically gave it them. The guards in Transnistria had many opportunities to take our possessions but only took what we gave. Of equal importance, we had noticed that once you passed one check, they would not stop you again and did not want to see those guards further down the line do better than themselves. Foxy had the idea of getting the customs guard back (to whom we had given nothing) to see if he could get the military guards to let us pass. It worked a treat. The military were told, by customs, to leave us alone and within ten minutes we were free to go. Everyone was more relaxed now and we had a brief chat (remember that neither of us spoke the other's language so as always this was actually two very separate, one-sided conversations, probably about the same things, although we'll never be certain) and established that a couple of other foreigners had passed through this border. We suspect that much of our problems were due to this, as they had no doubt caved in and given bribes, so setting the expectations of the guards (we later learnt that this was indeed the case).

Many of the problems with corruption at the borders are evidently borne of the fact that rich travellers happily hand over bribes, or pay false taxes, either naïvely or to speed up their progress. Once this has been done, it becomes the norm and the guards assume everyone will do the same. At this time, we decided to make a point of not paying anyone. Not just because we're tight, but it would be a challenge to try to beat their system and be very satisfying to do so. We would also get to experience a very different side to the borders – the side that the average person meets – rather than those who simply paid-up, felt ripped off and moved on.

Thankfully, after the huge amount of time we'd spent crossing Moldova, Odessa was not too far into Ukraine and we were soon there. The town was heaving with traffic, much like a city in the UK, and seemed even busier following the isolation we had experienced over the past few days. It was also the main holiday season in a very popular resort and we were having difficulty finding somewhere to stay. Odessa, it turned out, is as popular as any of the main Mediterranean resorts in the summer and we had arrived, without a reservation, in the middle of peak season. We had decided to get a hotel or B&B for the night, just something cheap, in the hope of a shower and a proper bed as a treat before our journey into southern Russia and central Asia, where we were unsure of what we may find. Before long we found a collection of hotels near the shore of the Black Sea, in a very respectable looking area made up of expensive looking mansions, restaurants and hotels with large, well kept, gated grounds. Very much out of the league of two unshaven, un-showered, tired travellers – but we were exhausted and had already spent long enough driving around the streets of Odessa in search of somewhere to stay.

A war memorial, Odessa

We took our chances at one of the hotels but were informed at reception that it was fully booked (or perhaps we just looked too dirty!). They did however suggest we try next door. Again, it was full, but the very helpful girl at the reception hesitated, then suggested that the suite was available if we wanted, as if apologising for offering something that would never be suitable or affordable. Hmmm... this wasn't really what we had had in mind. Out of curiosity, we asked how much it was and when we calculated the exchange rate and realised that the suite was incredibly only around the £10 mark we soon agreed. You can barely pitch a tent in the UK for that much! It was not quite the kind of suite you'd expect back home, with its sixties, communist-era décor but it had a huge bed, bathroom, living room with sofas, various painting and ornaments and two balconies over looking the Black Sea.

Upon our return to the buggy to get our bags, we were met by a man, looking like a security guard, who had been in the hotel car park when we had arrived. Predictably, he asked for some money to 'look after' the buggy. He seemed genuine enough and to not pay could well have led us to return to an empty parking space in the morning. We paid him the one pound he wanted, using the local money we had just acquired from the hotel desk, and went back to the suite for a shower. Later, we dined at an outdoor restaurant with a couple of £0.27 beers and got an early night. It had been an amazing day of worries, excitement and uncertainty and we were shattered.

28th July – Odessa, UA to Mykolayiv, UA

We had a great sleep and still managed make an early start out of Odessa. There were crowds of people on every street corner, again, thumbing for lifts. There was nothing we could do with all the kit in the buggy so we waved courteously. Predictably, no-one waved back. We drove for what seemed like miles along dusty, potholed roads, past row after row of giant, decaying blocks of concrete flats. There were no horses and carts in the city as we had seen in Romania; just battered cars, smoky trucks and old trams jamming the roads.

We soon realised that we had our usual problem of no local money and no petrol. None of the garages would accept dollars or credit cards. Why was nothing simple? In Ukraine, hotel suites are £10, beers are £0.27, smooth roads are priceless and for everything else there's bribery! So much for Visa and MasterCard being accepted the world over.

Luckily we had our own petrol for times like this

We filled up the buggy using our last jerry can of fuel and headed east. The next major town we arrived at was Mykolayiv and we were just slowing down to go over a level crossing at the far side of the town when we noticed a rotary clicking sound over the music. It didn't sound good, but neither did it sound too serious. We turned down the music, drove on and listened harder. The noise was only at low speeds, but clearly changed pitch with the speed of the buggy. We stopped and checked everything we could. I even drove slowly with Foxy running alongside so that he could listen underneath. We decided to carry on to the next town and by now had determined that the noise changed with the speed of the engine, not the buggy, so must be related to the engine or gearbox. That really was not a good sign. We speculated over what the problem may be, and the more we thought, the more terminal our ideas became. It was time for some professional advice.

We pulled over at a tin-pot garage on the edge of the first village we came to. I had no idea where to start with the man we found. The garage looked suitable, well, they had an engine block in pieces on the floor so he obviously worked on cars, but I found it impossible to communicate with the owner. I got him to listen to the engine, I pointed and gesticulated but he was very disinterested and I was getting nowhere. I should have expected nothing less, after all, I was in his country and didn't speak a word of his language so shouldn't have hoped for anything more, but you always do. He pointed back along the road we had just come down. We looked at the map and Foxy convinced me that it would be best to follow the mechanic's finger and head the 12 miles back to Mykolayiv. Once again, we were forced to retrace the route we had just come. Obviously, I was not delighted by this.

On the way back to Mykolayiv the noise became louder and louder. By now the buggy sounded to be terminally sick. We started to speculate further, to the extent that we even discussed what we could do for the next three weeks, should this prove to be the end of our buggy and our adventure.

Mykolayiv, just to the northwest of The Republic of Crimea, was much like any other eastern European town, with street after street of crumbling concrete apartments and featureless roads. We headed down the biggest road we could find, aiming roughly for the town centre. We pulled into the first garage we spotted and had the mechanic listen to the noise. He shook his head. We weren't sure if it was a problem he couldn't fix, or a problem that couldn't be fixed. Either way, it wasn't good. The mechanic then walked Foxy across the road to another garage where the mechanic knew a word or two of English, He directed us down the road to yet another garage. Apparently we wouldn't be able to miss it. We hoped so.

We crawled off down the road, waiting for the buggy to come to a final stop, the noise getting worse by the minute. About half a mile down the road we came to a brand new garage. It was big enough to almost be a superstore and looked like the chain garages we get in the UK. It was very modern and completely out of place in Ukraine. It also looked like the kind of place that would swap tyres, batteries and do general servicing – not major engine work. We didn't have much hope but tried all the same as they would hopefully be able to point us in the right direction.

As we pulled in to the forecourt, a group of mechanics were having a cigarette break in the shade so I pulled up alongside them and asked if they could help. Break-time is never a good time to ask for help and Ukrainian workers are no exception. I hopped out of the buggy to try and get some enthusiasm from them and gradually they moved round the buggy to take a look. To be honest, I think they were more interested in the stickers and race car appearance of the buggy than trying to fix it and still we were getting nowhere.

Then, a car pulled up onto the forecourt and a man jumped out and came across to look at the buggy. He seemed smarter and had an air of authority about him. Most importantly, he spoke broken English. Perhaps we were in luck. We explained the problem and drove the buggy back and forth so they could listen. Within five minutes they had decided, with some conviction, that the problem was the gearbox bearings. This really was bad. We were at a garage that wasn't suited to dismantling engines and gearboxes and we needed to get this done. More pressingly, we needed some Suzuki bearings from somewhere to complete the job. I started thinking about calling home to get the number of the man we had bought the buggy from, to see if he had any spares he could ship across. What I hadn't banked on was the resourcefulness and willing of the Ukrainians.

While these thoughts were going through my mind, the man who had pulled up in the car was ordering the mechanics about and having another car removed from one of the ramps, so that the buggy could be worked on. The other car was halfway through having the work completed on it, but that didn't seem to matter. All the mechanics seemed very subservient to him and there was a definite urgency about them, something I've never seen before at a garage and certainly not in the UK. At this point a smart man from inside the garage offices (I assumed he was the manager) came out to see what was going on, and began to stop the mechanics from removing the other car from the ramps. He couldn't understand why we were jumping the queue. The man who had been helping us walked over and exchanged some sharp words with the manager. Our fixer clearly had some kind of influence, although he appeared not to work for the garage. Soon the buggy was on the ramps being inspected. Within moments, they were draining the still-hot oil from the sump and while we watched on we could see slivers of metal flowing out of the gearbox in the oil. Then there was a clunk as a chunk of metal dropped into the bucket. Swilling the oil around we could easily make out chippings from the teeth of the gears and a short metal pin. This was serious and more than just bearings.

The repairs start, Mykolayiv

Our fixer was now on his mobile calling people and clearly trying to organise something, while continually telling the mechanics what to do and what to check. Soon enough he turned back to us and asked what year and engine size the buggy was (we sheepishly admitted that our 'race car' was just one litre, although he took some convincing of this!). More phone calls. He finished off and informed us that his friend could get some bearings but they would be €20 (£13) and we would have to wait until the morning. We couldn't believe it. In the UK to get a gearbox rebuilt could take days, even a week or so, and you would certainly have to book in advance, yet here we were, unable to speak the language, jumping the queue and within an hour or so, the parts had been sourced and the job was underway. We were still a bit dubious as to how he could be so sure it was the bearings, considering he wasn't a mechanic and hadn't even seen inside the gearbox (and that gear teeth were visible in the oil) but we were in no position to argue as we knew no better; we needed all the help we could get.

We were now left with the problem as to what to do with ourselves for the rest of the afternoon and the night; and we hadn't eaten all day except for a few dried crouton-like biscuits. As if on queue, a lady walked towards us from the street selling huge muffins. We didn't have a chance to buy them ourselves as our fixer must have sensed our hunger, got his roll of money out and had bought two for us. They were lovely, very sweet with a strange flavour. We tried to work it out for a while, but in the end had to ask. Opium we were told. Interesting. Apparently, the muffins were filled with the leftover opium seeds, once the oil had been pressed from them, and used by the street sellers to flavour their baking. Whatever the story was, they tasted great.

At this point our fixer's phone rang and he said he had to go but would be back later, and with that he drove off. It looked like we would have to wait at the garage until he returned. While he was gone we lazed in the sunshine chatting about how strange this guy was, and the way he seemed to have come from nowhere and yet have control over everyone at the garage – where he didn't appear to even work. Our conversation turned straight to the Mafia.

We had heard that there was a strong Mafia presence in Ukraine and how they look after businesses or run extortion rackets; the more we thought about it, the more this person fitted the bill perfectly. We weren't sure whether meeting him was a good thing or something to be deeply suspicious of. Deep down we hoped to spend the night as his guests with his family at some extravagant dinner – in future I'll learn to be more careful what I wish for. Anyway, it hadn't been our choice to meet him, it was too late now, and at least the buggy appeared to be being fixed. We'd just have to lie on the grass, wait for him to return and see how things panned out.

It was probably the uncertainly of not knowing what was going on and the situation being under someone else's control, but we seemed to wait for hours. The buggy was still on the ramps but no work was being done on it. We took a look around the garage to kill some time. It had six ramps, all with cars being worked on, modern extraction systems for exhaust fumes and huge tool chests. There was a large shop selling everything from barbeques, soft toys and chillers to wheels, radiators and lorry brake systems. They had everything. There was even a lady employed to continually walk around the workshop with a large squeegee-mop cleaning up any oils or fluids the moment they spilt. It was all immaculate. The only garage I have ever seen anywhere near as clean and organised had been in the pits of a Formula One race team. It really didn't fit in with the other garages or buildings we had seen in eastern Europe.

By mid-afternoon our fixer returned (we had now learnt that his name was Sasha) with an older couple in another car, and I'm really not making this up, but they were Italian. This wasn't doing anything to alleviate our suspicions and we smiled politely as we were introduced and shook their hands. Sasha hadn't, as we had optimistically hoped, returned with any bearings. Instead, he insisted that he would have them by the morning, or possibly the morning after (which sounded a bit strange considering that that would be Sunday morning) – either way he told us to get into the car with the Italians as he had somewhere we could stay for the night.

We really didn't want to leave the buggy behind; it seemed to give us some kind of security, and all our possessions, wallets, money and passports were in it, but Sasha was in a hurry and insisted we get in the car with him and the Italians. With that, we were driven through endless, high-rise concrete apartments. We tried to make conversation but it was hard given our limited knowledge of each others languages and the fact that Foxy and I were continually exchanging worried glances. We were trying to figure out just where we were being taken and what might happen when we get there. We've seen too many films where bad things happen to people in situations like this, and all we had to get ourselves out of it was a mobile phone that could send and receive text messages. Not very helpful in an emergency.

As we turned off the main road, our Italian driver swerved from one side of the road to the next. Looking out from the back seats we could see why. None of the manholes in the road had their metal covers; they were just great big gaping holes into the ground. Sasha realised what we were looking at and explained that they had been stolen as they are valuable once melted down – he then warned us to be careful when driving in Ukraine; thanks Sasha!

We went along a few more streets of huge, identical, decrepit concrete apartment blocks before stopping outside one. Surely we weren't staying here! A lady appeared from across the road and gave a key to Sasha. He took a huge roll of dollars, mostly hundred dollar bills, from his pocket and paid the lady a few dollars, she then disappeared. This was an incredible amount of money for someone in Ukraine, in fact it's much more than most people would carry anywhere in the world. We all went up the stairs, through the huge iron doors – much like you would see in a prison or on a bank vault – and into the apartment, behind two more huge doors, each requiring a gigantic six inch long key. This really was tuning into a surreal experience.

Foxy checks out the front door to our accommodation

The inside of the apartment was even more dated than the suite back at the hotel. It was perfectly clean but just looked as if there had been no work or decoration on it in the past forty or fifty years. It could have been part of a living museum. We had a bedroom, bathroom, kitchen and lounge and it would all be ours for the night – not quite staying with the Mafia, but not far off. We must have looked underwhelmed by the place, as Sasha asked if it was ok. Partly through not wanting to offend, and partly as we had no alternative, we said it was perfect. He hesitated as if he thought we were expecting more, and humbly offered us somewhere else if we'd rather; we had no idea what the other place would be, so agreed to stay with this one – though we would need a GPS to find our way back to it through the featureless streets and concrete apartments blocks. There was nothing of any architectural interest and everything looked the same.

Our accommodation for the night, Mykolayiv

Sasha showed us around the kitchen and told us of a market just around the corner where we could buy food, should we want to cook – he soon realised that we weren't up for this idea and quickly told of us a pizzeria around the corner – not that we had any money with us. He was about to leave but we insisted this time that we needed our bags. Ukraine is not the sort of place to be without ID or money, and we didn't want to risk losing everything we had. With that, we all piled back into the car and, thankfully, headed back to the garage and our possessions. Perhaps this wouldn't be as bad as we were thinking.

Back at the garage, we were pleased to see the buggy was busily being worked on again and appeared to have become a priority for the whole garage. Again, Sasha seemed to be in a hurry, so we only had chance to grab our money, passports and a few bits of clothing for the night – most of our kit was strewn around the buggy and couldn't be packed up in time. He got us into the car with the Italians and off we went. Sasha remained at the garage with our buggy. Close to our apartment, we passed a military barracks full of armed recruits and again wondered how safe this place really was. We were dropped off and left to our own devices – though not before being warned not to be 'showy' with our possessions. Nice. Inside the apartment, we rested on the sofas and drank some of our water, unsure of what to do next. We locked the windows.

It was just before 17:00 and we had just about decided to venture out for a walk around when there was a knock at the door. Reluctantly, we unlocked the door and there was Sasha. He came in and explained that the bearings needed replacing and that the clutch was worn out. We had half expected this, as when we had bought the buggy we had been advised to have the clutch checked out. As such, we had got a sponsor to donate a race-spec replacement, which we had stashed under the driver's seat just in case. We tried to explain that we had one, using actions to show him where it was. It was a funny few minutes then it clicked. He was straight on the phone to the garage to tell the mechanics where to find it and to get it fitted for us. The whole job would be about £80-£110, and thankfully, he was quoting us in dollars to make things easy. This guy was brilliant. He then reached into his pocked and pulled out a short, fat, metal pin – a bit like a roller-bearing. He explained that it had been found in the gearbox oil but that all the bearings in the gearbox were ball-bearings. He pointed as if it had come from the sky into the gearbox and pulled funny faces of confusion. It was unbelievable, but obvious where it had come from. When we had test driven the buggy, on the day we bought it, there had been no centralising spring on the gearstick as – we were told – the locating pin had fallen out. The guy selling us the buggy fitted a new one, but neglected to look for the old one. During our journey it had managed to find its way down the cowling from the gearstick, through the clutch and into the gearbox. It was this pin that we had been able to hear making the ticking sound as it minced its way through the gearbox, bouncing off the teeth of the gears as it went. We were lucky it hadn't destroyed the whole gearbox. Apparently, it had only chipped a few of the teeth which would be repairable.

Sasha gave us his phone number and said he would collect us in the morning. As he was about to leave, he looked apologetic and explained that this evening he had to entertain his 'comrades' (comrades being very different to friends as he explained at length) at a party and wouldn't be able to take us out, but pointed us in the direction of a local bar a couple of streets away. He asked if we had everything we needed which we said we had. He then stopped and paused, clearly having forgotten something and turned back and asked if we liked girls. We weren't too sure where this was leading but said yes. Then, as if it were the most normal thing in the world, he asked how many we would like for the night, as he would have some sent over later on. Apparently they would be very attractive and friendly. We declined.

We soon got bored of the apartment and did the only sensible thing two English people would do in this situation. We went in search of the bar. We left the safety of our apartment and, with the huge keys hidden away in our pockets, ventured into the suburbs of a very rough looking part of an Ukrainian town, while trying to look as Ukrainian as we possibly could. After only a few minutes walk we came to a collection of roadside bars, which were nothing more than a large fridge full of beers with a marquee over them and a few plastic seats. Overlooking them was an old Soviet tank, now forming part of a monument. Everywhere there were memories and memorials to the old Soviet rule. The bars may have been simple but they were perfect following the day we had had. More importantly the beer was only £0.35 a bottle, was ice cold and tasted great. We got some crouton-like nibbles and watched the world go by.

It's about time I discussed the girls. Now I'm not especially lecherous, but having seen the girls while crossing eastern Europe where they are renowned for being attractive, it was a surprise to find the girls in Ukraine to be quite simply in a different league. The girls in Prague had been exceptionally pretty but the girls in Ukraine were simply stunning. Walking down every street, in every queue at the tram stops, in fact everywhere you looked, there would be at least one girl who you could be forgiven for thinking was a model. The years of communist rule have led to the men wearing 1980's shell-suits, but the girls have embraced the modern fashions and most look like they have stepped off the catwalk. We weren't complaining.

Before we had finished our second beer, Foxy's phone rang and it was Sasha inviting us to the pizzeria for drinks and some food. Things were looking up. He was just around the corner so we finished our drinks and went to see him. He seemed very happy to see us, and got us some more beers while we chatted as best we could. He loved trying to use his English, which, to his credit, was actually quite good. He talked to us about his life, scrapes he had been in, and what it was like living in Ukraine – and the girls. We tried to find out more about his work but every time he skirted around the subject, but he did seem to have his fingers in many pies and often referred to the Mafia and the Costa Nostra. He also seemed very well connected.

After a while he suggested that we get some food so took us up to the counter to order. We had no idea what anything was but, pizza being pizza, couldn't really care less. By now we were starving as all we had eaten all day were nibbles and opium-laced muffins. Sadly, not been specific was not good enough for Sasha. He barked at the poor boy behind the counter and before long he had brought out every possible ingredient from the kitchen and had them lined up along the counter for us to choose from. We returned to our seats with more beers and chatted to Sasha in between his frequent phone calls.

At about 19:30 Sasha had to leave to go to the party he was hosting, advised us to be careful, to have a great night and to call him should we need anything. He once again offered us some hookers; almost as if he thought we were just being polite when we declined the first time, but we again declined. He seemed surprised, almost confused. We headed back to the collection of bars we had been at earlier. Feeling a lot more happy and confident with our situation, and our new friend, we got some more beers and sat down at one of the few remaining tables. We were clearly the only non-locals in the bar but felt welcome enough. Then we had a problem.

Being a street-side bar, there were no toilets. We did however notice a steady stream of people from the bars walking across the square towards the market, and returning soon after. It had to be the toilets so off I went. Unfortunately, once inside the market, the person I had chosen to follow decided to go shopping; just my luck. I went back outside, watched for the next person coming from the bars and followed them. This time it worked and I found a toilet at the far corner of the market. I queued up, managing not to blow my cover of being foreign by not speaking to anyone (this really was a very local place and I had no idea how they would take to foreigners; my cynicism taking over again). Then everything went wrong at the front of the queue when I was expected to pay a few pence. I hadn't brought any money with me so tried to blag my way through, but the attendant didn't understand a word of English and wasn't keen to let me in. Fortunately, the girl behind me realised my problem, understood a little English and spoke to the attendant, who reluctantly let me in.

Back at the bar, it was apparent that the group of four at the table next to us were talking about us, and I realised it was the girl who had rescued me at the toilets. They were fascinated as to why we were in Mykolayiv and what we were doing. We joined them and soon found ourselves drinking vodka with them. Being Ukraine, this involved very large, neat shots with a sip of fruit juice allowed to wash it down. We both realised that we were going to either have to leave, or get very drunk. We decided not to shun their hospitality and drank with them. After all, it could only be good for international relations.

We finished the rest of the bottle of vodka and moved onto the second. It should be noted here that these were full sized bottles and we're nowhere near as used to drinking vodka as our Ukrainian friends, but obviously we did our best. The banter got better and it was surprising how much English they understood and we were soon needed a third bottle. I was taken by the girl, Natasha, to a shop up the road where we could apparently get cheaper vodka than at the bar, leaving Foxy behind with the guys.

Buying more vodka with Natasha, Mykolayiv

At the shop I ended up paying for the vodka but at under £1.50 a bottle I was hardly bothered. Natasha was lovely and very friendly and we chatted for a while as we wandered along the street. We'd been gone for a while and when we got back to the bar one of the guys was quite agitated that we'd been away so long. So, Natasha got angry back at him while continuing to chat to me. Foxy also seemed to have lost his trust in the guys and it turned out that while I had been gone, one of them had threatened him because I'd gone off alone with Natasha. The tension remained for a while but soon enough that guy left, leaving the rest of us to enjoy ourselves again.

Drinking with the locals, Mykolayiv

We continued chatting, drinking, discussing our respective countries, life and drinking customs. After some time they suggested we go to a club with them. It was a great idea. We had nothing to do the next day with the buggy stuck in the garage, but there was a catch. They would pay for the taxi if we paid the entry to the club – and they said it was $20 (£11) each! That was a crazy amount to get into a club in Ukraine and we immediately suspected it was a scam. We thought of reasons why we no longer wanted to go, continuing to drink the vodka while we thought. Eventually, we made our excuses, said our goodbyes and staggered back to our apartment – which amazingly we managed to find without falling down any open manholes, getting lost or kidnapped.

It had been an unbelievable day and incredible to find everyone so hospitable and friendly. We really hadn't expected this in Ukraine, especially after the reception we had had only a hundred miles away back in Transnistria.

Back at the flat Foxy made a long, drunken phone call home; the cost of which he would regret later. We finally got to bed in the early morning, very drunk and knowing that we'd be in no fit state to meet Sasha in the morning – whatever time he might arrive!

29th July – Mykolayiv, UA to Mariupol, UA

We woke up just before 08:00, still completely and utterly intoxicated, and showered to make sure we were at least partially ready for Sasha's arrival. We both seemed to have huge blanks about what happened last night so we laid in the apartment and used the camera and each others memories to piece together the night before. The more we looked back, the more we realised how paranoid we were throughout the entire trip; thinking that everyone was out to rip us off or take advantage of us. The only people doing this so far were the border guards – the people we had met away from the borders had all been incredibly welcoming and hospitable – the only atmosphere was the one our imaginations were creating. Even so, we still remained very sceptical of the locals and the people we would meet as we went further from home. It was ingrained into us and small things, like the invite to the nightclub last night, were doing nothing to help. However, the more we thought about the night before, the more we laughed, and the more surreal it all seemed. We were staying with the Mafia, had a buggy that may never work again, in a small industrial Ukrainian town, unable to speak a word of the language, and with no idea what would happen next. Then the vodka caught up with us again, we both had a relapse and nodded off.

Foxy's phone bleeped. It was a text from Sasha who was waiting outside, in a taxi. Apparently, he had also had a heavy night on the vodka after he left us, so had wisely left his car at home. Bizarrely, he was now using a taxi as his private transport for the day. We had our packed bags with us, in the optimistic hope we would be reunited with a working buggy later in the day, but Sasha said to leave them. It was just after 09:30 when we got back to the garage and we were feeling seriously rough. So was Sasha, he could see we were suffering and immediately put two and two together and asked how we had liked the locals and the vodka. He ushered us across to the coffee machine and bought strong, black coffees for all of us which we drank in the cool of the air conditioned shop while we recounted the previous night and swapped stories.

The buggy was still on the ramps being frantically worked on and it was promising to see our new clutch was now in place. Sadly, the gearbox looked to be in a sorry state.

Major gearbox repairs, Mykolayiv

It was neatly laid out across an immaculate stainless steel workbench and the damaged teeth were clearly visible, as was the wear to the clutch plates. With both of us having an interest in engineering, we couldn't resist the opportunity to fiddle with the gears, bearings and shafts to see how they all worked and fitted together. Strangely, the bearings all felt fine. Sasha must have been watching this as he came over and picked up two of the bearings which he claimed were worn and demonstrated this to us. They felt fine, but we didn't want to offend him so nodded knowingly when he showed us. The teeth looked bad but he assured us that the mechanics would be able to fix, rather than replace them. The only problem now was that the new bearings hadn't arrived.

We needed something to occupy ourselves, and our hangovers, so got the tents out of the buggy to dry. It was already baking hot in the sunshine and the tents were still soaking wet from the early morning dew in Romania. We soon tired of this so went for a walk. Nothing was very appealing this morning. On the main road we came to a bustling market. It was teeming with locals; all scurrying about buying hardware for home building or improvements. The market must have had over a hundred individual shops, each selling a range of products from copper piping and baths to tiles and huge blocks of insulation. It was like a collection of mini B&Qs all selling the same goods and all next door to one another. And it was so cheap. Our thoughts turned to home and how we had to enter the 'real world' when we got back and start careers. Soon we were discussing how the way forward would actually be to restore houses using products from Ukraine. We even started to cost things and it all got quite serious. Then our thoughts turned back to reality, our hangovers, and the fact that we were stuck in a virtually unknown town, miles from home, still unsure if the buggy would be fixed today – or fixed at all. We went back to the garage to check on the progress.

The cleaning lady was having a field day; mopping up fluids from under our bleeding buggy and then chasing us around as we unwittingly stepped in pools of liquid and traipsed the mess around the garage. We apologised but she didn't seem to care – she was just happy to be mopping. Sasha joined us and seemed keen to show us around the shop. He took great pride in showing us all the parts they stocked and comparing the brands to those we had back in the UK. Many were the same or made by familiar manufacturers but re-branded while still using the original logo. He was very keen to learn the names of each of the parts and then tell us the Ukrainian version. It passed the time, doing actions and making sounds to describe the parts; we must have been in the shop for well over an hour.

It was now lunchtime and outside the mechanics were sitting in the sun eating their sandwiches. We wandered out and chatted to a couple of the younger ones who had learnt English at school and knew enough that we could have a broken conversation. They all appeared to be proud to work at this garage and much more dedicated than any mechanic I've ever met before. The talk moved to Ukraine, Russia, money and lifestyles. The mechanics earned about £160 a month at the garage, which we worked out, albeit very roughly, makes them no worse off than someone in the UK doing a similar job, when taking into account the differences in the cost of living between the two countries. In fact, given the cost of living – which we based on the cost of beer, fuel and pizza, might even make them better off. Perhaps not as accurate as other economic studies in this field but we were happy with the results.

We still had a hangover and had resorted to eating slices of the chorizo we had brought from England – the same chorizo we ate throughout the journey when things got dull – and some local peaches. Annoyingly, the peaches were now starting to attract giant wasps that we had to fend off. They really had no consideration for our 'delicate' situation. In an effort to get some peace, we left the peach stones and a chunk of chorizo at the far side of the car park to tempt them away and returned to dozing in the sun.

It was mid-afternoon and from time to time we wandered back into the garage to see the progress on the buggy. It was slow, and the mechanics seemed happier that we keep our noses out. Thankfully,

Sasha came back with the bearings. We thought this would be the catalyst to get the buggy back on the road in no time. Instead, he told us to get in his car, which he was using again in favour of the taxi. We had no idea where we were going, but he was smiling and seemed eager to go somewhere. Who were we to question him?

We drove from garage to garage, some were tiny ramshackle efforts and another was the BMW main dealer. At every one boxes were exchanged, rolls of cash swapped about, hands shaken and us, the Englishmen, pointed at. It was almost as if we were some kind of trophy he was showing off. At the final place we stopped at we saw one of the cars from the forecourt of the BMW dealership, now being worked on at a backstreet garage. It was all very odd, but was no doubt making money for all those involved. By this point we had been on the road for an hour or two, had been gifted a water melon and probably seen most of the garages in Mykolayiv. The driving was incredibly erratic, avoiding open manholes, huge potholes, rutted tram tracks and areas where there was no road at all – none of this mattered to Sasha as he tried to drive as fast as possible, darting from one side of the road to the other. As if this wasn't enough, every attractive girl he saw he kindly pointed out to us, almost turning around in the drivers seat to make sure we had seen, and believe me, there were a lot. It really was the kind of tourist trip you wouldn't get anywhere else. We drove past the bar we had spent the previous night, and Sasha seemed to approve, then on to the apartment to collect our bags. Our hopes lifted; it finally looked as if we would be leaving today.

Back at the garage the mechanics had the gearbox back under the buggy but were struggling to align it with the clutch. Thankfully, this was only a minor problem and the moment of truth arrived when the buggy was wheeled out of the garage for us to test. There had also been issues with the bearings – which were probably not a Suzuki part – but they too had been persuaded to fit. We were warned it would be noisy due to the damaged gears, but now that they had been fettled, should more than strong enough to get us to Mongolia. It was a huge relief that the buggy worked again, though with a strange clicking sound from the chipped gears. The new clutch was amazing (compared to the worn-out standard one that had been removed) and had a great feel – which it should have given that it was a full racing version!

Now all we had to do was pay.

Understandably, we didn't have enough Ukrainian money to cover this, as we had only intended to be in transit through Ukraine for a couple of days. We offered to pay by credit card but this was immediately dismissed. The deal was that part of the money was to go through the business, part to the mechanics as a bonus / beer money and another wedge to Sasha for his 'bearings'. It was all very dodgy, and we were paying much more than a local would, but we had a working buggy and had received the best service I have ever had, or expect I ever will, from a garage.

We spent some time explaining that the problem was not that we thought they were charging too much, rather that we had no other way to pay. After a while, it was decided that we would put the garage part of the bill through on a credit card and pay the mechanics and Sasha in dollars. Prices were discussed in Ukrainian Hryvnia's, converted to euros and then to dollars. It all worked very favourably for us, as inaccurate rates were used, and in the end we had to put $140 (£75) through the business, $40 (£21) to the mechanics and $30 (£16) to Sasha – all quoted in dollars. Amazing, considering we had had the full use of a crack-team of mechanics for two days, an apartment for the night and our personal city guide; in the UK the basic use of a mechanic would be about £30 per hour with none of the extras, consideration or care.

Annoyingly, the till wouldn't accept any of our credit or debit cards. We suspected it was a cunning trick so we had to pay with cash. Again we opened up the buggy to get the stashes of dollars out – to the amazement of the onlooking mechanics, who had no idea the buggy they'd been working on had been stuffed with wads of cash, and began counting it out.

We said our goodbyes and were finally ready to leave Mykolayiv and continue our journey. It had been an unexpected scare when the gearbox had given up, but had turned into an amazing and unbelievable stay in a town I doubt many English people have ever passed though, let alone visited. And the people had been genuinely helpful and incredibly kind towards us.

Sasha on the left, Foxy third from the left

We headed back out of town, trying to remember the way we had entered the previous day, passing row after row of identical, crumbling apartments. None of the petrol stations we passed appeared to accept credit cards and we were, as usual, worryingly low on petrol. We started to get desperate and began pulling into every petrol station we passed, waving our cards in the hope one would accept them. They didn't. Eventually, one gave us a lead to a garage down the road who would take cards. We found it, checked the situation with the cards and got them to fill up everything. At least by doing this we would have plenty of fuel – even if it did mean that we risked the wrath of customs at the next border. So far, customs had had a habit of checking the jerry cans; presumably in the hope of finding some fuel so that they could 'fine' us for importation costs.

I went inside, grabbed some ice-cold Coke and some crisps. By now the hangover had passed, we were starving and would have a long day of driving ahead of us, to make up for the time we had lost. Except the card wasn't working. We tried again. Foxy tried his cards. Nothing worked. We would later learn that the good old HSBC had frozen our cards due to 'suspicious transactions'! Now I'm all in favour of card security, but I cannot begin to describe how painfully irritating this was for us after such a long delay already and having had no warning of this. So much for being the world's local bank…

No-one spoke any English and it was clear they were getting annoyed that we couldn't pay for our bulk purchase, and the security guard was taking more than a passing interest. We had to move the buggy out of the way while we continued trying the cards and the assistant phoned the bank. They had no interest in taking dollars – which is fair as I assume the Shell garage down the road from me at home won't take Ukrainian Hryvnia's – but after about forty minutes one of the assistants seemed to have a plan. She walked me to the buggy and was about to hop in the drivers seat – then realised we had the steering wheel on the opposite side to that which they have – then moved to the passenger's side. We were off to the bank. She found our Russian phrase book on the seat, and took great delight in trying to direct me in English. A couple of miles down the road we came to a Western Union bank. I tried my cash card while the assistant was explaining what was going on to the clerk – or possibly having me blacklisted as a potential con-man. The card didn't work and nor did the credit card; I wouldn't have bothered trying them, had I known they were frozen. I decided to go back to the buggy and got some dollars from inside the doors. Obviously the petrol station assistant now thought I was trying to do a runner and scurried after me. She watched on in amazement as I pulled the huge wedge of dollar bills from the door. Now we really did look dodgy. She found the whole situation hilarious, and was in hysterics of laughter, pretending to cover her eyes to avoid watching what was going on. With the money changed, we headed back to the petrol station, following her English directions. I missed the last turn and, realising what I had done, tried to make a u-turn. She went crazy. Apparently, it's highly illegal to do a u-turn across a main road. Ah well, at least I knew now. Between us we had made loads in the previous few days and, admittedly, continued to make them in the following days. We had no choice with the useless signage and maps we were using.

Back at the petrol station, I swapped the now warm Coke for some fresh, cold Coke. While doing this I noticed that vodka was only £1.60 a litre, only ten or eleven times more expensive than water. No wonder they drink so much! Everyone at the petrol station seemed much happier now; I paid, tipped and left. Except Foxy was now missing. No-one seemed to know what I was asking, or who I was looking for. I was starting to think that everything that could go wrong today would, when I spotted him, sleeping in the sun across the forecourt. It was just after four in the afternoon when we finally left town, heading for the Russian border with the intention of camping up on the Ukrainian side, ready to cross early in the morning.

The landscape was incredibly flat and monotonous as we crossed mile after mile of farmland where they were growing all kinds of crops. To try and get some perspective on the landscape, I measured one of the straights and it came out at just over twenty-six miles without even the slightest hint of a curve.

Random Ukrainian monuments

The roads were very quiet and free of traffic, yet every couple of miles there would be people on the roadside selling huge melons and other equally oversized fruits. We passed a military base with loads of helicopters parked up and took the chance for a short break and to take a few photos. There really was very little to see in this part of Ukraine, so we were making good time, but as we set off again we were immediately pulled by the police. We thought back to the photos but there was nothing we could do now. Luckily, they hadn't seen us doing that and were really kind to us. They just checked our papers, we asked if we were on the right road and off we went, job done.

With so few towns and straight roads we were able to cruise at about 65mph. We were actually managing to overtake some cars – although most of the cars on the roads were ancient Ladas so it was hardly surprising or anything to be proud of.

The flatness of Ukraine

As we got nearer the border, the roads became much worse. They were still quite smooth, but littered with potholes up to twelve inches deep which we had to be on the constant look out for. The police checks also became much more frequent, getting stopped every few miles for nothing more than to check our papers. In one of the villages near the border we used the remainder of our Ukrainian Hryvnia's to top up the buggy with petrol as there was no point taking the cash with us.

We got to the border at 00:30 and decided to try and get through rather than camp and wait for the morning. As we queued up, a random woman asked us for our buggy's documents which we immediately thought was a scam. She had no ID, so after some heated words we managed to get rid of her and continued queuing.

30th July – Mariupol, UA to Volgograd, RU

While we waited in the queue we chatted to the occasional official who wandered by. Drawing in the dust on the buggy's windows had become the perfect way of communication with the curious locals and demanding officials. By doing this, we managed to establish that three rally cars had crossed the border about three hours ahead of us. Hopefully they'd got through without too much hassle and we'd be able to do the same.

At the Ukrainian exit check they found that we had four bottles of beer and several packs of cigarettes in the back of the buggy. One of the guards lamely tried to arrest us by pointing at us and shouting 'arresty! arresty!' to his colleagues, who were looking on. We saw straight though this and he was disappointed that we weren't taking him seriously, however loudly he shouted, so instead he demanded dollars or he would continue to try and 'arresty' us. We said no. He wasn't a patch on the guards in Transnistria and soon gave up, realising that he was onto a loser with us and was also losing face in front of his colleagues. If the midges were annoying him as much as they were me, he was probably glad to be rid of us and back in his hut. It had taken a while but we were now out of Ukraine and into the queue between Ukraine and Russia. We could see Russia. While planning the journey this had, in my mind, marked the point where I would really feel to be a long way from home and heading into a country very different to anywhere I had travelled before. Considering the things we'd seen in the past few days, I began to wonder how much stranger things could realistically become.

The queue, in no-man's land between Ukraine and Russia, was painfully slow. There didn't appear to be anything corrupt going on, just a series of very slow processes, but this was all ahead of us. We were still too far back in the queue to be doing anything towards getting through the border, so to kill some time we went for a walk, making sure to lock the buggy before leaving it.

We had noticed at all the border crossings that there was always a large amount of people drifting around, either trying to sell products or currency or just walking about as if they had nowhere better to be. We didn't trust them. None of the border towns or crossing points were the kind of place you would want to spend any more time than you had to, and we never felt particularly happy at any of them. Everyone was looking for some way to profit from the people passing through, and we were always their prime target with our sponsor-covered buggy looking very race-car-like. We looked much wealthier than two students in a £500 buggy on a mini adventure. But then all things are relative.

We got to the front of the queue and could see into the Russian compound where the officials were doing their checks and stamping papers. Worryingly, we could also see the three Minis that we'd been told were three hours ahead of us. Either this was the slowest moving queue we had come across yet, or the Minis were in trouble. We were going to be in for a very long, sleepless night trying to get into Russia – if they let us in at all.

After a while, we saw the owners of the Minis walking between the border huts and shouted across to them for a chat through the barbed wire. Things weren't looking good. They had been parked up, right where we could see them, for over six hours already, and they were still going through the processes to gain entry to Russia. They had paid the lady – the same one we had dismissed a few metres back on the Ukrainian side – and been issued some form of car insurance for £30. It all looked official and we would certainly need some from somewhere, but there was no way we could get back out of no-man's land to her now, even though she was only metres away. Worse news was that the guys didn't think we would be able to buy any until the huts opened again in the morning.

All along the side of the compound where the Minis were being held, was a collection of wooden huts with signs outside. We assumed these were there to sell insurance to motorists but, it now being almost 02:00 in the morning, none were open. We didn't want to be stuck at the border until they reopened, equally, with the speed the Minis were moving, it could well have been the case that we were still there when they did open. There was nothing we could do about it now, so there was no point worrying.

The guys had also paid a few small fees in the various huts, where they had had to get a form, pay for it, get it stamped, and then take it to the next hut where the process started all over. So far they had each paid £14 doing this. They all appeared very tired, stressed and irritable with the Russians, and to us it was evident that this was not helping their progress through the border. We both noticed this and decided to try to be as friendly and smiley as possible, whatever happened, in the hope we could get through faster.

We left them to it and went back to the buggy to eat some chorizo. For some reason, this had become our treat and it always seemed to make things better. It may sound pathetic now but it was great at the time.

The queue seemed to be moving faster than we had first thought. It could have been the impending challenge of getting through in less time than the Minis, or the fact that we were on the road again with a working buggy, but we seemed happy again and time was flying by. Finally we were allowed inside the Russian compound and had to go to each of the huts in turn, directed by stern looking Russian military personnel with huge-rimmed hats and equally huge guns. Obviously, at this point we still had no Russian money and played the usual trick in the huts; when asked for money, saying we only had credit cards. We were careful to do this only once we had completed the forms and had them signed and stamped, as by then it would be a waste of everyone's time to bin them. Surely somewhere as major as a Russian border crossing would accept Visa?

Nope.

This was again proving tricky. Then, the guard changed his tune and asked for less money. This rang alarm bells. If there was no fixed price, he was clearly trying to con us, or at least inflate the price to take a cut for himself. We decided to carry on with his game to see where it went. The more we protested that we had no money, the lower the price got until, eventually, we got it for free. We still have no idea what we got, but it had cost nothing. There were no prices on the forms, no indication that it should have cost anything, and no receipts; so I can only assume that the guard was trying to make some easy money – and this won't have been helped by the fact that the guys with the Minis had paid him only hours earlier. We moved on to the next hut. The exact same scenario unfolded and soon enough, now that we were well practiced, we were onto the next hut with two official bits of paper at no cost. In this hut, we recognised the papers as being the same as the one the lady on the Ukrainian side had tried to sell us, and also the same as the ones the guys with the Minis had. We knew we needed insurance and assumed that this would be genuine. The whole form was written in Russian, which uses the Cyrillic alphabet so we had no chance of understanding it, but it did have certain boxes and numbers we could understand – and it had the vehicle details printed into it instead of being handwritten. We were happy it was genuine and agreed to pay the required £21; £9 less than the Mini drivers paid. The official was eventually happy with dollars when we explained that we had no Russian money. Two more huts to go.

The next form indicated that we were to disclose how much currency we had. The last thing we wanted to do was to let on that we had a buggy stuffed full of dollar bills, so we did the only honourable thing to do in a situation like this, and lied. It was crazy. I'd never lie to a customs official in the UK, yet here we were, where the consequences could be undoubtedly much worse, and we didn't even think twice. Anyway, they were so corrupt that if we did get found out, we'd hopefully be able to come to some kind of agreement. In the end we put that we had enough to make it sound credible that we could support ourselves for the stay, yet without sounding rich. At the end of our journey we would discover that the idea of the form is, ironically, for our protection so that should any of the officials try to take our money, or if we were robbed, we would have some proof of what we had started with. We really were too distrusting for our own good.

The last hut again had an official looking form with pre-printed prices on it, so we assumed that it wasn't an optional fee and paid £1 each for this one. All the officials were very drowsy looking at this time of night; more interested in watching TV, snoozing, smoking or playing cards than dealing with us. This was clearly the best time to hit the borders and being firm and polite was saving us both time and money. And that was that. We jumped in the buggy, had our forms and passports checked one final time, had some friendly banter with the guards and we were off into Russia.

We had only been at the Russian part of the border for two and a half hours and it had cost us £23 for us and the buggy; the Minis were paying £58 per car and had been there for the best part of seven hours. Although the guards had tried it on, they were never aggressive and to be honest, they probably rely on small bribes to supplement their income. We were just trying to beat their system. Needless to say we were feeling pretty smug as we drove on into the sunrise, but once again fate was watching and decided that we shouldn't have it all our own way.

It was 04:15, the sun nicely rising directly in front of us to start a beautiful day in the Russian countryside, and I was at the wheel enjoying the quiet roads and beauty around me. I was driving at a good, constant speed for the buggy and the cool air, music and chat between us was keeping me awake, but my reactions and concentration must have been seriously lacking due to the tiredness – and the fact that I was virtually blinded by the rising sun. We hadn't slept at all the night before, and had had the night on the vodka before that, so it's hardly surprising; but being in high spirits we hadn't realised just how tired we were and naïvely continued to drive.

It was then that I ploughed straight through an armed Russian road block. I simply didn't see it in time, but was soon hard on the brakes trying to stop the heavily laden buggy. I couldn't believe it. All the time we were driving, we were both always on the lookout for police or other dangers on the road, but had both missed this. From the borders we had previously been through we both knew there were always police and military checks near to the borders, on both sides, trying to catch unsavoury people and to collect bribes from the rest, and I had just shot straight through one without stopping.

For a split second I considered coming off the brakes and driving on, but that was probably the lack of sleep again and was a crazy idea – I'll never know quite how that came into my mind but I'm glad it went as quickly as it arrived. Anyway, we'd soon have been found and then they would have genuinely arrested us. On the other hand, it was probably the sight and sound of the Russian guard running towards us, with his machine gun trained on the buggy, which convinced me to stop. I stayed on the brakes and we came to an abrupt stop in the middle of the road, one barbed wire road block now behind us and one more just ahead.

I'm not going to say exactly what I was thinking, as I expect this will be read by some people who don't need to know the details, but the sight of the machine gun coming towards me (and obviously the guard attached to it), knowing full well the gravity of what I had just done, left me in a cold sweat. This was the first time on the journey that we, or more precisely I, had got into a situation where we were actually in the wrong. And this was quite serious. I had all kinds of visions of being arrested and locked-up in the local police station, until I could find some way out and the embassy or Foxy could rescue me.

I was marched from the buggy and into the guardhouse, while Foxy was left at the buggy with another guard. My guard immediately started ranting at me in Russian, which I didn't understand a word of. This didn't impress him and the less I understood, the redder his face went. I tried to speak some English to him – we had found at other police stops that speaking was often a good way to calm situations down – but this had no effect here. He knew that he finally had someone in his office that had done wrong, and he was going to make the most of it. I was sent back to the buggy for my driving licence. Foxy seemed to be having quite a good chat to the other guard, who was a world apart from the one I was dealing with. Back in the guardhouse the guard finally put his machine gun down so he could confiscate my licence, which he then threatened to rip into pieces. He couldn't have known, but my licence was one of the most important things I had with me; without it my entire journey would be over. I needed it back in one piece. Predictably, he then started to ask for money. He wouldn't say how much – indicating that I should write a figure down. After a few minutes of negotiating, I got him to write a figure in dollars instead of roubles. We still had no Russian money and I had only a vague idea how many roubles there were to the dollar. Either way, he wanted $50 (£27).

Now looking back at this, if this had been in the UK, considering what I had just done, I'd have paid as fast as I could, before he changed his mind and I found myself in court with a huge fine and a driving ban. But this was Russia. We'd been travelling only a week but my mentality was now to argue back and assume everyone, official or otherwise, was trying to rip me off. Except this guard was quite serious and absolutely incensed when I disagreed. I asked him to show me the fine sheet or ticket he was theoretically going to give me. This took some doing, and the only way to get my point across was to lean over his desk and pick up some papers, indicating that I wanted something for the dollars. He got the idea and became even more irate. I suspected I wasn't going to get a receipt for my fine and that the official fine would be a fraction of the $50, which made me even more determined to pay less – although I was sure I'd have to pay something this time.

Throughout all of this, other motorists were being pulled over and filed through the room to see my guard who was processing them around me. None appeared to have done anything wrong, but all showed their licences, with a few roubles carefully tucked inside, and were sent on their way. The moment I tried to speak to them they were quickly ushered out of the room. I managed to see one of the bribes and it was for pence. $50 was ridiculous. Our arguing continued for some time and it was clear he wasn't going to shift on his demands. I was allowed back to the buggy to get the money. Foxy wasn't happy about handing over anything, which was understandable given how kind and friendly the guard he was speaking to was. So, just to be awkward, he counted out fifty one dollar bills for me to give him from our stash in the door panel. This in itself was tricky, as we had to do it out of sight of the other guards so they wouldn't know how much we had. Of the dollars we carried, we had taken about half of the money in one dollar bills, as we had been advised these would be the most useful. In reality no-one wanted such small bills, preferring larger fives and tens, as these apparently got them a better exchange rate. This guard would have to make do with ones.

I returned with the money and put it on the desk in front of him, and while still holding it, reached out for my licence. He wouldn't give it to me straightaway, but as motorists came into the office he was keen to hide the wedge of dollars from their view. I noticed his discomfort and played on this by waving the dollars to the motorists and indicating that the guard was doing wrong. With the motorists gone, he passed me my licence and took the money which he didn't even bother to count. Again I asked for a receipt; he understood this by now, and again shouted back and went red in the face. I was being ripped-off; I was tired and, more importantly, annoyed that I wasn't making any progress with this guard. With my licence safely in my hand, I reached over and took some of the dollars from the desk, thanked him and calmly walked toward the door. He shouted something and I turned and thanked him again. He made no effort to stop me and was probably quite happy with the money he had just made. Back in the buggy, I gave Foxy the $16 (£9) I'd managed to grab and we left. Overall, I didn't consider $34 (£18) to be too much for ploughing through an armed checkpoint. In most countries doing that would have left me, the buggy, or both, riddled with bullet holes.

I tried to explain to Foxy what it had been like but, given how amicable his guard had been, this took some doing. The issue was over $34, which, to put it in perspective, was only the cost of a bottle of wine in a UK bar – but money had taken on a different value on this trip. This had been a big hit. We still hadn't slept so we drove far enough away from the checkpoint to feel safe, and pulled off the road, down a dirt track and went to sleep in the buggy. It was 05:30 and broad daylight, but we were both too tired to bother with the tents, however uncomfortable it was sleeping in the buggy where we had been sitting for the past however many hours.

We woke again just before 08:30. The buggy was roasting now that the sun was fully up, so we decided it was time to hit the road again. First, as with most mornings I had a cereal breakfast bar for as a quick snack. We had brought about fifty of the things with us, and they were a quick alternative to preparing breakfast when there was nowhere to get anything else – they were also good food to nibble on when bored. I ate this while stretching my legs, walking around the area where we had parked. We were some way from the road, but next to six or seven quite large, part-built houses. They obviously had work begun on them several years ago, but would never be finished as they were now in a very sorry state, crumbling away. It seemed very strange at the time, but this would be a common sight all across Russia; people had begun projects and either the money had run out, plans had changed or bureaucracy had got in the way, leaving huge one-off houses and factories with no future, part-built and derelict.

Back at the buggy, Foxy was trying to get some music on the radio but it wasn't working. We'd had problems with the radio before we left and were worried it had finally given up on us – until we tried to start the buggy. It was dead. It wouldn't even try to turn over. Having driven through the night and then stopped after it had come daylight again we, or rather I, hadn't thought to turn off the headlights. It was going nowhere and I began to regret having driven so far down the track, away from the main road looking for somewhere quiet and out of sight to park for what had turned out to be only three hours of rest. We tried jump-starting using the second battery we had installed in England but for some reason this wouldn't start the buggy either.

It was roasting. The buggy was about seven hundred metres from the road, it was on a rough, sandy, uphill track, and I was tired, hadn't really eaten and was being blamed for the situation. I was pushing the buggy. We tried bump-starting; we argued the merits of whether to use first or fifth gear (or to compromise with third!) but nothing worked, so I ended up pushing it all the way to the road. I was nearly sick given the heat and my lack of sleep. There was the occasional car on the road but none were willing to stop. Hardly surprising given that we were two un-shaven, un-showered Englishmen, in the middle of the Russian countryside, jumping up and down manically waving a pair of giant jump leads at the passing cars. They probably thought we wanted to hang them. After what seemed like forever, though probably still less than thirty minutes, a car with two men stopped and reversed back to us.

We hooked up the buggy to their car and tried. Nothing. The Russians looked to be losing interest then we suggested they try with their car running. Once they understood what we were getting at, they reluctantly tried this and gradually the buggy's engine turned over. A few moments later it was running. We thanked them and tried to offer them some cigarettes, but they misunderstood and they ended up offering us some – it was great to find kind people after the guard – even if we didn't smoke.

The buggy was running rough and weak and it was a worry that it would stall again before we got back onto the tarmac of the road, leaving us stranded trying to flag down another passing car, but we made it and were on our way again. Well, for the next ten minutes.

There was a police roadblock and predictably they pulled us over. Having a foreign car covered in bright sponsorship stickers, trying to look like a race car was doing us no favours with the law. We would spend the rest of the journey to Mongolia being stopped several, or rather many, times every single day. It almost became routine after a while. The police would see us coming, or be expecting us from their colleagues who had stopped us a mile or so earlier, and wave us over with their batons (at night they had luminous light-sabres!). They would then ask where we were from, (although it took us several days to realise this was what they were asking) take our passports and whoever was driving would have to get out, sign some forms and produce the buggy's documents. This would usually coincide with being mildly hassled and asked for dollars, though we never gave them any. A stop like this could take anything from ten minutes to an hour or more; it really depended on the official who stopped us and how lucky he was feeling. The longer stops, however, were often more due the curiosity of the police who were trying to find out just what we were doing and why we would want to. It was impossible to even begin to explain, but we tried all the same. They simply had no concept of holidays or travelling, unless it had a clear purpose.

After a few of these stops, we learnt that it was imperative to take the lead, so as soon as we were pulled over we would have the map ready and ask for the next town and whether we were going the right way. This always seemed to give us the upper hand; giving us more control of the situation, meaning they were less likely to search the buggy and waste our time. Confidence was the key.

But this stop was one of the awkward ones. We were still near the border crossing and stops in these areas were always harder work. Firstly, we had to explain that we couldn't stop the engine as we had a flat battery and the engine would never start again. With that issue eventually covered, we established that the policeman wanted the engine number. This should have been reasonably easy but Foxy, the

124

policeman and I looked everywhere for more than thirty minutes and still couldn't find it. We looked in the Haynes manual, but that had no clues as to where we could find it. The policeman was suspecting us of having removed it and presumably therefore driving an illegal car. I considered phoning the man we had bought the buggy from to ask if he knew (after all, he was a Suzuki enthusiast and could probably have helped) but given the time difference he would certainly have been in bed. Instead we just kept on looking. I was starting to recognise the grease patterns on the underside of the engine as I'd been looking at it for so long when the policeman's superior walked over and talked to him. They must have decided that we were genuine or were just admitting defeat, but with that we were on the road again. To this day we never did find where the engine number was.

Once again we had our usual problem. No local money and very little fuel. The first major town we got to was Rostov-na-Donu and we started looking for anything that may be a bank or a cash machine – not that we held much hope that our cards would be working. Very soon we spotted the word 'bank', which looks very similar in Russian to the English, but it was beside the door to the hardware superstore. Very odd. Anyway, we went in and asked the security guard for directions by pointing at our wallets and asking for roubles. He pointed us to the back of the store, past the baths, sinks and fitted kitchens to the foreign exchange desk. We couldn't believe it. Not only was it in the most unlikely place but we were actually having some good luck for once. We changed some of our dollars and left. On the way out I spotted an ATM and tried my card. Even that worked! Happy days.

Trying to leave Rostov-na-Donu was not so easy. The only map we had of Russia was in the Lonely Planet guide, with a scale of approximately 300 miles to the inch. It only showed major cities and no road numbers. When we bought the other maps we dismissed buying maps of Russia due to the choice available. We would have had to buy about fifteen separate sheets to make it worthwhile, any less would not have shown much more than the map we had; we couldn't find anything in between so did without. You could call this a slight oversight in our pre-rally preparation. You could call it an absolute disaster. I liked to think of it as a challenge. What it meant in reality was that, rather than cut across Russia directly to Astrakhan, we would have to aim northeast to Volgograd which was big enough to feature on our map. In theory this was fine, but there were no signs to Volgograd or Astrakhan; hardly surprising given that as I write, the map I'm looking at calls Volgograd, Zarizyn, and prior to being Volgograd it was Stalingrad (I've also seen Tsaritsyn used) – and all that's before you throw in the Cyrillic letters used on the almost non-existent road signs (here's Volgograd in Cyrillic, Волгогра́д, so you can see what we were up against!). This would be another issue to dog us from here to the end of the journey – why couldn't they just have one name, written using the Latin alphabet?!

For the first time on the journey we pulled out the GPS. It felt like cheating but we had no choice and anyway, it had no map uploaded so was little more than a glorified compass; simply giving the coordinates of our position with a digital compass bearing. We found a main road out of town and decided to stick with it for a while. It was going to Moscow and we knew Moscow was roughly north so we couldn't be too far wrong. The hope was that soon we would find a main road heading east that we could take. There was one about 80 miles north of us that we decided was the one to go for (assuming we were on the road we thought we were at this point in time).

Thankfully, we soon came to a police checkpoint, got pulled over and were able to check we were going the right way. Had we not been stopped I doubt we would have volunteered to stop as it would be more hassle than it was worth. We quickly hid the GPS as we had been warned that the Russians are still suspicious of foreigners with GPS – we didn't want branding as spies – and got our passports ready. We decided to try out our Russian. Throughout the morning we had been reading the Russian phrase book we had brought with us and this was the perfect place to see what we knew. He loved it. Our accents will have been terrible but he appreciated the effort, confirmed we were on the road to Moscow and sent us on our way.

All along the roadside were stalls, as there had been since Romania, but these were now selling dried and smoked fish as well as fruit. They were just hanging on wooden racks at the side of the road and wherever there was one stall there would be at least eight or nine others nearby, all selling exactly the same produce. It was strange given that none of them were busy and you would have to travel a few miles to the next group of stalls. I always thought they'd do better if they spread out a bit. Anyway, we picked one stall and after some haggling, and insisting we didn't want or need his biggest, prized fish, we came away with whole twenty-inch-long smoked mackerel, complete with head and eyes, and a bag full of giant peaches. It all cost less than £1. We dropped the peaches into the only remaining space in the buggy, between the seats (we'd come to regret this later when we found two had escaped, demolished themselves, and started to rot under the seats) and ate slivers of mackerel, cut with a penknife, while driving on towards Moscow. It tasted great, but in the heat the smell was pretty intense.

Foxy buying fish

Whilst still looking for the turning for the road to Volgograd, we came to a huge roadside market, miles from any town. Parked amongst the trucks I spotted another rally car – the first we had seen on the road since the Church of Bones. It was a Mini Scamp – a kit car built around a classic Mini. I woke Foxy up and we did a quick u-turn to go back for a chat. There were four other cars waiting with the Scamp while it was having its suspension repaired by a welder in the market. They had been there for some time and, at the request of the welder, half of them had been drinking vodka together since they'd arrived. The other half would be doing today's driving. The Scamp was now pretty much good to go; the welder having been able to weld it back together and make a new threaded bar, apparently fixing the problem and he hadn't even charged them. I walked off into the market with one of the guys who had been drinking to meet the welder, as we were assured he would be delighted to see more English people. He was. The moment I was near enough, he started shaking my hand and, as they had already drunk the four bottles of vodka he had, he dispatched his sidekick to buy some more so that I could drink too.

We had barely slept, hardly eaten and wanted to make some progress. The last thing we needed was to sit drinking neat vodka all afternoon. I don't even like neat vodka. I tried to explain this, to no avail. He passed me the remainder of his food which was a cross between a hotdog and a burger stuffed with molten cheese. It was actually really good but I was all too aware that his mate would soon be back with the vodka. I made my move and left, leaving him chatting to the other rallier. Back at our buggy someone had bought a stack of hot flatbreads which we all ate before setting off, in convoy, in search of the road to Volgograd.

Other ralliers, on the road to Volgograd

We soon realised why we had decided not to travel in convoy. We had only travelled ten miles and in this time we had to stop once for the toilet and once for one of the guys to be sick – too much vodka –

although we had by now found the road that would take us all the way to Volgograd. Then the suspension on the Scamp broke again. Of all the cars in the convoy, the Scamp was the most heavily laden and probably also the weakest; we couldn't see the logic. We all pulled into a petrol station to look at the damage.

Effecting repairs to the Scamp with Foxy on the right, advising

The half of the people who were sober enough to be useful set about trying to fix the Scamp, us included. It didn't look good for them. The suspension arm was being overloaded and kept bending. It was the kind of part that would need replacing rather than bending back into shape now that it had been weakened, but that wasn't possible here. It would have helped to remove some of the kit from the over-laden Scamp into the other cars but no-one seemed to see the benefit of this except Foxy and I. We decided to stick around for a while to help, also taking time to sort our kit, which by now was starting to get lost all over our buggy. Noting the condition of the Scamp, we also decided to throw out everything we thought we didn't need, in an effort to get our weight down.

We didn't want to end up like the Scamp and were aware that there were things we hadn't used on the journey so far, and probably never would.

A couple of the guys we'd just met had come over from Chicago for the rally and had been parked near to us in Hyde Park. They were great guys and planned on following a similar route to ourselves into Uzbekistan. We decided to stick with them in the hope of travelling together for a while, but we doubted the Scamp's chances when the tarmac roads ran out further east. With the Scamp now botched back together, we set off again.

Not more than five miles later and the Scamp was limping as we pulled into the next petrol station, its suspension broken yet again. We had spent almost five hours at the previous petrol station and didn't want to spend as long at this one. We had only met these guys about seven hours ago and didn't need to be caught up with their problems.

It may sound selfish, but for us the rally was never about travelling in a convoy. It would have been great at night to share a few beers and chat together, but it also meant that we would have to stop whenever any of the others broke down. Police checks would take many times longer, as would border crossings. The others would have to stop for us too, which we didn't want, and we would have to debate routes and stop when the majority wanted, rather than doing our own thing. We wanted to be able to sort any problems ourselves and if things went wrong we'd just have to find a solution ourselves. We wanted to have independence on this trip and fend for ourselves. We exchanged phone numbers, wished them luck and left.

Volgograd was looking a long way off; we had wasted most of the day and it still looked to be five hours or more away. We had hoped to be beyond the city before we stopped for the day. The roads were incredibly quiet and there were only a few towns, but we still got lost at every one we came to.

Our first evening in Russia

The wide, main road would go almost into the town centre, then deteriorate into a tiny potholed lane with no signs and no indication of where to go next. The GPS was a help but we were never sure if we'd picked the right road out of town, driving for several miles before deciding if the heading we were on matched the approximate direction of the road on the map. This just created unnecessary stress as I was always expecting that we would have travelled thirty minutes out of town only to have to backtrack to find the right road. Thankfully it never happened. Perhaps we just have a good sense of direction.

It was getting late, and we were driving through what could have been a ghost town it was so lifeless, when we came to another police roadblock. They were great guys. We had a bit of a chat, showed them where we were from and where we were heading to, and they seemed impressed and glad to have seen us. It just confirmed my earlier thoughts about the officials at the borders being a different breed to the ones on the interior.

It was now raining and we were dangerously low on fuel. We really should have filled the jerry cans at the last place, but had foolishly assumed that fuel would be easy to come by in Russia, and we also didn't really want forty litres of fuel sloshing around in the back of the buggy with us unless we really had to. Then, as we were about to run out, we came to a small village which had an incredible eight petrol stations. Typical. We just filled up the buggy and didn't bother with the jerry cans, confident again that we'd find a petrol station sooner next time. We never did learn.

Foxy drove on some more while I dozed in the passenger seat. It must have been a good snooze as before I knew it we had just passed Volgograd. We pulled off the road, to the side of a field and slept in the buggy. It was early morning and we were shattered, but it was still dark and we had no intention of getting out of the warmth of the buggy and into the midges to put up the tents.

31st July – Volgograd, RA to border region, KZ

We awoke early and started driving at 06:30. It's impossible to have late mornings in a car with the intense heat of the sun burning through the windscreen. Astrakhan, our first town on the historic Silk Road and situated on the delta of the river Volga, was now 210 miles to the southeast. All we had to do was follow the river to get there and we could see for miles now that it was light. Having covered so much distance through the night, the morning had brought us into a completely different landscape. There was nothing but flat, parched grasslands as far as the eye could see in all directions. This hardly made for the most inspired driving but at least it was quick. We were making good time and with our visas for Uzbekistan being valid from the 3rd, we still hoped to reach the border on time, even with the incident in Ukraine delaying us. The intention was to get to Astrakhan in time for lunch and have a leisurely afternoon there before crossing the Russian / Kazak border late at night. We were travelling at about 60mph so in theory we could have been in Astrakhan by about 10:00, but that didn't take into account driver swaps, police checkpoints or the rapid and unforeseen deterioration of the road ahead.

The road here was very remote and was not much more than a single track surrounded by arid, sandy scrubland and dried-up salt marshes. It was to be expected that the road was deteriorating, as all that lay ahead was one town before the border so the Russian authorities probably didn't see it as a priority. It was also baking hot, the sand almost burned to touch – and it was still only morning. We pulled over for some water and to have a walk about. We were spending far too much time in the buggy; all day and sometimes all night. It was good to wander over the sandy mounds, surrounded by nothing for miles around. It was also completely silent; there was no traffic, buildings or people to be seen in any direction. We had some more of the mackerel and threw the rest of it away – it was really stinking now and probably turning putrid in the heat.

Taking a break in the desert on the way to Astrakhan

We were stopped by the police a couple of times and used our broken Russian to great effect, having no problems and they all seemed very friendly, and we got to Astrakhan by about midday. We parked up by some kind of huge, ancient fortress with a palace beside it, and the Maria Ascension Cathedral towering over the buggy. The palace was beautiful, while the fortress was in the process of being completely restored. We walked around the grounds and down to the river Volga.

Some of the buildings were gorgeous, with a Parisian feel, and it could easily be a huge tourist destination, but I guess years of communist rule have stifled that so far. In a few years I'm sure it could become an international tourist centre, but at the minute it has all the beauty and attractions, without the crowds.

Parked up in Astrakhan

At the river we found an outdoor bar overlooking the Volga and stopped for a drink. I went to the bar and chatted with the barmaid; me in English, her in Russian. She was trying to tell me something, possibly that she had seen some other ralliers passing through (we were both wearing our rally t-shirts) or possibly something, or, for that matter, anything else. We had a good laugh at our situation and, once I'd returned to Foxy with the beers, all her friends were soon talking about us. We stayed for a while and read in the Lonely Planet that there was a bar they recommended within walking distance, just up the river from where we were. It also had air-con and we decided that it would be good to be somewhere cool to get some food.

We walked up the river, past a busy swimming pool built into the river itself and to the bar. It was much smarter than the rest, had a 'Wild West' theme and the clientele were wearing suits. We hadn't shaved or showered in a couple of days and had been sleeping rough in the buggy; we can't have looked as good as we usually do. Anyway, we were welcomed in, given a table and ordered two large beers. They came in ice-frosted glasses and were perfect Czech beers – just what we needed. In London these would be costing us an arm and a leg, but this was Russia so, with no real foundation, we assumed it was bound to be cheap. At the time, we were so glad of the comfort of the surroundings that the thought never even crossed our minds – to the extent that we ordered food without even seeing a menu. The waitress came over and spoke enough English for us to be able to order, or rather accept what she offered us; apparently we were having a green salad to start, followed by a pork steak each. When they arrived, the steaks were absolutely incredible; it was the first proper meal we had had since Odessa and we were starving. We got another ice-frosted glass of beer; well, they were good and looking at the map we might not see another good beer for some time. We were also starting to have our suspicions about the cost. We stayed sitting around for a while, enjoying having no worries and no rush to be anywhere, but when the bill came we worked it out to be almost £40. We couldn't believe it, it was extortionate! So, to make it better value we each went to the bathroom. It was a lovely bathroom, nicely scented, with a choice of soaps, pristine, folded white towels and playing gentle music so we had a quick shower in the sink.

The problem in our minds was that just a day or so earlier, for only twice this amount, we had had a team of men work on the buggy for two days, the gearbox repaired and a place to stay. We felt seriously ripped-off. We knew we should have checked the prices before we started but it was too late to worry about it now. We joked about how we would laugh about how petty we were being when we got back home; then continued being petty. We both had the same outlook and this was just another thing that wasn't worth worrying about. Like the problems at the borders, it was just something that happened and we had to get on with it as there was no point getting stressed about it – but next time we'd be sure to check the prices. The irony was that the true cost was actually less than half than we had, as we had got the exchange rate completely wrong, but we didn't discover this until weeks later!

We walked out into the hot sun and looked around the town. The intention was to spend the afternoon doing nothing much, then cover the last forty miles across the top of the Caspian Sea to the Kazak border in the early morning, just after midnight, when the guards would hopefully be less demanding. There was no point getting there sooner, as all we would do was spend longer in the queue and longer with the guards. We'd much rather spend that time in the sun at Astrakhan. We stopped at a shop and bought some bread, bags of crisps, biscuits, fruit, loads of bottled water and other nibbles for our time on the road, then dropped them back at the buggy. While repacking the buggy, a soft-top Suzuki SJ pulled up at the side of the street in front of us. Two ralliers jumped out and we chatted about our experiences for a while. They'd had a few problems but nothing too serious and wanted to travel with us for a few days as they were heading down a similar route.

Following yesterday's problems, this was something we could do without, but this being only one car it might not be too bad and was potentially useful to have two extra people at the Kazak border. We really had no idea what to expect at this border and guessed that it wouldn't be as straightforward as the ones we'd come across so far. Then they told us that they were only driving at a maximum of 55mph to conserve their car. We were doing 65mph.

They left to find some food and we directed them to the riverside, ill advisedly suggesting they avoid the place where we'd just eaten, and we went to sunbathe in a park and look through the maps. We decided that we'd travel with them through the border and then see how things went. We needn't have worried; when they came back a couple of hours later, they were set on getting a hotel for the night so that they could have a shower. Apparently they'd had hotels most nights so far and didn't want to be crossing the border late as they wouldn't be able to find a place to stay. The idea of a hotel was very tempting and we had even talked about it earlier, but now we were set on getting into Kazakhstan. There was something more exotic and exciting sounding about it than Russia. Then the guys told us that the Russian border was open all night but the Kazak side shut at some point and didn't open again until 07:00. That sealed it. We decided to leave there and then, otherwise we'd have no chance of getting through. The guys decided to stay in Astrakhan to get to the border at first light.

Getting out of Astrakhan was easy but within minutes we were again in the hands of the police. Nothing much happened and we were off almost as soon as we had stopped. As usual we were short on fuel and, from looking at the maps, suspected there was no fuel on the Kazak side for about 180 miles, exactly the distance we could get on a full tank of fuel. That's not entirely true, as there probably was somewhere to get fuel, but certainly not to get Kazak money in the middle of the night and we couldn't rely on using dollars to buy fuel in small villages. We pulled off the main road at the border town and spent half an hour or so driving round trying to find fuel. We filled up the buggy, but only one jerry can as we couldn't afford to fill the second with the roubles we had left.

Nearing the Russia-Kazakh border

With the fuel bought, we wasted even more time looking for the last bit of road to the border. There was no 'Kazakhstan this way' sign and we simply couldn't find it. We were wasting time we didn't have if we were to stand any chance of getting through the border. We had been driving round for about an hour, so went back to the same petrol station and managed to buy another eight litres of fuel for the second jerry can (I know it's not good to have a part-filled can, but by now we just wanted the extra fuel). There was no point saving the money and the way things were going, we would need the fuel just to find the border!

We were into early evening and had no idea when the border would shut. Eventually, we found a road that seemed to be going the right way and not far along it we found the familiar sights of the borders; the people milling around with nowhere better to be, the guards with huge hats and huge guns and the scattered queues of cars and trucks. We got out of Russia without any major hassle but it was still an excessively long winded process. We filled in forms, got them stamped, showed our passports, then moved to another office and did it all again. Several times. We couldn't tell if the Kazak side was still open and no-one would tell us. We thought it was just visible down the road, but that transpired to be yet another Russian checkpoint. We were waved across, showed our growing collection of paperwork and passed through. We weren't a hundred percent sure if this had got us into Kazakhstan and we were once again on our way, or if the Kazak border was still to be negotiated.

We drove down the dirt track, the tarmac having ended at the last checkpoint, and on into the dark. It seemed strange that we had entered Kazakhstan without any checks, but then for all we knew the last set of guards could have actually been Kazak, we couldn't tell. It had all been too easy. We also realised just how poor our lights were, now that we weren't on tarmac and needed to see the road and the potholes clearly. We needed some flat track on which to stop to re-align the headlights if we were to stand any chance of making progress, but it was too undulating where we were.

We came to a river where there were a couple of cars queuing for a rickety cable-driven ferry. We joined the queue, even though we had no money, as there was no alternative route to take.

Queuing for the ferry at dusk

On the ferry our buggy was soon surrounded by people demanding money; it could have been for the ferry but no-one else had appeared to pay and too many different people were asking. We locked the doors and tried to ignore them. Reluctantly, they let us off at the other side, but as we thought back, we realised that everyone else had in fact paid one of the first men stopping the cars. We just hadn't realised it at the time and assumed they were pulling a fast one. We never would lose our scepticism, but that wasn't a bad thing as it was certainly saving us money! We drove up the muddy river bank and continued along the dirt track when, after a mile or so, we came to a queue of cars. Then it dawned on us. All this time, even on the ferry, we had been driving though no-man's land, and had only just reached the Kazak part of the border.

We joined the queue, locked the buggy and went for a walk around. Someone shouted to us in English. Ahead of us were two guys in an old Volvo, driving a similar route to us but heading somewhere in eastern Russia to end their journey. They were being held in a compound because they had no Kazak insurance and couldn't buy any until the morning when the offices opened. They had got to the front of the queue, had been sidelined and were now stuck. We chatted over the razor wire (this border looked a bit more severe and had razor wire instead of barbed wire) and established, as we had feared, that the Russian car insurance we had bought was not valid in Kazakhstan. They had implied when we entered Russia that it was valid, but we had been doubtful they had understood what we'd been asking. We had no desire to spend the night at the border, they really do attract the most awful people – the decent people get let through in a few hours rather than days – and we had no intention of spending a night amongst them. We decided not to mention the insurance and see what happened, then try and buy some in a town in Kazakhstan in the morning.

Eventually, we got to the front of the queue at 22:00 and could start the form-filling process. Everything seemed above board and we were finished and back in the buggy at 23:15. We were waved forward and, as usual, went through the rigmarole of showing our documents, moving another twenty metres, showing our documents again and confirming that we had nothing illegal. We did however, have twenty-eight litres of petrol in the back of the buggy and we knew that this was something they would try to use against us if they found it. They would certainly try and fine us or confiscate it; every other border had tried but this was the first time we actually had any. They had us open the back of the buggy but just looked in from a distance with their torches. It was piled high with kit and we could easily have had another two people in there and still be left with room for a good amount of drugs and guns, but they didn't seem bothered. We got back in, the gates opened and we were through. I asked the last couple of guards when the border shut. They spoke a tiny bit of English, everyone seems to learn some at school, and said 00:00 which they confirmed by pointing on their watches. It was now 23:45; no wonder they couldn't be bothered with us. Best of all, no-one had mentioned the insurance. Another stroke of luck. We felt sorry for the guys in the Volvo, for a second, then drove down the dirt track into the vast, darkness of Kazakhstan...we were in! Into a country as large as the whole of western Europe, yet only fifteen million inhabitants. This was the start of the real wilderness for us.

We decided we would reconsider our insurance options at the next town, Atyrau, 180 miles away, and hoped we didn't get stopped in the meantime.

The road was terrible. It was plenty wide enough for two cars to pass safely – about as wide as any normal two lane road, just without the tarmac. On top of that, it was littered with deep, sharp-edged potholes. These were almost impossible to spot in the dark, and the way the shadows fell meant that you couldn't judge if the hole was two inches deep or two feet; and several were at least two feet deep. We know, we hit them. We stopped, adjusted the spotlights by wedging some straw underneath them and taped them down as tightly as we could. It was painful work. To do it, the lights had to be on so they could be aligned, but that in turn attracted huge, dense swarms of hungry midges. The adjusted lights helped a bit and we could get up to 45mph where the road allowed. Any faster and you simply couldn't avoid the potholes in time. The buggy was bouncing everywhere and was hard to control but we were keen to cover some distance. If the roads from here on were similar, we'd have no chance of making Mongolia for weeks – and we had no idea if they got worse or better; we suspected that Uzbekistan and Kyrgyzstan would be much worse. The road we were on was little more than an access road, probably gouged out of the landscape so that the labourers could get to the railway, which we were now driving alongside, while they were building it.

The driving was incredibly hard work as we tried to concentrate enough to see the potholes and react to them in time. As we got more and more tired, the worse we got at avoiding them. Then we came across the famous Kazak horses.

Suddenly, there were wild horses all over the road. They came from nowhere and for some reason were hardly visible in the lights. I narrowly missed one, slamming on the brakes and swerving off the road, and we carried on, slightly shaken, but happy not to have hit anything. Then, while my concentration was down again, there was another. I hit the brakes, veered off the road again and just missed it. It didn't bear thinking about what would have happened had we hit one; it would have come straight through the windscreen and with the border shut, there would be no more traffic along this already desolate road for hours, so no chance of being rescued. The buggy was taking a hammering and getting airborne more and more frequently. It was time to call it a day; it was almost 03:00, so we pulled off the road to get some sleep.

It had been a really draining day and a night sleeping laid-down under canvas would have been great, but we were too tired, we couldn't see in the dark and frankly couldn't be bothered with the tents (even though we could get them up in a couple of minutes). We got our fleeces on and settled into the buggy's seats. I knew I should get my sleeping bag as within hours it'd be freezing, but that would involve getting out of the buggy to get the bags out of the rear. I was really that tired I couldn't be bothered, even though I knew it made sense to do it now rather than wake up freezing cold later on. Whichever way I looked at it, it was going to be another uncomfortable night in the buggy's seats.

1st August – Border region, KZ to Eastern KZ

We were on the road at 06:30. As predicted, the night before had been far from a good night's sleep. It had been freezing and I'd been stuck with the driver's seat. Definitely the short straw. Even though neither seat would recline with the piles of kit in the back, it was much worse on the driver's side, with the steering wheel and peddles getting in the way.

The road seemed much better in the daylight, as it was possible to see the lay of the surface ahead and take evasive action that bit sooner. The road was made of hard-packed rubble, cutting its way across the Ryn-Peski Desert in the Caspian Depression – an area rich in oil, natural gas and huge flats and domes of salt. The surface itself was very loose, causing the buggy to randomly skid and buck about, even whilst going in a straight line. It was also clear that the shock absorbers weren't working as they should, with the buggy bouncing around wildly through the potholes. As we launched out of a hole the buggy would dramatically snake from side to side as it landed, and there was nothing we could do but ease off until the snaking stopped. We checked and found a significant amount of oil leaking from three of the four shocks. There was nothing we could do here and (so far) the snaking always sorted itself out without incident, although it was pretty unnerving. To try and fix the problem, we reluctantly engaged four-wheel drive. It worked to an extent, making the buggy more stable, but the downside was that it would use a lot more fuel. As we didn't really want to crash out here we decided it best to run with the four-wheel drive.

Alongside the road there were occasional herds of cows and wild horses, grazing, on whatever scrub they could find in the wilderness of the steppe. And camels. The camels appeared to have no concern that they were on a road, and simply lay there as we approached with absolutely no intention of moving, so we had to come off the road and drive around them. Although there wasn't much difference between the road and the desert it crossed.

Kazakh camels

Then, without warning, the road ended. I'm still not sure if they were still in the process of building the road, or repairing what they had, but there was a barricade and nothing more than a path leading into the sand of the desert, looking as if it had simply been created by vehicles that had passed in the weeks previous. We followed, the going getting even slower, and after a few miles joined the original, hard-packed road again. To the south there were oil fields, their rocker-pumps lazily and repetitively extracting the oil, and then we came to a small town of a few hundred buildings. The road through the town was tarmaced, but only as far as the extremities of habitation, where it reverted to hard-packed rubble. There appeared to be nothing in the town and no people around,

I assume they must have been working the oil fields or sheltering inside from the intense heat.

The melting road on the way to Atyrau

Gradually, as the miles passed by and we got nearer to the town of Atyrau (formerly Guriev), the road started to get better. Compared to the places we had been recently, it was huge, which, given that it is Kazakhstan's main harbour city on the Caspian Sea, is hardly surprising. The city is considered to be half in Europe and half in Asia as it straddles the Ural River. This is widely accepted to be the boundary between the two, so was another marker point on our adventure. It's also quite an important city, though somewhat at risk from the rising waters of the Caspian Sea. Atyrau is situated in the huge Caspian Depression, which is far from a good thing, considering that the city is some twenty metres below sea level – some of the lowest elevations on Earth. We didn't know this at the time, but it does explain why we never even saw the Caspian Sea, even when we were less than ten miles from its shores.

A shame really, that we came all this way and missed the world's largest lake – although called a sea, it is, apparently and technically, a saline lake. It's also the main producer of the exceptionally rare Beluga caviar which, at 'just' £120/kg locally, is an incredible bargain compared to the prevailing price of £9,400/kg charged for Royal Beluga in the UK (although almost cheap in comparison to Golden Almas caviar, also from the Caspian, which at this time was fetching prices of up to £18,500/kg) – the smuggling potential is quite evident!

As usual, we were completely unprepared and without any kind of appropriate map, although Foxy was muddling through with the central Asia Lonely Planet. It was inadequate to say the least and made worse by the fact that we were reading a book written in English and looking at signs written in Cyrillic. We found the words for 'town centre' and headed down the road in search of it. Little did we know that this was virtually the same name as a region some kilometres to the south, to which we were now en-route. We wasted the best part of two hours finding the wrong way across town and through an industrial centre, only to have to turn back from the shanty-suburbs to get back to the modern glass buildings of the centre.

Being back in the centre was surreal. In the past few days we had been in the most remote places I've ever seen and had now arrived in an oasis of a town, rich from oil, with Western investment banks, familiar City firms and huge modern office developments. There was an enormous amount of money being spent here, much of which looked to be new wealth, and is considered by America to be one of the quickest emerging, strategically important regions in the world. Even the cars were new and for once the Ladas were outnumbered by other makes of modern vehicles. It had a feel much like Las Vegas or Dubai, but on a far smaller scale and still in its infancy. Worryingly, there appeared to be far too much building work in the centre and I had to wonder who was going to work there to support it and make it viable. As usual we were struggling to find a retail bank to get some cash when we spotted a Western Union in one of the newly built glass tower blocks. Sadly, our cards weren't working again so we had to exchange some more of our emergency dollars from inside the buggy. At this rate we would be completely out of cash in just a few days time with, potentially, no way to get any more.

With money in our pockets, we ventured into the brand new shopping mall next door in search of some food and drink. The place was immaculate. It had restaurants, music shops, a huge food store and a leisure centre with a pool perched on the roof. Perfect. We decided to get some food then relax for a while in the leisure centre – it would also be a chance to get clean, have a shower and a well earned rest. Our hopes were dashed when we realised that the mall was so new that neither the leisure centre nor the food store were open yet; they were both due to open at the end of the week. We would have to settle for lunch in one of the bars and a wash in the toilets. It was quite a let down – with everything being so new and sterile, it had no character and felt very Western; we could have been back at home.

After a couple of hours we had had enough of waiting around and wanted to get back on the road. There was not much of any interest to see in the town as it was very commercial, so we headed in the rough direction we needed to get out of the town. We aimed for the Ural River and used that as a guide to get a bearing out of town. We had no chance of finding the places we were looking for on road signs, and assumed that there was only really one 'main' road going the way we wanted. We were right, and having negotiated the sprawling shanty towns that surround the perimeter of the main city, we were back beside the railway and back on the right route.

Railways and rivers were a great way of finding our direction as they were the most accurate features on the maps we had. Roads were often hit and miss, would randomly change direction or end, and the towns were usually called by different names to the ones we had, or even turn out to be in a different location.

The tarmac ran out and the camels became more prolific

All we had to do now was follow this railway to a junction at Beyneu, then take the south-eastern fork into Uzbekistan. There appeared to be only one junction, and this seemed reasonable considering where the only other towns lay on the map. We would be following the railway southeast to Beyneu, where it had to split, with one branch heading to the only other town, Aqtau, to the southwest on the shore of the Caspian and our branch heading southeast to the border. Easy to say, but this amounted to, in a straight-line, over 280 miles to the border, which would probably be more like 300-350 miles on these tracks; and the tracks were atrocious. It couldn't even be classified as a road and beyond Beyneu, there wasn't even a road marked on the map – it was simply denoted as a path – and no indication of a passable border crossing. The worry now was that we would follow this road and find that we were stuck at the border.

This was as good as the sand track got

There were several possibilities and most weren't good; at the border there was the chance that there would be no actual border post and thereby we would enter illegally, causing problems when we found civilisation as the police would inevitably check our passports and arrest us – not to mention further issues trying to exit the country; the border could be patrolled and our entry denied (some borders only permit trade crossings and not tourists – which were the type of visas we had) forcing us to travel more than six hundred miles to circle around the north of the Aral Sea to get back on course; we could get hideously lost, breakdown, or crash in the middle of the desert, following a non-existent, never travelled path with the associated consequences; we could meet a group of understanding border guards who would greet us, give us some tea and biscuits and send us on our way. We hoped for the latter.

There was little traffic to worry about

Assuming we got through the border, we would still be on this 'path' beside the railway for another 250 miles until we came to the next marked village. At this village, assuming we could get money or use our dollars, we would be in desperate, desperate need of petrol. The last place we assumed we could fill up would be Beyneu, 50 miles before the Uzbek border, leaving us with potentially 300 miles to travel on the petrol we were carrying. The buggy was good for 180 miles on a tank and we would have a little bit more in the jerry cans, giving us just enough fuel to get to the next village. But we were now off-road using four-wheel drive. Looking back, it may have been worth the extra twenty pounds for a third jerry can. Anyway, it wasn't something to worry about now as we had little alternative, and should we run out we would just have to set up camp, hold tight, and wait for a passing truck or nomad to help us out; assuming anyone else even used the route we were heading along. We talked about other things and carried on, it was supposed to be an adventure after all, and this had always been marked as the point where we were expecting things to get interesting.

This was the beginning of the unknown, the real wilderness, mile after mile of non-policed, off-road driving with no towns, no roads and probably no means of contact with the outside world – and consequently for us, the potential for massive problems.

Dust was an ever present problem

Now that we were once again in the desert, the road was terrible because, as always, the tarmac had run out at the edge of town. We were sharing the track with huge dumper trucks, each of which was carrying several spare tyres (although we only had two), and the very occasional car all of which were throwing up huge plumes of dust, making overtaking both difficult and dangerous. Not only could you not see the potholes for the dust, you couldn't see any oncoming traffic – although that was a rarity. Often the track, though vague to begin with, would simply end and our tiny buggy and the huge trucks would take to the soft sand of the desert for a few miles, until we could find the smoother gravel of the main road. That said, even though it was smoother, it had a corrugated effect on the surface where it had been compacted. This was literally shaking us and the buggy to pieces. We experimented at various speeds and found it smoothest at just over 40mph where we seemed to almost float over the ruts. The problem with this was slowing down in time when we saw potholes, but it was worth it for the added comfort. The result was that we'd get up to speed, spot the track deteriorating, slam on the brakes as hard as we could – hopefully without skidding – and dart towards the smoothest looking area of the track (which was now as much as six cars wide, as over the years it has expanded through people moving further to the sides to avoid the worst bits). This obviously made the buggy very unstable, with its broken shock-absorbers, as it pitched about on the broken track. Sometimes we were too late and piled into the potholes. When this happened, we had to virtually come to a standstill to pick our way out of the minefield of deep potholes and get back to the smoother areas. When we got to areas like this, it could take several minutes to negotiate the holes to find the smoother, more drivable sections again. Sometimes there were some very worrying moments as the buggy jarred to a halt, before literally firing itself out of the potholes and becoming seriously airborne. The side-effect of this was that all the kit in the boxes in the back of the buggy was doing its best to fly into the front with us. Large boxes, rucksacks and bottles of water repeatedly smashed into us as they made a bid for freedom, no matter how well we tried to tie everything down. We used bungee cords, towels tied over the kit and packed everything down. It was hopeless, so the passenger now had the added job of trying to catch these projectiles, wedging them somewhere before they got in the way of the driver.

The potholes were getting larger and more frequent. Some were easily bigger than a small car and would have caused the end of our journey, should we have fallen into one. Luckily, we only ever seemed to hit the 'smaller' ones. However, it was taking its toll on the buggy and it was both mentally and physically tiring for us. We still hadn't slept properly in days. There was no chance for the passenger to catch any sleep, as he had to hold on with both hands at the same time as bracing with his feet, while the driver had the same issues but with less hope of bracing. Both of us were intently watching the road to shout warnings of potholes, and to try to pick out the best route to give the driver a chance of making it through them. Should the passenger let go, they risked a bruised head, which happened more than a few times.

If we had to carry on like this, our estimations would be miles out. We had expected to be spending about a day and a half on this part of the journey. It was now looking more like three; assuming the buggy didn't simply collapse around us. We pressed on, passing yet more groups of camels that would surround the buggy out of curiosity whenever we stopped near them.

The road continued relentlessly like this and we thought back to the other cars we had seen at the start in Hyde Park – the Minis, the

Pandas and the Metros and realised that they stood no chance if they had picked this route. They simply didn't have the ground clearance and would be looking at a detour of several days to get around the region.

We were really struggling with the road as, once again, we had to leave it and take to the makeshift sand tracks beside it, when we had a moment of inspiration. To either side of track were dried out lakes which had formed mile after mile of crystalline salt-flats. They stretched as far as the eye could see and were perfectly smooth. There was absolutely no reason we could see to be on the main track, so we took to the salt-flats. It was the perfect solution and we should have thought of it earlier, but it was one which almost ended of our journey.

As Foxy drove into the salt-flats we gradually started to slow down and a few moments later it was obvious that we were sinking deeper and deeper and grinding to a halt. We were stuck in deep mud. We were in the middle of the desert, the temperature was almost 50°C, and yet we were sinking into wet, clay-like mud.

Sinking in mud – in the scorching desert!

This was the last thing we had anticipated out here. I jumped out to take a look. We were about 70m from where we had entered the salt-flats, and completely stuck. The buggy wouldn't move forward and even if it could have done, it would be a long way to arc back to the track so we tried reversing. The buggy was still stuck, all four of its wheels spinning, and very much out of the reach of any other vehicles that might happen to pass by. This really was the worst thing that could have happened to us, short of rolling the buggy. Then we tried selecting the low ratio on the gearbox and reversing again. Gradually, with a push, the buggy slithered awkwardly and moved back along the tracks it had made coming in. With his foot to the floor, to get enough speed up to get back over the raised edge of the salt-flat, Foxy powered the buggy back to the safety of the track and we were strangely relieved to be back in the bone-shattering track.

We drove on until early evening, deciding to stop while it was still light to camp and actually cook some food for once. The previous few nights we had pretty much missed out on dinner due to the driving and border crossings, so we were keen to get some cooked food. Not that we'd ever been particularly hungry, probably due to the heat and also the sugar-filled, isotonic sports drink we were mixing from powder to drink as we drove. So, at about 18:30 we simply turned to the right, off the track, drove a few hundred metres and stopped. We had the tents up in a few minutes, it would be a real treat to sleep in the tents after three nights in the buggy. We then realised just how hot and isolated this place was. Even in the early evening sun it was astonishingly hot now that we didn't have the breeze from driving. The nearest village was tens and tens, possibly even hundreds, of miles away – and the only thing visible, in any direction, was the railway line some miles to the southwest.

Camping in the desert with nothing for miles in every direction

Foxy, dinner and some hot beers

I've never known isolation, peace and quiet like it. It was beautiful, stunning even.

Foxy cooking dinner

Foxy set about cooking a chicken curry from some of the tins of food we had brought with us, and we drank a couple of the warm (hot, actually) Kazak beers that we had in the buggy. The railway was just visible on the horizon and a goods train was lazily making its way towards Uzbekistan, with over fifty trucks on it – it was huge, though I suppose once it was moving there would be nothing to stop it here, with no towns or hills to negotiate. The landscape was almost perfectly flat in all directions, the only notable feature being the curvature of the Earth, and it was a perfect place to have a night off from travelling and appreciate where we were. The ground was half white with fine sand, the other half covered with dead-looking grasses, and there was the occasional salt-flat sprawling out with its white crystalline formations. It was, and probably always will be, the most isolated, inaccessible and remote place I have ever stayed. The sunset was incredible and when the sun went down the night-sky was truly amazing.

Pure isolation

2nd August – Eastern KZ to Eastern UZ

We were up just before 07:00 and began packing the tents away. This was a quick and simple job and we grabbed some snack food from in the buggy while we worked. I was almost finished, kneeling on the stone-sheet while rolling my tent, when I spotted a white scorpion, motionless on the mat. It must have been crushed in the night after crawling onto the mat and getting trapped under me as I slept. Then, it suddenly came to life and scuttled towards me, tail-up, heading straight for my knee. Now I'm not the most energetic person straight out of bed but this certainly got me moving! I jumped up, grabbed an empty water bottle and 'gently' swatted it into the desert. I anxiously finished packing the rest of the kit away, now checking everything for scorpions as I did. We had a good medical kit with us, containing everything from plasters to intravenous drips, but neither of us had any idea how to deal with a scorpion sting, or how serious they might be from this type. I later learnt that by night this part of the desert is rife with scorpions – which is something I'm glad I didn't know when we had been sitting out and walking around, in just our shorts, the night before.

Back on the road, we occasionally came to half-heartedly tarmaced stretches, which were actually worse and harder work than the gravel, and sand sections. The tarmac simply gave the potholes sharper edges, making the going even tougher. Where we could, we actually avoided driving on these bits, picking our own route along the side; the going was just as tiring as yesterday. Further on, the road split into several tracks leading off in slightly different directions with no indication where any went. We could still see the railway a few miles to our right, so picked the one running the most parallel to it and hoped for the best.

With our concentration slipping as the day wore on, we were hitting the rough sections harder and harder, with the buggy becoming fully airborne several times and up on two wheels much more often than we were happy with. Before we left the UK I'd expected the going to be rough but this was beyond anything I'd imagined. We really were beginning to think more frequently that some critical part of the buggy would snap soon and there was no hope of getting it repaired out here. Rolling or crashing simply wasn't an option.

We had to make the decision whether to carry on as we were, or slow down and try to preserve the buggy. As it was, we were already travelling slower than we wanted, with a huge distance left to cover. If the buggy did break at least we'd have had fun breaking it; we had enough food and water for a few days, which would give us time to, hopefully, sort the situation or hitch a lift out of the desert. More importantly, we would almost certainly never get the opportunity to do anything even remotely like this ever again, and we didn't want to look back and think that we had been too cautious or avoided risks because we worried about things going slightly wrong. I can't think of anywhere closer to home where there's a landscape even slightly like this where we could do this in such a vast area – it is pretty much the size of England with nothing in it but us and the buggy.

Even though the driving was hard work, and looking back quite dangerous, it was incredible fun to cover such vast distances off-road. We could drive how and where we pleased, with no restrictions, no traffic and complete freedom – it was almost a challenge to see how fast we could go when we had the smoother patches, and how well each of us could get through the potholed patches. In the areas of deeper sand, the track would weave its way over and around hillocks and as the buggy drifted and snaked sideways, it would catch on the edge of the tracks, grip again, and usually carry on in the right direction. Sometimes it didn't, but the result of that was just a quick, bouncing detour through the rough, to get back to the sand-track. It was a true wilderness. We decided that if things were going to go wrong, they would, and we'd have to deal with it when it happened, rather than trying to mitigate all the risks. We opted to carry on as we were; driving to the limits of our, and the buggy's, abilities. This was after all why we had come, and it was such a long way to get anywhere round here that we had to press on – and it was so much fun!

Again, the heat was painful and there was nowhere to hide from it. Outside, in the direct glare of the sun the heat was scorching; inside the buggy was like an oven but at least when we were moving there was a breeze which, even though it too was baking, managed to cool us a bit. A few years ago, in 2002, I crossed Death Valley in the midst of a Californian heatwave and I remember the temperature had hit 52°C, but the temperature here was in a different league. Then we got stuck. Again.

Tarmac was long forgotten as we ploughed on through the sand

Any tarmac was now a long way behind us and we had been in nothing more than sand for miles now. In all, it was the best part of 200 miles along a deeply sandy track, devoid even of any hardcore and it resembled little more than a bridleway. The track appeared to be there for no other purpose than to have provided access for the workmen who had laid the railway and power lines some years ago. The tracks themselves meandered around the larger mounds of sand and from time to time, we would drive through the scrub to switch to a neighbouring track that looked smoother or straighter; although it was very much a case of 'the grass being greener' and we rarely benefited from this. Except this time we got wedged trying to get onto the next track. The buggy was half onto the next track and half in the scrub, grounded, the wheels spinning in the sand. We tried pushing, but in the end it was switching to the low-ratio gearbox that saved us again, and we were on our way. We thought for some time that we could see a better track, which almost looked like a gravel road, on the other side of the railway. We looked at ways to cross the rails and considered using some wooden sleepers we found to create a ramp to get over unusually high rails (possibly to keep them out of the constantly shifting sand) but decided against it in case we got stuck – and to be honest, driving in the sand was too much fun to leave in favour of a gravel track some miles away.

It really was great driving. With our off-road skills improving, we were able to get up quite a good speed and drift the buggy round the curves in the track, occasionally going too far or too fast, only to be saved again as the raised sand at the edge of the track brought us back into line. We'd slow down for a bit, worried about the potential consequences of rolling the buggy out here in the desert, soon forget, and start racing again. Luckily we both had an implicit trust in each others driving and a very similar outlook on how to approach this adventure. We had also both been quite involved in kart racing for several years in our teens and this seemed to us to be a progression of that; pushing as far as we could and only slowing down when things started to go wrong – possibly not the best way to approach this but it was some of the most adrenalin-filled driving I've ever had. More importantly, there is nowhere else I can think of where you could behave like this for such a prolonged period without getting arrested, or paying a fortune to have a go on some pre-laid, Mickey Mouse off-road course.

The sand got everywhere

And that was another thing that had crept up on us, or rather left us behind. The police. For days we had had constant interest and grief from the local police, yet out here, obviously, there was no-one to stop us and we were free from the worries and more importantly, the expectation, of getting stopped. We were able to relax and get on with what we had come for; travelling, carefree, in the one of the most amazing, untouched, landscapes left in the world. And the driving was incredible.

Finally, we reached Beyneu. It had been a torturous journey across Kazakhstan but we were now into the final 50 miles. What lay after was probably no better, but at least we could see that we were making progress and it wasn't far until we'd know the situation regarding the border crossing, if we'd be back-tracking for miles along the track we'd just come, and how the rest of the journey would pan out.

Driving into town was nothing to be excited about. The place was tiny and apparently deserted. It probably only existed as a staging post for the workers who had built the railway or worked on the sporadically occurring oil wells. Chevron has a huge plant many miles to the north, but there was little evidence of that here. Beyneu also marked the point where the thin line we'd been following on the map stopped and turned into what was marked as nothing more than a path.

Buying supplies, Beyneu

Soon enough we found a fuel pump in the dusty sand by the side of the road and, through a tiny window, we were able to give some money to an old man and get the fuel we desperately needed. We had the buggy and both jerry cans filled in the hope we'd have enough to get across the border and to the next village somewhere in Karakalpakstan, the autonomous desert region of western Uzbekistan. Opening the jerry cans was a hazard out here; the cool fuel used to fill them would expand in the heat and when opened, the caps would literally explode against our hands, trapping misplaced fingers. We also stocked up on water and crisps through this window, quite a slow process as the opening was just big enough for one bottle at a time and we had to keep sending him back for more, time and time again, until we had six bottles and several packs of crisps. I got the impression from his face that most people just bought the one bottle. We now had about twenty litres of water in the buggy so mixed some of it with our re-hydration salts. We must have been dehydrated for days, as we had been drinking pretty much constantly, yet hardly ever going to the toilet. It was just impossible to drink enough in this heat.

Just up the road we found a bland concrete building with a 'café' sign outside – all the buildings here were low, square, decrepit, single storey, concrete buildings with tiny, deep-set windows to keep the searing heat out. Luckily, like 'bank', the word 'café' in Russian looks very much like the English. It was about 14:00 so we popped in and were greeted by the sounds of the Backstreet Boys playing on the radio; not exactly Russian, but it gave it a familiar feel. In keeping with the rest of the town, the café was deserted so we picked the table near the one electric fan. A girl came out of the kitchen and looked suspiciously at us before handing us two menus and saying a few words. She didn't speak a word of English and the menu was incomprehensible. We chose three items almost at random but using a technique we had picked up. We'd found the best way to determine starters from mains from desserts was by looking to see how the prices change as we moved though the menu. This is fine if, like us, you aren't too bothered what you eat. And at this stage we'd have eaten almost anything. Except that we weren't allowed any of the items we picked. Perhaps we had selected a bad combination, perhaps we had picked things they didn't have, or perhaps she had some food to get rid of. We'll never know. Instead, she quickly pointed to some other items and being unable to understand, answer back or suggest alternatives, we agreed. Soon we were presented with a bowl of noodles in soup with a basic side salad. Hardly gourmet dining but this was pretty much standard for the ex-Soviet states, basic, filling food, presented 'as it comes' with no pretension.

We finished and took a look at the maps, taking advantage of the tables and the floor space to spread out and see just how far we had to go and how little distance we had covered in the past few days. I spent a few minutes catching up on my notes but soon Foxy was keen to get going. I tried to delay leaving and wind him up by writing more but it wasn't working as I was as keen as him to be on the move again.

We drove back to the railway and found the junction where it split. Half was turning southwest, staying within Kazakhstan, the other fork heading southeast into Uzbekistan. We headed southeast. Just outside the town we were met with a strange sight. Tens and tens of redundant steam trains parked on a raised sideline, leading nowhere, rusting away in the desert where they must have been abandoned years previously. I'm sure train spotters or restoration fiends would have had a field day, but we weren't either and had a border to find.

The road was much better now; it had obviously been maintained to keep good access between Beyneu and the border and was about the width of a dual carriageway, only without the tarmac. It was looking promising that the border here would be open to traffic – and hopefully this would include tourists and not just commercial vehicles.

Without the potholes we soon covered the 50 miles and arrived at the border just before 16:30, only to find we had a slow puncture in the right rear tyre and it was now virtually flat.

Foxy changing our first flat tyre

In all fairness, it was incredible that we hadn't had one sooner given the terrain and our driving style. While swapping the wheel we were constantly hassled by a lady trying to sell us Uzbek money. We had no idea what the exchange rate was, so tried to fob her off. We would try to get some later when we had more idea. She was having none of it but we eventually got rid of her by promising to go to her hut to see her once we had dealt with the wheel. Again, the work was harder than it should have been due to the intense temperature, and pumping up the tyre seemed to take forever, but at least there was a gentle breeze to take the edge off the heat. Added to this, the foot pump decided to break part way through pumping up the tyre which didn't help anything.

Foxy with the broken pump

I set off down the queue of five trucks waiting ahead of us at the border in search of a pump. None of the trucks looked to have moved for hours, days even, each with their drivers lazing under them in the only available shade, chatting amongst themselves. Either nobody understood or they didn't have one. It wasn't looking good, but the tyre seemed to have enough air in it to be useable so we decided to make do. In the meantime the inpatient money selling lady had returned and Foxy had bought $40 (£21) worth of Uzbek money from her. The nearest town that looked big enough to have a bank, or consider accepting dollars, was further away than our fuel was likely to take us so we had little choice at the time. To our surprise we would later find out that we had actually got quite a good exchange rate too!

It appeared that the trucks were going nowhere and there were no officials to be seen, so we drove right around the trucks to the razor wire covered gates at the front of the queue in the hope of getting some attention. Possibly a bold move but there was no point hanging around. It worked and a guard came across to look at the buggy, took our passports and invited us to walk through the gates to the office to fill out the required forms. It was all relatively welcoming. The forms looked very similar to those we had filled in at the Russian borders, and on entering Kazakhstan, so we just copied the information across verbatim. It must have worked as we had no problems, no demands for money and before we knew it we were though and heading across no-man's land to the Uzbek border.

In keeping with the rest of the trip, our good fortune had to be countered by some bad luck and this was to be no exception. We realised that having made such good time throughout the day, especially on the road from Beyneu, we were now in fact ahead of ourselves. Our visas wouldn't let us enter Uzbekistan until the next day. Had we thought of this sooner we could have stopped in the desert before the border and had a rest rather than now being stuck with the traders, beggars, unsavoury characters and filth of the border post. It was too late now, we were at the border and with no-man's land not being the kind of place to hang about we drove on to the queue at the Uzbek border to see if they'd kindly let us in.

Here the cars and the trucks were in separate queues – not that there were enough of each to make a real queue – and we pulled up some way behind six Italian luxury 4x4's, all fully kitted out with sat-phones, GPS, tons of spares, extra tyres, roll-cages, modified suspension, survival kit, a trained medic and four motorbikes. We got out and went to chat to them and thankfully a few of them spoke perfect English. They had left Rome a couple of weeks earlier and were heading for Beijing in China which they hoped, at a push, to reach within four more weeks. We told them our route and that we had about four weeks for the entire journey, they sounded suitably impressed. Then we explained that it was just the two of us, that we weren't in fact waiting for the rest of our team to arrive, that we had no support crew, sat phones, survival training or team medic. This seemed to surprise them and they looked a little doubtful. They were somewhat older than us and had apparently done such journeys several times before so were acutely aware of the potential pitfalls and the terrain that lay ahead; this worried me slightly. They were clearly thinking we were mad or stupid or, more likely, both. Then we took them to look at our buggy. I think some of them saw the funny side of our immeasurable optimism that it would make the full journey while the others seemed genuinely and quite seriously concerned for us. However, meeting them was good for us as thanks to their meticulous preparation they had an electric compressor which they loaned to us so that we could pump up the rear tyre. Annoyingly, the cables weren't long enough to reach from the battery to the rear wheel but we soon fixed this with our resourcefulness by using our jump-leads to extend the cables. Always thinking. The local truck drivers and waifs and strays found this fascinating and all gathered round to watch our efforts. It was then that we realised why our pump had broken. The pressure gauge on ours mustn't have been working correctly as the tyre was already somewhere over 60psi, well over what it should have been and considerably above the safety level for the tyre. We subtly let some out and returned the pump but not before pretending to put air into the other tyres so we didn't look completely stupid in front of our now expectant audience. They had clearly never seen an electric tyre pump before so we had to demonstrate it in action.

Talking to the Italians some more, it transpired that they had already been parked exactly where we had found them for over six hours. This concerned us until we got the full story. Of the nineteen Italians at the border, only eighteen had Uzbek visas. The administrator who had sorted all the pre-expedition documents for them had forgotten to get one of the visas (they had an admin person!? We had nothing like this – just the two of us running around London between various embassies and queuing up for hours. We had clearly missed a trick somewhere during our prep!). As a consequence, their group leader was now somehow trying to blame the Uzbek border guards and demanding his group cross the border such that they could resolve the matter in the capital, Tashkent. This was a fundamental mistake and all it did was make the guards far less cooperative and the argument built and built. The sat-phone was out, tempers were flaring and the gates remained shut. Our problem was that we were becoming associated with the Italians as we were all speaking English – English seemed to be the universal language that all the foreigners used when speaking to other foreigners, who didn't speak the other's mother tongue.

While I had been over with the Italians, Foxy had befriended an Uzbek guard and was tucking into a watermelon while showing him our buggy. He seemed quite impressed and most importantly, friendly. We had considered accepting that we had no chance of crossing the border until the next day, but now we were here we had nothing else to do so decided to try our luck at getting through – it couldn't do us any harm and would kill some time. We made it clear that we had nothing to do with the Italians and he took us down to the front of the queue, past the razor wire, into the compound and into an office. Our passports were checked, without any problems, and Foxy sent back to the buggy. This was looking good, but as the named owner of the vehicle I now had the job, the long drawn out job, of completing the documentation for the buggy.

One of the more friendly guards with Foxy

I was handed a form, which I was delighted to see was in English, except it was the only one they had so I couldn't use it before it had been photocopied. The military had given it to me but it was the customs officers who had the photocopier, hence, somehow, the job fell to me to get the copies. I was pointed in the direction of a different hut-like office where there was supposedly a photocopier, although I couldn't believe something that modern, or for that matter anything powered by electricity, would be in any of the huts out here. Contrary to my doubts, it transpired that there was actually a dedicated photocopying person with a room all to himself. I handed him the form and immediately got the impression that he was going to make my life hard. He started indicating that he wanted money. I didn't have any with me and was sure I shouldn't have to give any. After a few minutes he gave up and disappeared into the back room. He was gone for ages, I tried to ask his colleague what was going on but he just shrugged. Half an hour later he eventually came back with the copied forms, and a wry smile. They were all in Russian and the English version was nowhere to be seen. I protested but he acted dumb and then the two officers started laughing. They had never had any intention of copying the form. It really was exasperating. I was tired, hot, getting hungry again and ultimately felt I was wasting my time as our visas weren't even valid yet. I walked out after insulting him in English, which he seemed to understand.

I headed back to the military office and found the guard I had spoken to earlier and handed him the forms with a look of disgust and confusion. Instantly he jumped up and practically dragged me over to the customs office, barging the queue of civilians out of the way to get into the hut while holding the forms out in front of him. The copy guy was looking smug while the guard barked at him. I caught a word that sounded like 'Italian' from the copy guy then the guard saying 'English'. At this point the two moved into the back room where the argument intensified and nationalities were debated. It was clear that the Italians had managed to really aggravate everyone at the border post with their arrogance and now as a direct result we were suffering. With the issue apparently resolved the guard reappeared with the English copies of the forms; the customs official looking genuinely sheepish.

I filled in the form and queued to get it stamped. I was then handed another form to complete. I found that the guards were actually being quite friendly towards me but the mood changed whenever any of the Italian contingent were in the vicinity. With these completed and stamped by another person in another office I received yet another form. This happened two more times. The Uzbeks, Kazaks and Russians must have huge data storage costs with everything being in duplicate. Even with all these forms completed I had seen nowhere to buy car insurance. We had managed to get through Kazakhstan without any, but it would be a comfort to get some for Uzbekistan, especially as we were going to be here for a few days and travelling through all the country's major cities. But with no option to buy it, there was nothing much we could do. I got the feeling I was near the end of the process and I was right. I was taken to a cleaner, more official room and asked for our passports again. With all the paperwork complete, all we needed was a stamp in the passports and we'd be off – assuming they didn't check the date on the visa. Which they did.

I started by acting surprised and pleading ignorance. A nice idea but it didn't wash with this guard who was one of the highest ranking military guards at the border; although being on border duties he was probably quite low in the overall military. He wasn't budging and kept pointing to the date on the visas and an ancient flip-calendar on his desk. It was just before 20:00 and I had no idea if, or when, the border shut for the night. Whether it would or not was irrelevant now. I could give up and fight my way through the midges back to the buggy and try to get some sleep until the morning – when no doubt we would have to redo all the forms as they would then have yesterday's date on them – or continue to try and change the guard's mind. I had nothing to do back at the buggy and was strangely enjoying the challenge so decided to carry on and see what I could do. I went for the sympathy vote.

While I had been doing the forms I had learnt from one of the guards that some other Westerners had crossed the border earlier in the day so I said we were with them. I said they were waiting in the desert thirty miles from the border and drew pictures of tents to indicate they were camping until we caught up with them. I drew pictures of broken cars to imply we had been delayed with car problems. I basically lied through my teeth. It was great fun. With more pictures and gestures he explained that he would lose his job and get shot if anyone found out (though I'm still not sure if he actually would have actually got shot). I explained that there wasn't a single town for the best part of 250 miles so no-one would know we were even there. With more pictures I explained that the police were never going to venture 220 miles into the desert to find us where we would supposedly be camping. He seemed to like this and started to smile. Then the Italians arrived.

They were being aggressive again, when it was them who were in the wrong, and complaining they had been waiting eight hours. Not wishing to be outdone I chipped in that I'd been waiting nine; the lies were coming naturally now. The guard had the Italians removed from the room and I remained with him. He seemed to be being sympathetic and was now toying with his rubber date stamp between his fingers. He glanced at another guard who was waiting in the room, they exchanged a few words and he rolled the date over to 3rd August, stamped our passports and, looking away, hurriedly gave them back to me. Job done. I couldn't believe it.

Outside the room the Italians were waiting and one of them complained to me that I was wasting his time as we didn't even have visas that would get us in until the morning. I smiled, explained that we were ready to leave, had the stamps, would be gone in ten minutes and sarcastically wished them a good night at the border. They were not impressed and without one of their visas they knew as well as I did that they would probably be there most of the next day, if not longer. They really would have to change their attitude if they were going to get anywhere.

I walked back to the buggy and took great pleasure as the guards had the Italians move their 4x4's to let us though. We drove into the compound waving to the irritated Italians, and now friendly guards, only to be stopped by customs.

The usual questions followed about if we had guns or narcotics. This time I decided not to joke about it and Foxy was led off into a room to pay some form of emissions tax – a classic method of asking for a bribe. After pleading ignorant this came out as just 100 roubles (£2.00). They seemed happy with the Russian roubles, which suited us as we didn't want to waste our Uzbek money, and we didn't want to push our luck too far considering we had what were now effectively forged visas. Customs and the military seem to have very different agendas at the border posts and work very independently so it's not worth assuming that what one says the other will accept and we didn't want to have to find out the hard way and have our visas refused at this juncture.

In the meantime, I was chatting with the officials and showing them all the gadgets we had; the cameras, the iPod, all the switches for the spotlights and extra engine fan and letting them sit in a right-hand drive car; they loved it. They especially loved the iTrip (an FM transmitter that attaches to the iPod such that it plays remotely through the buggy's radio) and they soon got the hang of changing the music and selecting their favourites and singing along. They were all desperate to have a go and so we had to stay a while longer until they had each had their fun – and it was good to be there with them now it was more relaxed and less formal. We gave them a few cigarettes and it was great to see how the very formal officials in their huge brimmed hats, with machine guns and stern faces could become much more human.

When we were ready to leave one of the guards leaned in the window and pressed five roubles into my hand – for luck he said. It was a really nice touch.

With that we shouted goodbye to the disgruntled Italians and drove into the darkness waving goodbye to Kazakhstan and the Uzbek guards.

It was just after 21:00, three hours before our visas were due to begin; a small victory and a great feeling.

The road was still unsurfaced and where it had been compacted was like driving across a shallow-ploughed field with the ruts running left to right across the road. I drove on as long as I could. To begin with, Foxy was awake and we were chatting away when we came up behind a truck travelling in the same direction as us. The first we knew of it was being engulfed in a seemingly impenetrable cloud of dust as if we had driven into a sand storm. The truck came from nowhere, like the horses in Kazakhstan, completely invisible until the last minute with its lights blocked out by the plume of dust it was throwing up. I pulled back and we could just make out the shadows being cast by the headlights on the rocks some distance up the road.

It was seriously dangerous trying to overtake as there was no chance of seeing if anything was coming the other way or where the edges of the road and the huge potholes were. It was highly unlikely that there would be any traffic, but had there been we would certainly have hit it head on. The potholes and the edge of the road were an equally great issue and could easily have wrecked the buggy. Just as dangerous was the risk of the truck swerving across us as we came alongside if the driver tried to avoid potholes himself. We decided that we had to pass it, we were confident that nothing would be coming and our speed had now dropped massively. We shut the windows and drove into the dust cloud, using the horn and hoping for the best. I had to drive straight into the dust to be sure that I wasn't heading off the road into the desert. The cloud got thicker and thicker then suddenly dim red lights appeared and we were literally on the tailgate of the truck. I had massively misjudged how slowly the truck was going and had to dive on the brakes to avoid plunging under its tailgate. I pulled out of the dust cloud and had a few moments to recompose before trying again. This time it worked much better, I pulled out just in time and got past. My palms were sweating and I didn't want to have to do this many more times.

We drove on and soon Foxy was asleep; I had the music up and the windows down in an effort to stay as alert as I could. I had overtaken another three trucks, some of which I had been stuck behind for ages waiting for a chance to get by and even then having to make several attempts. It was dangerous, I was getting sleepy and we were making pitifully slow progress. It was 01:20 when I pulled off the road into the sand, driving a safe distance away from the road to make sure nothing would hit us while we slept. It was going to be another night in the buggy, we swapped seats and like last time I couldn't be bothered to get my sleeping bag. We had been on the move for four hours since the border, passed just four vehicles and had covered only 100 miles. Driving at night was always slower than the day but an average of 25mph was ridiculous.

3rd August – Eastern UZ to Khiva, UZ

Throughout the night I woke several times from quite vivid nightmares. I would imagine that Foxy was driving and had fallen asleep. As I was in the passenger seat I would find myself reaching over to grab the steering wheel, dozily panicking, to try and guide us in a safe direction until I could wake Foxy. This whole period was incredibly lifelike and would only come to an end when we were both fully awake and I could realise that we were in fact still safely parked. This happened several times throughout the night and made a bad nights sleep infinitely worse; I really would have to stop sleeping in the buggy.

By 05:30 we had had enough of trying to sleep and dealing with my nightmares so got out into the cold morning air, put the last of the fuel into the buggy and set off. We were now starting to pass through a few very tiny villages and, predictably, with them came the police checks. There were several of these, but they were harmless enough and we never got stopped for more than a few minutes. Our progress was probably helped by the fact that everything was now thick, really thick, in dust and sand. The dust had come in through all the door seals and the windows and had penetrated its way into absolutely everything, even our bags. Everything was sand coloured – even us! The police had no interest in getting filthy while poking around our buggy, so the searches tended to be far from rigorous.

We were still travelling on a dirt track (with the exception of a one and a half mile stretch of tarmac laid in the middle of nowhere for no apparent reason) and at 10:00 arrived in Qonghirat, the most westerly town in Uzbekistan. Fortunately, our fuel had just lasted but we really had to find some quickly. There was no obvious filling station so we asked some men at a junction for benzene. They sprang into life and dispatched one of their boys, who was soon running back from a hut with two plastic water bottles full of fuel. We had no idea what quality it was, or for that matter if it was even petrol or diesel – most people assumed the buggy was a diesel – and we didn't want to take the risk. We also needed about fifty litres rather than the five or so the boy had. We managed to get away without having to buy it and drove about the town looking for fuel. All we could see were more people, usually children, with containers of fuel on the roadside selling it out of plastic containers and water bottles. We wondered if there was some kind of fuel shortage or if this was common practice. About twenty miles back up the road we had just come along, we recalled seeing what had looked like a deserted filling station on its own in the desert. We decided to chance it and head back there, in the hope they had some kind of fuel we could properly identify. It was quite a big risk as we had virtually no fuel and potentially a forty mile round trip to make to get back to the town if they had none, but we decided it was better than risking putting in diesel or watered down petrol. We stuck the buggy back into two wheel drive and steadily drove back to conserve fuel. Incredibly, the deserted garage was open and sold us the fifty litres of fuel that we just could afford, filling the buggy and one of the jerry cans. At these garages it is only possible to buy fixed amounts of fuel, unlike in the UK where you can simply put in as much as you want. This was always a problem as we were never sure just how much we would be able to get in the buggy without it overflowing everywhere – they have no auto cut-off and simply pump it in! However, by the end of the expedition we were pretty much able to guess correctly to within about half a litre or so.

Driving back through Qonghirat there were a few cars but mostly donkeys and carts. The carts were all piled about eight feet high with straw and this overhung the body of the cart by about three times its width. This was all very precariously balanced and on top would be perched a young boy to whip and direct the struggling donkey, which seemed far too small for the job in hand. Still, however dodgy it looked, it seemed to work. What was also strange was that all the buildings were single storey and constructed of wattle and daub. It really was a step back in time but at least the road was tarmaced, though absolutely riddled with potholes. There was nothing much to stop for, so we headed north to the ex-port of Moynaq, our first real diversion of the whole adventure so far.

Moynaq was once on the shores of the Aral Sea before the Russians diverted the river that fed the sea to irrigate their cotton fields, reducing the sea to twenty-five percent of its original area. Presently the shore is now some 30-35 miles from Moynaq and receding by the day. This has left many fishing boats and cargo barges rusting on the dried-out seabed, and some forty thousand locals lost their livelihoods with the sea disappearing and the fish dying; they had no alternative but to abandon the ships where they lay. Even the remaining water is useless due to its increased salinity and high levels of toxicity from chemical run-off. A more worrying side-effect of the receding water level is that the bio-weapons facility on Vozrozhdeniya Island has now become dangerously connected to the mainland with the risk of the anthrax remaining on the ground following weapons testing by the Russians, spreading.

A further effect of this is that the rains never come and a whole new arid and unnaturally hot micro-climate has developed. Poisonous dust storms are formed in the strong winds which blow over the dried-up seabed, resulting in many of the remaining residents of Moynaq now suffering from chronic and acute illnesses. We hoped to get to some of the safer areas and take a look at the ships before they corrode away, becoming lost under the sand forever.

Driving north to Moynaq the inevitable finally happened while I was at the wheel. I had my arm out of the window, tanning in the hot breeze, when a wasp shot down the sleeve of my t-shirt and got lodged between my back and the seat, leaving its sting firmly embedded in my back. I stopped pretty sharp-ish and Foxy extracted the remains of the dying wasp from my back.

At Moynaq, after a good half an hour of searching, having crossed the town twice, we found the rough area where we thought the ships were supposed to be. From a high point that had once been the edge of the sea, we could see out into the distance to where the rusting hulks of about ten ships lay.

Looking out over the bed of the Aral Sea

The seabed ahead was flat as far as the eye could see, except for the curvature of the Earth, and was now littered with sand dunes and patches of parched scrub. We drove down to the seabed and set off in the direction of the ships. Even in the low ratio gears, the buggy was soon bogged down in the sand dunes and going nowhere. We decided not to risk getting too stuck so set off to cover the remaining mile or so on foot.

Not really thinking, we set off as we were; no t-shirts, no water and no sun cream. Down on the seabed was certainly the hottest place we'd been so far – nudging towards an almost unbelievable 60°C – and the sand was actually burning our feet as it flowed into our flip-flops. I actually felt like I was gradually being cooked. It was a long job as the searing heat soon had its effect on us and walking in the sand was slow going.

At the ships we posed for the obligatory photos and had a look around them. I had hoped to find some huge container ships, their hulks trapped in the sand, but we had to make do with some fishing boats and some slightly larger barges.

Posing by a rusting ship at the Aral Sea

It turns out that the larger container ships are near the town of Aral, on the northern side of the sea, but we were 250 miles south of this. The ships we did find were all half-submerged in the sand and corroding rapidly. We soon found the true extent of the corrosion while walking on the decks and discovered holes rusted right the way through which creaked and moved under our weight – we clambered back down to the sand before we found ourselves falling through. It was all very surreal, and a little sad, walking around ships like this with no water for tens of miles and a disused port just a couple of miles away. But then that's the Russian attitude towards progress I guess, after all, it wasn't their towns they ruined.

Getting back to the buggy and our water was a bit of a relief, so we got up some speed and, with all the wheels spinning in the sand, made it back out of the sea and to the old shoreline. A few miles south of Moynaq, we stopped to eat some of our tinned fish and nibbles beside a large pool in an irrigation channel we'd spotted on the way north in the morning, where some farm workers had been swimming. We had hoped to swim too but the water was horribly stagnant and full of algae so decided against it – though it was tempting just to cool off. Back on the move and the buggy's engine was now pinking (when the timing is out and the valves hit the pistons) and running extremely hot even with our additional fan permanently turned on. We tried to ignore it and found that by accelerating more gently the problem went away. So that's what we did and successfully ignored it.

We had almost got to Nukus, which was back just south of where we had been earlier in the day, after our 170 mile detour to look at the ships (at the time it didn't seem worth it but looking back I'm glad we did), when we were stopped by the police. We couldn't tell what they were saying but they were clearly using the word Italian. The Italians from the border had obviously got ahead of us and were causing chaos that, again, the police thought was to do with us. We explained that we were English, smiled loads, asked for directions and used a couple of words of Russian. We also blamed Kazakhstan for the filthiness of our buggy and clothes – apparently they hate the Kazaks – they found it amusing and started laughing and soon we were on our way.

In Nukus we located the Bank of Uzbekistan using the tiny map in the Lonely Planet. It was a huge, beautiful place made of granite and marble and would have fitted in well in central London. When we went inside, past the hefty security guards, the difference to my expectations was incredible. Behind the grand doors that fronted every room was nothing, absolutely nothing, each room looked derelict and deserted. We followed the hand written signs, sticky-taped to the walls, to the room where they took Visa. Inside this room things were not much better, but at least there were two members of staff. Once they had established that we wanted to withdraw some cash, the process began.

The Visa machine was unearthed from a drawer in a desk where it appeared to be stored for special occasions and we had our passports checked. A printer on the desk was unplugged so the Visa machine could be plugged in. Once it had 'warmed up' they swiped my card several times, each time it was rejected. They then tried Foxy's card. This too was rejected. Then, being the technical geniuses we are, we politely pointed out that they hadn't connected the phone cable to the Visa machine such that our cards could be verified. The next challenge was to connect the phone cable which had no plug on it. They shaved the insulation off with a pocketknife and poked the bare wires into the phone socket. It really was pitiful watching them have to work like this in such an impressive building. Again, no joy (thanks once again to our bank for having put a potential-fraudulent-usage-block on our cards –

surely they could have phoned us to tell us this by now?). The staff then phoned various people (once they had re-made the makeshift connection with the bare phone cable to the socket) and after more than an hour, had no solutions. We left. Back down the grand stairs, past the neglected rooms, along the ornately decorated, marble floored corridor and out into the baking heat.

We had just 8000 Uzbek Som (£4.50) and $30 (£16) left in cash. We were convinced we had lost some somewhere but that was irrelevant now. We had virtually no money and absolutely no way of getting any. The only option left we could see would be to find an internet café, open an account with Western Union and transfer some money to ourselves that we could then collect at the Western Union office in Urgench or Khiva (however, with our accounts frozen this too would probably not have worked; though at this point we still didn't know this to be the case!).

On the road we passed several villages. At each one, children on the street would stop and wave at us as we drove past and wherever they could, they would come over and look and point excitedly at the buggy. They were clearly expecting us and must have heard of the rally in the press. We later found out that the rally had made the front page of the national paper a day or so earlier and being one of the first cars through made us appear to be mini-heroes. It was like being a famous rally driver. In all fairness, the buggy did look the part and could easily be mistaken for a race car in a country that didn't actually have any race cars to make a true comparison against. We accidentally helped the façade as we both happened to be wearing our matching rally t-shirts and matching sunglasses.

Just outside Urgench we came to a vulcaniser. On the outskirts of every village there would be a number of vulcanisers ready to fix the tyres of cars coming in from the desert – a sure sign of just how bad the roads were. We handed over the flat tyre, jacked-up the buggy and removed what had been the spare, ready to fit the repaired tyre once it was fixed. This way we would once again have a matching set (our spare, which we were now having to use, was narrower and a slightly different type and certainly wasn't helping the handling). All the while, a crowd was gathering from the nearby huts and from inside the vulcaniser. Here we also noticed that metal fatigue had set in on the rear windows, the hinges now just hanging on by the smallest piece of metal so we mixed some more of the liquid metal and botched them back together, taping them shut to allow the metal to cure. With the tyre inside the hut being repaired, Foxy spotted a hand-pumped well next to a drainage ditch, where some locals were bathing, and went across to wash his hands. As soon as he got there one of the fascinated locals was straight on the case and started pumping the well for Foxy and before long he was having a full shower under the tumbling well water.

Foxy showering in the well

I threw the soap and shampoo across. I spent my time showing-off the buggy to the curious locals, who had never seen anything like it, before going for a shower myself. I felt a bit guilty using the fresh, clean water from the well whilst the locals bathed in the ditch, but then again it was the locals treating us to the well and tipping the water over our heads, so I guess it was ok. Making the most of the situation, we filled our bucket and washed some clothes, the buggy's windows and as much of the interior as we could. The thick dust had penetrated everywhere.

Everyone was incredibly kind and helpful and they even insisted on fitting the repaired tyre for us now that we were clean. And all they wanted for this was $4 (£2.15). We gave them $6 (£3.20); $4 was way over the odds, but they knew it was nothing to us and that we'd be happy to pay it, and we felt we should tip just for the extra service. Having said that, we were hardly flush ourselves at this point!

It was a great feeling, driving off as the sun set, feeling clean and having both spare tyres serviceable again. It was one thing less to worry about. As we left we realised we were lost, being followed and extremely low on fuel. We had driven out of the village but had to turn back. As we did the car following us waited, then turned back itself and followed again. This happened a few more times as we tried to find our way and we became ever more concerned. We headed back to the vulcaniser. They were worried to see us again but we made it clear there was nothing wrong with the tyre and asked for directions, put some of our fuel in from our jerry cans and kept an eye on the car which was now waiting some way behind us up the road. There was nothing we could do, so we drove off in the right direction as quick as we could. Even though the buggy was pretty slow we were still driving quicker than most of the locals, who seemed to creep everywhere, and we managed to lose the car, or it may have just got bored. It could be they had just been curious to see one of the foreign rally cars covered in race stickers and wanted a closer look, but with it now being dark we had obviously started to think the worst and came up with all kinds of theories as to what they wanted to do to us.

We were trying to get to Khiva, a few miles away, to find somewhere to camp for the night but were now in a relatively built up area with a few shanty huts and some more substantial buildings thrown in. We were stopped several times by the police, all thinking we were Italian, but got away quite quickly once they realised that we were English. We also kept getting lost and had to ask for directions several times. At Urgench it was getting late and there was nowhere to camp – all the land to the sides of the roads was fenced off for farming or full of crops – so we asked at a couple of restaurants if they knew of anywhere to sleep. They didn't, or didn't understand my poor sleeping actions, so we headed on to Khiva. We were tried and getting lost more and more often. It was like trying to drive across London with a hand drawn map, no signs and just knowing that you needed to head roughly in a certain direction to get to the other side. Being immensely tired and not being able to communicate to ask anyone the way wasn't helping either. It was virtually impossible.

Then a local car, about the size of a Ford Fiesta, pulled along side us at a junction with about six excited men crammed into it. They were waving and desperate to talk to us so we showed them the map and asked for Khiva. They started waving and pulled ahead of us leading the way. We followed them for a couple of miles around the streets and began to wonder if we were on a wild goose-chase and we were about to give up when we identified some words on a sign that looked a bit like 'Khiva 8kms'. The packed car pulled over, we thanked them, and they all waved and cheered us on. They really did seem to think we were in a serious race and that they were helping one of the lead teams. Not that surprising given it was late at night and we were one of the few cars still on the road so, in the minds of the locals, had to be trying urgently to get to somewhere; it was a great feeling and probably made their day.

The next five miles were pretty hair-raising. It was a good straight road but it was littered with donkey carts stacked with straw and pedestrians. The carts didn't have lights and it was impossible to see them if, when we came up behind them, a car happened to be coming the opposite way, due to us being dazzled by the headlights of the on-coming car. The pedestrians had no concept of pavements and never bothered to move off the road. The next moment we would get involved in some hasty braking and a quick swerve to avoid running into the back of a cart, which would be doing less than six miles and hour, or mowing down a couple of people walking in the dark. It wasn't good and we discussed what we would do, should we accidentally hit a person or animal, and the consequences of our decisions in each of the countries with their respective legal systems and punishments. We made a plan and decided to stick to it, whatever happened.

Arriving into Khiva was incredible. We had seen that it was possible to stay within the walls of the citadel, Itchan Kala, a UNESCO World Heritage site dating from the tenth century in the heart of the old town and, as there was no chance of camping anywhere, we headed there to see what we could find. Sadly, it was too late in the day and everywhere appeared to be shut. We took a walk within the citadel along the deserted streets by moonlight, which has been completely restored and now people actually live in the ancient buildings inside. The walls, mosques and minarets were truly amazing and stunning to look at. Considering how old they were it was extraordinary how good they looked and how vivid the blues were.

We found somewhere which was just closing and stopped in time for a local beer, within the citadel walls, before wandering back to the buggy. A great place, steeped in history and the perfect way to relax after so long on the road. The main street and open area outside the walls was clearly the area intended for visitors to park but was now completely deserted, so we parked the buggy beside the walls, hoped we didn't get moved on later in the night and went to bed, in the buggy.

The citadel by night, Khiva

It was too late to look for anywhere to stay and the buggy had the best views in the whole of the town, probably even the whole of the country.

4th August – Khiva, UZ to Bukhara, UZ

We woke before 07:00, facing the walls of the citadel from our sub-star rated buggy-hotel with the kind of view that even the best hotels didn't have, so we could hardly complain however cramped our legs and sore our necks were.

Inside the citadel, Khiva

As it was, as always, a gorgeously, warm, sunny morning we went for another walk within the citadel. It was clearly a huge tourist venue yet at this time in the morning there was not a soul about. The minarets were amazingly detailed with stunning, vibrant colours and mosaics decorating them.

Early morning in the citadel, Khiva

As we walked on, there was the occasional local person coming out of their house in anticipation of the tourists arriving or just to go about their daily chores. They all knew the word 'hello', confirming our suspicions of the popularity of the place. One man walked with us a while asking if we wanted to see his house. We were in no rush so accepted and soon we were taken inside one of the thick, mud-walled buildings through a tiny door into the cool air. He sat down on a bright, woven rug

197

and started to point out things of minimal interest around the room. It was interesting to see inside but to be honest we would have been happy staying for just five minutes to get a feel for the place, rather than looking at every item in turn. We made to leave and, predictably, he started asking for money and looked offended, then started demanding it. I wouldn't have minded giving him something but he had hardly done anything to justify it and, with his sudden change in attitude, he certainly wouldn't be getting anything.

More of the citadel, Khiva

As we walked further, the locals were starting to set out their stalls of rugs, paintings and tourist tat, jostling for the best spots. The scene was changing from one of a genuine old city to that of a tourist trap. We had been lucky to see it this early in the morning but it was now the time to leave as the stall holders were now starting to try and sell us their wares. At the main gate out of the citadel we were stopped by a security guard who had now installed himself to collect money from the entering tourists. Money we didn't have as everything was in the buggy. We explained this but he was asking for more than we even had. We didn't see that there was any reason to pay to walk around a town now that we were leaving and that had been free to enter, but he insisted we stay until 08:30 when the he could phone the bank to somehow authorise our Visa payment.

Even more of the citadel, Khiva

We knew this wouldn't work considering our cards hadn't worked the day before and it would just waste more of our time. We had twenty minutes to kill before half past eight and decided to make our getaway.

We persuaded him to allow us back to the buggy to get our credit cards and surreptitiously started the engine to allow it a moment to warm up. It had a nasty habit of stalling if we got the position of the manual choke wrong in the mornings. Once we were happy it would work, we jumped in and drove off as quickly as we could. This wasn't easy as we had to go pretty much past the guard but he didn't seem too bothered. By the look of things he would have plenty more tourists to get money from throughout the day.

Further through the town we were stopped by the police while trying to make our way back to Urgench to find money. This was where the guard had told us the bank was and being a bit touristier than Nukus, and bigger than Khiva, we hoped that we may have more luck getting money out, assuming we could even find Urgench and the bank. We pointed to Urgench on our map and the policeman started pointing to the sky, then straight on. It made no sense. Then we saw the overhead power lines for the trams which assumed must run between Khiva and Urgench. We thanked him and shook his hand.

Shaking the hands of the locals had become a great game throughout the journey. We would get a different reaction almost from town to town. Some would be slightly confused and hesitant, others overly keen and smiley, but most somewhere in-between with a look of excitement, confusion and pride. It was great and really made a difference when we did this while using a couple of the Russian words we'd learnt.

Amazingly, we followed the power lines and they took us the whole seventeen miles right to a bank at the centre of Urgench without a single hitch. Annoyingly, it didn't take Visa but we soon found another nearby which did. Having no cash left we decided to try for $300 (£160) so we'd hopefully be able to get most of the way to Mongolia without needing more (in hindsight this was a little optimistic!). This was an incredible amount of money out here and the assistants immediately looked shocked and suspicious that two young men could ever have so much money. The best thing was that they seemed, in principal, to be able to deal with the request and began phoning various head offices to check that they could in fact do this for us. We feared the worst considering our cards hadn't worked the day before, but then the assistant stopped calling people and collected a manual Visa machine from another room. This was perfect. We'd easily be able to get the payment authorised like this as there'd be no need for them to contact our bank directly and so discover the block on our cards (we still didn't know this at the time but by now certainly had our suspicions). Realising our good luck we asked for $400 (£215). This stalled him for a moment then he simply agreed, swiped my card and handed over the money. We took the dollars downstairs to another room where, without too much hassle, we were able to exchange some of the dollars for Uzbek Som. It was such a relief to have money again and even better when we were presented with a stack of Uzbek Som about 5cm thick – and that was only $100 (£54)! We'd noticed that everyone out here had an amazing ability to count money at an astonishing rate which was evidently due to the number of notes needed to buy even the most basic of things. It was a superb feeling walking out of the bank, our shorts pockets literally stuffed with wads of cash. It was like having our freedom back and had seemed so simple, although to get this freedom we had wasted most of the morning, but taking the previous days as a benchmark, this had seemed painless. It was amazing that we were thinking like this as I get impatient queuing for just five minutes at a cash machine! All we needed now was some fuel.

We were almost back at the buggy when we were pounced on by some street kids trying to force flatbreads into our hands. Admittedly, we did want some breakfast, but to be honest we didn't fancy our chances with this. However, there was no getting rid of the kids even once we were back in the relative safety of the buggy and able to get the wads of money safely into our bags.

If only it was worth anything like as much as it looks!

It was then we realised that there were about twenty more kids behind a fence to our right. With some teachers. They were school kids. Suddenly we felt very stupid for being so dismissive and cynical and, again, assuming the worst. One of the older girls spoke a small amount of English and explained that they had just baked the breads in class that morning and they wanted us to taste them to see what we thought of their traditional food. They had never had the chance to try them out on foreigners and, on seeing the buggy parked up, had waited for our return. She loved having the chance to speak some English and the teachers seemed thrilled too. We tried the bread, which was still warm, and it was gorgeous. It was like large pitta bread, but crispier on the outside with cumin seeds inside.

By now all the kids had joined us and were leaning in the buggy's windows to get a better look at us and the buggy, touching and pointing at everything they could. One asked for an autograph and soon they were all jostling to get their school books signed by us. It was all very strange but we were definitely welcome in Uzbekistan. We had nothing much to give them in return so left them some tennis balls, a football and cricket bat – they seemed happy but to be honest they just seemed happy to have met us. As we started to drive off we were stopped again by one of the kids who had run back to the school and got two more of the breads for us to take on our way. It was brilliant, not only was it fantastic to meet them but now we also had breakfast.

Finding petrol stations was easy enough. The problem was the fact that they all had massive queues and only 80RON fuel available. We bit the bullet and joined one of the queues. It seemed like there may be a fuel shortage so we had little choice and filled everything up. This took some time as various people shoved their cars in front of ours while we tried to work out who to pay and how to get them to fill our buggy instead of the other cars.

All that was left to do was find our way towards Bukhara. Instead we found ourselves on a huge, four-lane, tree-lined and practically deserted road which lead to an airport which itself looked, but wasn't, disused. This had been a common sight on the journey so far, that government buildings and installations would have the most impressive surroundings and transport links. Millions of pounds must have been spent on such buildings, and the infrastructure to go with them, purely for the purpose of impressing officials and dignitaries on their visits. It was a dreadful waste of money but then that was the way the system had worked under Soviet rule. Not that I know if it's any different now, but it was certainly that era when the infrastructure we saw had been built.

We found the road out of Urgench and headed for Bukhara; 260 miles to the south-east across nothing the scorching Kyzyl-Kum desert. The road had some form of tarmac but over the years the intense heat had taken its toll and it was in a bad way. Even so, we were able to get a good speed up and simply pound through must of the potholes. Only occasionally would the buggy hit one big enough to throw us off line and for a few moments the buggy would be in control of itself until the snaking and bouncing stopped and we could regain control.

There wasn't a single town along the entire length of this stretch of road with the exception of a couple of huts and one tiny village. Then we came to a military checkpoint, miles from anywhere with the obligatory collections of machine guns and other weaponry. The check was very thorough but they were kind enough, seemed excited to see us and waved us on. It seemed odd to have a checkpoint out here but looking at the map we saw that the road here was running parallel to the Turkmen border just five miles to the south. Turkmenistan and Uzbekistan aren't the best of friends and are probably keen to check who might be sneaking through.

As always with the checkpoints, it was a massive panic to scrub off the entire buggy's speed without making it look like we had just slammed the brakes on in guilty panic. We suspected that most of the time we were speeding but with no signs and no other cars to gauge our speed against we were never sure. Running up to a checkpoint too fast would probably result in a fine or getting shot and too slow would make us look nervous as if we were hiding something so we'd just slow to about twenty miles an hour for the last quarter mile or so – assuming we spotted the checkpoint in time, which we often didn't!

Crossing the baking desert

With over 120 miles left to go we spotted an impossibly bright turquoise lake just to the south. It looked too inviting so we pulled off the road, engaged four wheel drive and worked our way down a track towards what was in fact the banks of the river where it was running slowly and easily a couple of miles wide. The baking dry desert air was proving hard going, but a couple of hours in the river would sort us out. Part way down, the track ended and we started to worry as we were surrounded by very hardy looking, low-laying, cacti with huge, stiff spikes that would no doubt puncture the tyres if we were unlucky. We picked our way through and came to the dried, cracked mud, metres from the edge of the river. It was here that the buggy started to bog down as the dried mud changed to wet silt so we had to accelerate, with the wheels sinking, and make a big arc back towards the sandy bank hoping the momentum would keep us free. We were out of sight of the road which was now quite a hike away and, as in Kazakhstan, we certainly didn't want to get stuck here.

Stuck at the water's edge

We left the buggy on the sand and headed to the river on foot. Almost at the shore we were engulfed by large, black, buzzing flies and the mud underfoot was too soft even to walk on – almost like quicksand. Even if we did get to the water, when we tried to get out again we'd end up caked in mud. We went back to the buggy, defeated by the flies and the mud. Looking back it was probably for the best. On the map the other side of the river was Turkmenistan and to anyone patrolling the border it could easily have looked like we were trying to swim across. Never a good thing.

Not much further along the road we came to a café, a bit of an oasis in the desert. The dining area was outside, under a canopy, with bench-like tables in the middle with two raised seating areas at either end where it was possible to sit cross-legged or lounge on the cushions. As these raised areas were both in use, we went for the benches. We had barely sat ourselves down when we were beckoned over by two men drinking tea at one of the seating areas. We went over and joined them on the cushions around their table. We spent the next couple of hours drinking tea and Coke and chatting to the men.

Lunch with the locals

They didn't speak a single word of English and us not a word of Uzbek yet somehow we had a full conversation for all this time and even managed to share jokes over the tea, which was a bit like green tea served in delicate china cups. We were in need of some food so I wandered over to the other end of the café where more locals were sitting to see what they were eating. As soon as I approached the table they were smiling and one held out a piece of the deep fried fish for me to try. Of all the countries we were to travel through, I'd expected Uzbekistan to be one of the least hospitable toward us, yet the complete opposite was proving to be true. The fish was very meaty and quite fatty with some herbs mixed in the batter. It was perfect. I talked to them for a bit and, at their request, brought the buggy around right beside their table so they could have a closer look while they ate. The rally really was big news out here.

I ordered some of the fish from the owner and went back to our table. Behind the café they had a small pond, though where the water was from I have no idea, and a small vegetable patch with a puppy playfully running around. While we waited for the food we showed the Uzbeks some of the English money we had; they were fascinated by it and wanted to see the different types so we left them some as they were keen to show it to their friends. When the food came it also had more of the now familiar flatbread, salad, hot chilli dip and a bottle of water and the whole thing, including the tea and Coke for the four of us, came to less than £2.50. We lazed on the cushions for quite a while but felt we had to be on the move again. We were permanently restless to see what lay ahead. But as we got to the buggy the café owner's young son leapt out with a bucket and started to wash the buggy's dust and fly covered windows. He was happy to be doing it, but looked to be making a big job of it as he didn't even have a cloth and was just using his bare hands. We gave him our sponge and he carried on with even greater enthusiasm. He grabbed the hosepipe from the pond and started to wash the entire buggy. It was incredible, here we were in the middle of the desert and this boy was using their precious water to hose down our tin-pot buggy while we watched on with his proud father. To be honest, it was in desperate need of a clean but using a three inch square sponge was making it quite a long job and we had already become restless when we had first wanted to leave, but the kid was being a perfectionist and seemed too happy to be stopped.

Having a wash in the desert

Once he was done he tried his luck by asking for money, smiling cheekily and writing the amount in the sand. His father glared at him as the amount he asked for was clearly excessive for what he had done but all we had was a much larger note, five times more than he'd asked for but we agreed to give him that instead. By the look on his face it must have made his day, yet it was only twenty pence. Lunch had been a great experience but it was good to be back on the move through the featureless, blisteringly hot desert again. Then we nearly crashed.

It was a perfectly straight, flat road and we were doing about 65mph with Foxy driving. This was about as fast as the buggy would go (without being on a downhill slope) and it was a good cruising speed to cover these large distances until we hit some potholes. The buggy launched awkwardly into the air, crashing down on the front left wheel before bouncing back into the air only to land on the rear wheels, slightly sideways. This kangarooing continued for a few hundred metres and there was nothing we could do but listen to the squealing tyres and hold on until the buggy had slowed down, allowing Foxy to steer us back onto our side of the road. Luckily there had been no traffic coming the other way. The obvious worry was that should this happen again we could easily be thrown off the road or hit other traffic. We really needed to get the shock absorbers looked at, as we knew that having at least three of the four not working was ruining the handling of the buggy. We slowed down for a bit while we recomposed, but as there was nothing we could do here we simply set off again at full speed, trying to keep a sharper lookout for potholes. We'd had moments like this many times before, but this had been a huge one and really made us think, for at least a minute, about the risks.

It was also at this point that we realised it was always me driving when mechanical things broke and Foxy when we had near misses with crashes.

For the second time since lunch we were stopped by the police so they could check our documents, we gave them a couple of cigarettes and they seemed happy enough to let us carry on. We had a brief chat and learnt that there were two Mongol Rally cars about an hour ahead of us, but the chances of catching up with them were slim – although we were pretty sure from what we had discussed with the others in Prague that we were running our buggy quicker than most. If the cars ahead hadn't had any breakdowns and were taking the same route as us then there was a fair chance we would see them on the road in the next day or so. It began to feel like a race, there were cars ahead and the locals thought we were stars.

Continuing through the desert we could distinctly hear the sound of a jet engine quite nearby. Thinking we had stumbled across an airbase we stopped the buggy and jumped out to get some sneaky photos.

Standing on the buggy's roof we were disappointed only to be able to see a pipeline with a jet engine being used to power a pump. Our disappointment was short lived though, as we then discovered the skeleton of a creature about the size of a cow half-hidden in the sand. Not wanting to miss out on a photo opportunity now that we'd stopped, we scooped it together and proceeded to do some primitive archaeology to recreate a shortened, comedy version of whatever it had once been – it's the little things that make you laugh at times like these. Taking the idea further, we then tied the largest parts of our skeletal creature to the spare wheel on the back of the buggy as a trophy. We needed something to brighten up the day and the bleached white of the bones against the matt black of the wheel looked pretty artistic, though we did wonder what the police may make of it. We should have realised that it would just give them something else to use against us, thus creating more grief – and it did.

For the next couple of hours we found ourselves travelling at roughly the same speed as a long distance coach which, from a scrap of card in the window, was apparently on its way to Tashkent. Whenever we stopped, to fill up from the jerry cans, take photos or to change drivers the coach would pass us again with the passengers, all grown men, with their smiley faces pressed against the windows waving manically at us. Once on the move again we would overtake – which was a long process in the buggy – and as we did the crowd of men would move along the coach watching us until they were all crammed around the driver, still waving. They loved us and we loved the attention. We felt as if we were in the Paris-Dakar race and really did feel to be developing our stardom and the matching t-shirts and sunglasses helped endlessly.

At the next police roadblock the coach had arrived just ahead and was waiting. All the men had got off and came running over as we pulled up beside the guards ready to hand our documents over. Instead of the usual checks we spent the next fifteen minutes or so showing off the buggy, posing for photos and shaking everyone's hand, several times over. It's a good job we couldn't speak Uzbek or they would have soon discovered the reality of who we were. The national newspaper, with typical journalistic licence, must really have hyped-up and sensationalised the rally.

Our new friends packed on the bus

Eventually, we were out of the desert and heading into Bukhara. The area has been inhabited since 3,000BC with the city founded in

500BC, famous for being part of the Persian Empire and being a main centre of Iranian civilisation and a trading post on the Silk Road. It was much like Khiva, also a World Heritage site (I've lost count of how many of these we saw on the trip) and everything was centuries old, although not as fully preserved or restored as Khiva. For once we were able to locate ourselves on the mini town centre map we had and aimed straight for an area where a couple of hotels were marked. It was early evening and we had decided that we should stop here and have a proper bed and shower for the night. The last few nights in the buggy had been hard going and looking ahead there would be many more like this to come.

Foxy was navigating and I was at the wheel. I don't know whose fault it was (I'd like to think it wasn't mine), and this happened a few times, but left was supposedly shouted but I went right. The classic error. We had both done it from time to time but I got the blame for this one. Not wanting to admit that I was getting us lost, I carried on, I had a thing about turning back as it was clearly a waste of time to cover the same ground again. Foxy managed to pick a new route that would get us through the back streets and to the centre with the hotels. But remember, this was a map designed for people on foot and the streets had been built sometime before cars, probably even carts, had been invented. We carried on through streets of wattle and daub houses which were all identical and it was impossible to spot a landmark to use as a reference, but we felt to be going the right way and our hunches tended to be right. Except this time the road got narrower and narrower to the point that it was no wider the buggy itself. We were literally getting wedged in the street and it was impossible to continue forwards. I tentatively reversed back, trying not to demolish the adjacent, historic mud houses although it felt like I had taken a bulldozer into an art gallery. We paused and considered our options.

While waiting, trying to decide the best way to get out of the maze of identical baked-mud lanes, a taxi appeared from nowhere and waved us to follow him. He was clearly much more skilled at driving these streets and occasionally had to wait for us to catch up but he guided us, without even asking, right to where we had been trying to get. We parked up in an area that would probably hold the morning market, right beside another huge, restored citadel, the Ark Fortress, and wandered across the road to the Hotel Caravan (just to keep up the camping theme). It really was quite a surprise to find that the hotel was such high quality considering the state of most of the buildings we had seen over the past few days. It had air-con, which was absolute heaven and the lobby was decked out in polished marble with huge, ornate ornaments dotted around, and the staff were friendly. It had the feel that a place on the Silk Road may have had back when it was still the world's most important trade route. We were filthy. It was unavoidable. The buggy was full of dust and wherever we drove the roads kicked up more all over us, so our hands, faces and clothes were all now a uniform dull brown colour. Anywhere else and I expect we would have been swiftly escorted off the premises, but here they welcomed us in. We had read in the Lonely Planet that the rates were about $40 a night (£25, not bad for the quality and astounding location) but we expected that this would by now have increased, or at least that they would try to ask for more. As it was, forty dollars was exactly what they asked for. Deciding, lamely, that we weren't in the mood for haggling and keen for a shower, we accepted straightaway. However, our general state and appearance must have made us look despondent and downcast and immediately the receptionist looked surprised and asked, or rather suggested, that he was asking for too much. He was actually encouraging and expecting us to haggle and was almost apologetic for suggesting we pay the rack rate.

I couldn't believe it. Clearly having no interest in doing this today we haggled a little and ended up at $35 (£22) for the room with air-con and two breakfasts thrown in; barely much more costly than camping in the UK.

The room was great, noting special I guess, but it had two large beds, clean sheets, air-con, a TV, a good, hot shower and views over the tranquil inner courtyard with its ornamental gardens and waterfalls. Everything we needed. It was lovely to get a shower and to feel fresh and clean again, the first proper one since the night way back in Odessa – even if it did take two attempts to get the dirt to stop coming out of my skin. 'Showering' in the well yesterday had been a treat at the time but nothing compared to the real thing.

While we made the most of the air-con we realised that the only things that were stressing us and causing any issues on our adventure so far were the continual lack of money, lack of fuel and lack of water. All simple things but every couple of days we'd seem to run out of all three at once and usually this could all be attributed to having run out of money. Anywhere else these should be easy things to fix but out here it was a different story and was becoming pathetically stressful. At least we could see the funny side of it, so we headed out to see the town and find a restaurant and any nightlife Bukhara might hold in store.

Bukhara was very much like Khiva, but larger and less well preserved, and for this it looks a whole load more authentic. We wandered around the ancient buildings with the huge, mosaic covered madrassahs – the biggest and best of these being the Mir-i Arab madrassah – through the markets and ended up pretty much back where we started, at one of the few restaurants in the town. Everywhere seemed that bit 'too quiet'. It was like we had arrived in a holiday resort out of season, as the town appeared to be geared up, to a small extent, for tourists but there were none to be seen.

Bukhara by night

At the restaurant, we were the only people there but they were still happy to serve us. Again, we had the low tables and cushions to laze on in the hot evening air and after a quick scan of the menu, ordered. Except, as we had found at several other places, nothing we wanted was available. It seemed commonplace for the menus to contain everything the restaurant is able to produce – or has probably ever heard of – even if they don't have the ingredients or skills to produce it at that point in time. Had I been able to read Uzbek I'm sure I would have been able to find roast beef and Yorkshire pudding listed somewhere; not that they would ever serve it. We settled for what was pointed out to us by the cheery waitress, got some local beers and hoped for the best.

When it came it was gorgeous. I got a chunk of beef wrapped in chicken then baked and served with couscous, a simple side salad and the now obligatory flatbread and water. For the both of us, including drinks, it was all well under £5.

The moon rising over Bukhara

We didn't stay out particularly late – the town had been pretty dead when we arrived and there wasn't a soul about – so went back to make the most of having a bed for the night.

5th August – Bukhara, UZ to Tashkent, UZ

Predictably, we woke early and just after 07:00 headed downstairs for breakfast. The dining room was decked out with numerous antiques and central Asian artefacts but had a serious lack of any other guests. Until halfway through breakfast we were the only people there, save for the ever attentive staff, when a Japanese family arrived. We finished helping ourselves to the buffet and went for another walk around the town. All along the streets were locals selling their wares, which ranged from general goods to the more touristy items. The dyed cloths and paintings they were selling were actually great quality and had we not had so far to travel in these dusty conditions I would have loved to buy some to bring home, however, there was no way they would survive the remainder of the journey intact so sadly, it would have been futile. This didn't seem to bother the man who owned the stall we chose to stop at who kindly gave us a quick talk on the paintings followed by the majority of his life story using gestures, actions and Uzbek; none of which I understood. Free from the merchants we fuelled up and headed for Tashkent, via Samarqand. By this point it was getting far too hot for walking around these confined and airless alleys, even though it was still early.

The road to Samarqand was pretty good. We were back into a relatively densely inhabited part of the country, with not far to travel between each of the small towns. The downside of this was that we were well and truly back in the land of the police checkpoint, and had already been stopped five times this morning alone. None were anything major, but added together they were wasting hours of our time.

As always, when we got to Samarqand, we aimed straight for the centre of town and, being one of the oldest cities in the world, it was simply packed with sights. We dumped the buggy right beside the

Registan, one of the most the most awesome collections of buildings and madrassahs in central Asia, probably in most of the world, and also the centre of medieval Samarqand dating from the fifteenth century, and went for a look around. A very serene place, although this has clearly not always been the case, as Registan, meaning sandy-place, got its name from the sand dusted on the ground to soak up the blood from public executions, which continued until as recently as the twentieth century.

The Registan, Samarqand

Having exhausted the Registan we drove a short way up the road to a bazaar just on the outer edge of Samarqand. We hoped it would be more genuine than the ones situated directly in the centre which were more geared around tourists and when we got there we weren't disappointed. There hadn't been many Westerners at the Registan but here there were none and we got the feeling that there rarely would be. The market was huge with entire sections dedicated specifically to spices, fruits, vegetables, hardware, cloth and biscuits. Biscuits seemed like an odd one but would prove to be very popular in most of the towns we passed through from here to the end of our journey, often presented simply in large card boxes for each flavour.

Outside the bazaar, Samarqand

The place was buzzing with locals rushing about their daily business, far too busy to notice us, and we made it through to the far side where we found some stalls selling flatbread and kebabs. They were baking the breads there and then in clay ovens, which were glowing red on the inside, and cooking the kebabs over charcoal filled troughs. The smoke and smells were filling the air so, not wishing to miss out, we stopped to indulge.

Me, on the right, awaiting my kebab

Foxy and some friendly spice sellers

The man cooked our kebabs while a girl chopped onions, the same onions she wouldn't stop chopping until we left some thirty minutes later. The food was simple and nothing amazing, but the atmosphere was great. The plumes of smoke coming off the barbeques, the scent of the spices, the wheelbarrows of produce being carted around and people shouting and bartering. Then there were the vibrant turquoise domes of the mosques and minarets in the background, rising into the perfect, deep blue sky.

Foxy with his food at the bazaar

We decided to try and take some photos inside the main market where the spices were being sold. This attracted the attention of a group of guys who were now trying to get us to buy their spices, and each time we said 'no' to one type they offered us the next type and so on all the way down the stall. As they realised they were fighting a losing battle they changed their tact and actually gave us an assortment of spices. The hard sell had changed to generosity and they handed us small packets of various spices and teas while excitedly posing for photos. They even ran down to the next stall to get the other traders involved in the photo-shoot. It was great and once we had explained we were from England they started saying the words 'Tony Blair', 'David Beckham' and 'Margaret Thatcher – Iron Lady'. That was pretty much all they could say in English but they had immense fun doing it and made a great thing about the 'Iron Lady'. It was unclear exactly what they thought of her, but she had clearly created quite a stir in the ex-Soviet states and we had heard her referred to warmly at several of the military checks we'd already been though. It was a wonderful place but we wanted to get to Tashkent in the hope of finding our last hotel of the trip before nightfall, so we said our goodbyes and hit the road again.

We were starting to get the hang of navigating the towns even with the next-to-useless maps we had. The passenger would hold the GPS out of the window (annoyingly it didn't work in the confines of the buggy) get a bearing and match it to our map. We'd then travel a couple of miles, stop and ask whoever was nearby for the direction of the next town by pointing ahead and saying the name of the town in various ways until they understood or just pointed in an acceptable direction. The fortunate thing was that there were always people on the street corners chatting away and often the police would help us, the downside was that when they did they always wanted to talk and we couldn't understand a word!

We would repeat this process time and time again until we were out of the built up areas or certain that we were on the right road. It never failed us.

The roads here were much better and there were even some tarmaced dual carriageways; in fact a short stretch of road out of the centre of Samarqand was better than many in the UK. Obviously, this was too good to be true, so to make it that bit harder and more dangerous, the locals would drive their cars, donkey carts and motorbikes along either carriageway, in either direction, in any lane, although we never once saw an accident. Now back on a decent road, for the first time since Ukraine, we were aware that the buggy was running smoothly but seemed very down on power. It just felt tired and worn out. We hoped it was nothing more than a result of low octane fuel, as we were running on 80RON, and decided it was yet another problem best ignored unless it became more serious.

We soon started to run out of fuel again, on a stretch of road miles from anywhere, and pulled into a one-man filling station. It had once been as big as any modern multi-pump station but was now, like much of the infrastructure of the ex-Soviet states we had seen, decaying and a shadow of its former self, with just two working pumps. The attendant wandered over and we went through the rigmarole of explaining that we wanted the tank full rather than a fixed amount of litres, before having to settle for fifty litres as, typically, it had to be agreed by the litre before he would start filling. This would allow us to fill a jerry can and have the remainder pumped into the buggy, hopefully without it overflowing as the attendant would simply pump in the amount we had ordered regardless of whether or not the tank could take it. Then, having steered him away from the diesel that he wanted to give us, we asked for the 92RON petrol he was advertising. He worked out the price, took our money and then insisted that we move to the 76RON pump, which was not only much cheaper but also far lower quality than we had used, or wanted to use. The 92 was 565 Som (£0.31) per litre while the 76 was 510 Som per litre (£0.28) – it seemed a lot at the time! After much protesting, drawing in the sand and arm waving, we reluctantly moved to the 76 pump. After all, we had to get something or we'd be going nowhere, though it would do nothing for the already dwindling performance of the buggy.

While he was filling the buggy he was persisting with his claim that the fuel was 92 even though the pump and the mechanical counter both said 76. We must have spent a good half an hour arguing with him, demanding our refund. The poor guy didn't speak a word of English and soon we started making up crazy stories about how important the money was to us and how much trouble we'd be in for having overpaid. At the time it was good entertainment for us, out in the desert on the road to Tashkent. He was adamantly sticking to his story when Foxy decided that he had had enough and, rightly, started to question the value of our time. It was then that we both realised that the cheap cost of living, continual scams for money, heat and tiredness were getting to us; we were arguing over nothing more than £1.50! We drove off pretending to be angry but honestly couldn't care less, and by now we were trying hard not ruin our act by breaking out into fits of laughter.

Back on the road we laughed some more about it and wondered how the attendant had taken it. We laughed even more when we noticed how well the buggy was going. Evidently, the attendant hadn't been lying and had in fact given us the best fuel we had used in days. It had all just been another quirk of this country to have only one operating petrol pump that dispensed something completely different to the label on the pump it came out of.

We were now making our way along quite a good dual carriageway that had recently been built, so had not yet had time to crumble, and we were making good time. Though it did come as a surprise to find trucks and cars coming straight for us on our side. In places they were still building the road, and from time to time there were contra flows, only they never thought to put any cones or signs out as a warning. If you spotted traffic heading for you, you were in a contra flow. Keep as far right as possible to make room, and be ready to swap to the other side of the carriageway, without warning, if the roadworks started in the lane you were driving in. Simple really.

Soon we were in the hands of the police again, only this was proving to be a long stop and the demands were sounding serious, in a persuasive, rather than threatening, manner. They wanted to look at everything and were particularly interested in our English money. We chatted about Blair, Bush and Putin with everyone pulling appropriate faces at the appropriate times. We were all actually getting on quite well and one of the policemen asked for an English twenty pence piece from us which we had been showing him as he wanted to make a medallion. Naturally, we assumed this would be the start of the demands for money but to our surprise he offered us five hundred Uzbek Som for it, which was actually more than its true value. We wouldn't have taken it but he was insisting we take it 'for luck' and not wanting to offend, we accepted. It seemed very odd, almost unsettling that the police were now giving us money. We might have been overly sceptical at times but this time we were right to be dubious.

About five minutes down the road we were stopped by some more police who demanded, oddly enough, five hundred Uzbek Som to cross a bridge. There was no toll sign and no-one else was paying so we claimed not to speak Russian or Uzbek. They seemed confused that we couldn't have any money but they weren't too interested and soon let us go. I think the guy at the first checkpoint knew these guys would try to rip us off and had taken pity. For the second time on the trip we had managed to have, in effect, a reverse bribe! Value wise it was next to nothing, but the principal counted and we felt pleased to be beating the system.

Many police stops later we arrived in Tashkent, the capital of the country in the far east of Uzbekistan, and headed for a hotel we had heard of. Tashkent, with a population of around two million, was far and away the biggest city we had actually driven into since London and was much more cosmopolitan than other cities we had seen since Europe, with many modern buildings and offices, possibly helped by the major rebuild following a huge earthquake in 1966. We were negotiating the one-way system quite well when a modern car pulled alongside us and asked, in broken English, where we were looking for. Again, worry set in as we assumed he was after money or planning to kidnap us but we told him and he insisted we follow him. He seemed to be heading the right way and eventually stopped right outside a hotel of the same name but on the wrong street. Looking in our guide book it was a fair mistake, so we thanked him and after a few moments he drove off. For some reason we were still uneasy about it so once we were sure he was gone we drove on to the hotel we had originally been looking for. I was worried that now he knew where we were staying he would come back in the night and steal the buggy or its contents. I never did like the fact that we had to leave so much of our kit in full view in the buggy whenever we stopped, especially now we were in a major city which would be sure to have its fair share of common criminals. Having the buggy stolen was no major financial loss but would spell the end of our journey which would be an absolute disaster.

Sadly, the hotel we had wanted was full, but fortunately just down the road there was another one and after a little haggling we got a twin room with air-con for $30 (£16), right in the heart of the city. We took a taxi into the central nightlife area with its bars, restaurants and some form of summer fair and settled into a street side bar. Foxy had a huge wad of money with him but we counted it out only to find that we had less than five pounds to last the night. Such huge wedges of cash were proving very misleading. Having walked round all the street stalls we went to another bar only to discover that all the bars in Tashkent shut at midnight. We had barely got into town and already our hopes of a night out were being dashed as it looked like everywhere was closing around us. A quick look in the trusty Lonely Planet, which we had learnt seemed to come with a fifty-fifty chance of misleading us, recommended a bar literally just around the corner that was open until 03:00. Off we went.

Considering that Tashkent is in the capital of a very devoutly Islamic country, steeped in centuries of history where the majority of people don't drink alcohol, it should have rung alarm bells that there would be somewhere serving that late at night, but we wanted a beer so we decided to give it a shot. The bar had a reasonable amount of security but, for once, we were looking quite respectable having found some clean clothes so made it in fine, ordered drinks and sat ourselves at a table while our drinks were served. It was then that we realised that we were in fact in a strip bar.

This really defied belief to think that this was such a religious country yet we had been able to find alcohol late at night and not only that but the bar was full of half-naked ladies. It really went against everything that we thought they believed in that two of the most forbidden things would be openly available on the high street.

The taxi back to the hotel was slightly over a fifty pence and even including that we had had a night out for less than £2.50 each.

6th August – Tashkent, UZ to Jalal-Abad, KG

For once, we had a late start, getting breakfast and leaving at about 09:00. Driving out of Tashkent we were stopped numerous times by the police before joining the road that would take us the next 300 miles, past Qoqand and into and through the infamous Farghana Valley.

The Farghana Valley was another region we were a little, well quite, apprehensive about travelling through. The valley is a thin stretch of Uzbekistan surrounded by Kyrgyzstan to the north and Tajikistan to the south and is very much under military control. The valley is also renowned for its extreme religious views, heightened political tensions, sporadic civil unrest and general lawlessness. As recently as the pervious summer, 187 unarmed civilians were massacred in the region following protests and civil unrest – and that's according to the government, nearer one thousand or more were slaughtered according to news agencies – and this was just the one event large enough to be newsworthy in the UK; the smaller events going largely unnoticed by the West. The effect of this is that the area remains pretty volatile, banditry and kidnap are a realistic threat, arbitrary arrest takes place and torture is not unheard of, added to this, the landmined borders are often inexplicably shut. Considering this, and especially the landmines, we decided to stick only to the most main looking roads we could find, not that there were any major roads to speak of. It sounded like Transnistria all over again – except here we had time to think about the region before we got there, had chosen to travel this way and the danger seemed much more tangible.

As we neared the valley, the police checks were noticeably more frequent and gradually replaced by military personnel who, rather than holding their guns casually as we were used to, had their machine guns constantly trained on us as we passed by. In Transnistria the feeling had been very different as, in all fairness, it was quite close to home which somehow made it a bit more comforting, but here we were in a region with a serious and current history of violence and our every move was being tracked by several AK-47s. There were also many more things we didn't understand about this region. In Moldova it was clear that greed and political views had lead to the fighting and the formation of Transnistria, yet here the reasons were both political and religious; the latter something we had no experience of, so could easily do the wrong thing without realising. The only advice we had been able to gain was to wear a t-shirt and trousers rather than shorts; advice we'd completely forgotten with the distractions of the adventure.

Several more of these armed stop-checks followed before we started climbing into the mountains before finally dropping down into the valley below. As we drove through tunnels, rough cuttings in the rock faces and over rickety bridges, we could see heavily armed and camouflaged soldiers crouching in the scrub to the sides of the road. I assumed they were there for protective duties rather than for offensive reasons, but it did nothing to make me feel any more comfortable. Dropping down steeply out of the mountains we came to a collection of huts and buildings with a number of soldiers stopping and rigorously searching every single vehicle, not that there were many. There were in fact very few vehicles and mostly all we saw was the odd truck transporting goods.

We approached slowly, literally crawling the last hundred metres or so, and were directed to stop just before the razor wire blockade by a soldier waving purposefully at us with an AK-47. The whole arrangement looked like a border crossing, yet we were still several miles off the true border. Instead we were to be checked and registered into the Valley. In effect moving from state to military control and having to register so that our whereabouts in the Valley could be monitored. I waited with the buggy while Foxy, who was driving, was taken to a building to register. There was a metallic tapping on the door beside me and I turned to see a soldier tapping the door with the barrel of his gun which was pointing straight at me, his finger resting on the trigger. He indicated that I should get out. I wished they could just point with their hands instead.

I got out and thankfully all he wanted was to have a search around and inside the buggy. He asked the now familiar questions, by pointing and speaking Russian and Uzbek, about the switches in the buggy, looked at the cameras and tried to figure out the GPS. Thankfully, nothing seemed to interest him too much, but during his thorough search I did notice that there was no longer any oil leaking from the shock absorbers, they were clearly now completely empty of oil and utterly useless. As I waited, different soldiers came and went, each looking over our kit. To pass the time, and there was plenty to pass, I took to trying to take covert photos of the soldiers by using the wing mirror of the buggy, although after I'd taken one and noticed another soldier sneaking up on the other side of the buggy, I decided it was probably best to stop.

I was called into the room where Foxy was still being processed to show my passport and sign my life away, and with that we were off, into the Valley. It had taken the best part of an hour and had effectively been an additional border crossing we hadn't planned for.

The road climbed steeply up and down the mountainsides and even though tarmaced we still had to use all of its width to pick a line through the roughest bits. Due to the heat, the steepness and the occasional heavy trucks using it, the surface was in an appalling condition and I expect the harshness of the winters here wouldn't help either, with the temperature frequently dropping below minus twenty.

Added to this was the fact that the condition of the shock absorbers did nothing to help us on this terrain.

We were now driving right alongside the Tajikistani border, denoted by the huge and very imposing razor wire fences with guard posts and machine gun turrets, and by us getting stopped more and more frequently with each of us having to enter a hut and register our presence while having various weaponry pointed at us. It was almost like we were being tracked through the Valley, which we probably were.

Attempting to photograph the guards in the Farghana Valley

The Farghana Valley itself was a strange place. The mountain sides were barren, jagged, sandy and incredibly steep whilst down beside the river, in the basin, was a stark contrast of flat, fertile land with vibrant, green vegetation. And all this was interspersed with the guard posts and razor wire which tore the valley in two. Further up we came to a narrow canyon with sheer sides towering hundreds of feet above us while we drove beside the lush, green paddy fields either side of the river. In places the river would be more than half a mile wide, weaving lazily across the plain, and then further on it would be just metres wide, a rough torrent enclosed by the walls of the canyon. Having spent the previous few days in the desert, it was a welcome change to have greenery around again, even if it was restricted to the valley floor. We stopped at the top of a cliff overlooking the river below to have a rest and take some photos and I found myself chasing some goats. I needed some relief from the confines of the buggy but, as I expected, failed miserably in catching one. Not that I would have known what to do with the thing had I caught it!

Before long we were lost. It shouldn't have been hard. All we had to do was keep the Tajikistani border to our right and we should have arrived at the border crossing with Kyrgyzstan, but instead we found ourselves on a hugely impressive road leading up to a hydroelectric dam. Like most of the roads that led to places where government officials or influential people may visit, it was several lanes wide and will once have had the feel of an exclusive tree-lined boulevard, except that the trees had long since died from years of neglect. It was a sorry sight and also somewhere we shouldn't have been. We turned around before anyone had time to arrest us under suspicion of scoping out the weaknesses of the border security or the technical capabilities of the dam; we were now travelling literally feet from the primary border fence.

Exiting Uzbekistan was amazingly easy and having filled out the forms, had the usual chat about what we were doing, visited the appropriate offices and shown off all our belongings we moved onto the Kyrgyz side.

We were relieved to be greeted by smiling guards who were genuinely interested in us. It turned out that they virtually never get Westerners at this crossing – from the looks of things they rarely got anyone crossing – and as such they were fascinated by us, everything we had and everything about where we had come from. I doubt they had ever seen an English car before, and they set about looking at every part of it. They wanted to know and see so much, not for official reasons but purely out of curiosity. It was a welcome change. It was also a relief to be out of the Farghana Valley intact. That might sound a bit dramatic, but the amount of military personnel and activity we'd seen hadn't been there for fun, and having researched the region more upon my return home it remains as volatile and dangerous as ever. We'd just been lucky and picked a quiet day; it was a Sunday after all.

The area we were now waiting in didn't even look like a border crossing as it was right on the edge of the town; we could actually see the locals on the other side of the high fences going about their daily business. The border post itself was nothing more than a group of guards sitting and chatting in the shade on the roadside beside a very rickety wooden hut. They had an impressive, if random, collection of Kalashnikovs, AK-47s and pistols but were thankfully carrying them very casually and were perfectly happy to show them off to us. The apparent tensions of the Farghana Valley seemed miles away.

The downside to the curiosity was that we seemed to be making no progress. It was more like we'd stopped by for a social rather than trying to cross a border. All that was happening was that we were trying to understand the questions, about our journey and lives back home, and then trying to find actions or creating drawings in the sand to answer them. I went into the hut to complete the vehicle forms but found myself chatting to the guard and sharing a bottle of his water rather than getting any details written down. Outside again they spotted our cigarettes and showed an interested in them, rather than blatantly asking for them, so we offered them around which went down a treat. We shared more of their water and flatbread and played music from the iPod while trying to have a political discussion about the 'Iron Lady' and the Cold War – everyone we met seemed to love Thatcher and I began to wonder if they still thought she was still in power today.

While I had been in the hut, Foxy had been playing with one of the guard's pistols and posing for photos with it; the same guard was now trying to sell me the very hat off his head, complete with its regimental silver badge, for just $5 (£2.70). In comparison to the crossings we had seen earlier this place was a world apart and I was actually enjoying being here, socialising with the guards. They were so much more relaxed and never tried to coerce money out of us and the fact that they were prepared to let Foxy play with their gun was a sure sign that they trusted us and were genuinely as curious about us as we were about them.

They loved the buggy and having checked everything about it they quite seriously made an offer to us of $7,000 (£3,750) if they could take it there and then. We'd only paid £500 for the thing. It would have been a brilliant return on what we'd paid for it but sadly we needed the buggy so had to decline. They simply couldn't get such cars out here in any condition we were told.

After more than two hours with the Kyrgyz guards it was apparent that they would never ask us to leave. While we had been there only two other cars had arrived and both had now passed through some time ago, it was amazing just how quiet the border was. There had also been a number of pedestrians crossing in both directions. They had carts of fruit and other produce which they had been selling at the markets on the opposite sides of the border and were now heading back to their home side of as the day drew to a close. We started the long and drawn out process of saying our goodbyes and preparing to leave. It was clear that they were in no rush to see us go, so it ended in us having to get in the buggy and actually start the engine to make our intentions clear. This allowed us to move all of twenty metres to the customs check, who were just as welcoming. Soon the formalities of the check were over and the curiosity got the better of them and we went through all our stories again, but this time we didn't wait quite as long until we asked to leave. They obligingly un-padlocked the gates and let us through, shaking our hands and giving us a small amount of money for luck as well as a huge watermelon. We gave them some more cigarettes and drove through into the chaos of the ramshackle market beyond and on into Kyrgyzstan. It had been a change to meet such friendly guards and no doubt they will be talking about us for as long as we talk about them. They really were delighted to have something different coming through their border and we were happy to oblige.

We were now heading into our first real mountains of the journey and they would dwarf anything we'd seen already, for that matter, anything I'd seen in my life. The Tian Shan mountain range dominates much of Kyrgyzstan and from the 350m (1,150ft) lowlands of the Farghana Valley which we were now leaving, it rises to a colossal 7,439m (24,406ft) in eastern Kyrgyzstan and we'd be cutting across a good part of it. We headed toward the town of Jalal-Abad, a couple of miles from the border, to look for the start of the mountain pass. We hoped to join the pass on the far side of town such that we could set up the tents before dark, off the road and out of sight.

On the near edge of the town we started looking for somewhere to pick up some local currency. Deciding not to waste time, we stopped to ask a group of policemen – all casually wielding machine guns – and they indicated that we'd find money at the local bazaar. We parked up and walked around the maze of stalls, shaded under a canopy of brightly dyed cloths. It looked like an unlikely place to find an exchange bureau. We passed stall after stall selling of every type of fruit, biscuits and food and miraculously stumbled on a tiny window, in one of the only permanent buildings, offering foreign exchange. The man was adamant that he wouldn't take our one dollar bills, which we were now keen to get rid of, so we reached a compromise, giving him some single dollars and also some larger notes. No-one wanted small bills and they were proving to be a pain for us. With $40 (£21) of Kyrgyz Som we headed back to the buggy, picking up some huge peaches on the way and also a crackpot local beggar who was now walking with us and getting a bit too close for our liking.

The market at Jalal-Abad

It was 18:30; we'd seen the centre of town so we fuelled up at 22 Kyrgyz Som (£0.27) a litre and set off again, leaving us a good amount of time to get out of Jalal-Abad to find somewhere to camp. The route ahead was very sketchy looking. There were no road signs anywhere. This had been the case for much of the journey but usually we'd come across at least one, eventually. Not here. We knew we were roughly on the correct side of the town and picked up the river – hoping it was the only major river – as from this we would be able work out where we were heading. We took a couple of roads and thought we were about right, but the first two ended in tiny dirt tracks and the third climbed into the hills before turning back on itself to the south, when we wanted to be heading north. Jalal-Abad was quite a small town but we had spent ages trying to find the way out and it was now pitch-black. There were no signs and no landmarks in the dark and no-one we asked could point us the right way. It was going to be another night in the buggy. A real let down after the recent hotels. We drove back past some of the locals who must now have seen us pass several times, but they just stared at us as if they were trying to fathom the antics of these strange foreigners. We pulled over to ask them the way and they spoke back in what sounded like grunts and coughs – it was unrecognisable and much like I imagine people may have communicated thousands of years ago. It was nothing like the language of the people we had met in the middle of the town and they showed no interest in the map. It was useless.

It was now 21:00, almost three hours of going nowhere, as we took another road that looked like it may go the right way but once again the already-poor tarmac ended in a narrowing dirt track. As we started to turn the buggy around a few local men came over so we tried, again, to ask for directions, pointing at our map and saying the name of the next village some hundred miles or more away over the mountains. They didn't seem to understand but did seem helpful and friendly. We got out of the buggy to see if we could get some useful advice. By now there were about five men all trying to help, and they all seemed to think they knew better than the next man. No sooner had the first started trying to explain the way than the next had come up with a better idea. One had taken my notepad and was drawing a map for us but never got a chance to explain before the next person stepped in with his theory. It soon broke down into chaos. Fortunately, one of the men's daughters appeared at this point and she spoke some broken English. It was brilliant! She was eighteen, had learnt at school and was keen to help us and test out her English. She took me to one side of the noise and chaos to establish what we were trying to do. When we got back, Foxy had disappeared but everything seemed a lot calmer. The girl briefly spoke to her father then explained to me that we were to stay the night and he'd show us the way in the morning. Worryingly, she also said that no-one thought our buggy stood a chance of making it over the mountains. This was the only thing that everyone seemed to agree on. It didn't look good. Now we were in Kyrgyzstan there was no other way to go. We couldn't get back into Uzbekistan and there was no chance of driving through China. The only way out was over the mountains. I looked for Foxy to see if he liked the idea of staying the night, but didn't even need to ask. He was sitting in the sand at the edge of the road with the other men drinking vodka. The father opened the iron gates to the yard outside his house and I pulled the buggy in.

The other men left and Foxy, the daughter, the father, another younger man and I went into the house. We met the girl's mother, a Russian lady – who looked more than a bit surprised to find two Englishmen being ushered into her house – and her younger brother. The mother was cooking and the daughter, who now introduced herself as Aselay, showed us around their house, which in reality was more of a small-holding, while their dinner was being prepared. We really were being made incredibly welcome. Outside they had fruit trees, pens for rabbits, pigs, ducks, a cow, cats and a pile of month-old puppies falling about with their surrogate mother who was looking thoroughly worn out. The toilet was a wooden hut in the corner of the vegetable plot consisting of a deep hole in the ground with a couple of very unsteady planks over the drop. I played with the rabbits and cats for a while, chatting to Aselay and commenting on how nice one of the rabbits was. She had a surprisingly good grasp of English, though not quite conversational, and it was a welcome change from the struggles with the locals we had met over the previous days. She was interested to know what we were doing, and why, and about the places we'd been to, but like most of the people we met she couldn't understand why we would be on such a journey with no real purpose. Shouldn't we be working? Couldn't we have just posted the money to the Children's Hospital and given a cheque to Cancer Research UK? How could we afford to leave a perfectly good car after the journey was over, and why would we ever consider such an extravagant option? They were all good questions and none of my answers satisfied her.

Back inside, Foxy was chatting to her brother, who must have been about ten years old, and he was fascinated with our digital cameras and loved being able to take photos and then immediately see the results on the screen. We had to go though every single one of our photos so far, explaining what they were of and where we had taken them. Then we did it all again for the other man who was there while Aselay translated the cities and counties for him. It turned out he was the son-in-law. He was married to Aselay's elder sister and also lived with the family in the house. Aselay's sister was currently at the local hospital in Jalal-Abad, heavily pregnant and due at anytime. However, the arrival of two Western travellers had cancelled any notion of visiting her that night as, apparently and we were told this, we were far more important and exciting than the daughter's first child and the first grandchild for the house. It truly was unbelievable!

The house was a simple one storey building with hundreds of books on shelves in the sitting room and, to my surprise, they had a large screen TV and DVD player. It didn't really fit in with the relatively primitive nature of the place that they would have such modern technology as well. Speaking more to the daughter it turned out that the father was a physics lecturer and so had quite a high standing in the local community, and had travelled extensively throughout Russia where he had met his wife. It also transpired that he had also written most of the books on the shelves in the sitting room. It was clear that they were quite well-off for the area.

With our unexpected arrival the mother was now short of food for the dinner, which was now apparently being cooked to include us, so Aselay was dispatched to the local bazaar to get some bread. We went with her as it was easier than trying to make conversation with the others and would be good to have a look around the outskirts of Jalal-Abad. We bought the bread and some chocolate for her brother, which was the least we could do, and walked back up the sandy track to the house chatting about our lives and listening to the silence of the hills.

Back at the house the father took me roughly by the arm and half-dragged me to the outbuilding which we entered through the cloth-sheet door. The building was made of wattle and daub with an electric light bulb hanging precariously from the roof and a wooden bench along one side under which was a trough of water. I had no idea what the father was getting at as he tugged at my shirt and gestured with his arms. All kinds of thoughts went through my mind in the fifteen minutes or so we spent there ranging from being challenged to wrestle to him, him wanting my shirt for himself or the beginnings of a murder scene from a horror movie. It finally clicked when he handed me a bar of soap. I was in the bathroom! The realisation brought smiles all round and he left me to it. A couple of minutes later the son arrived with fresh towels for me. Even though the water was icy cold it was really refreshing in the sweltering night air to be throwing it over my head with a wooden ladle. Back in the house the table was being set for dinner so Foxy went for a quick shower.

When the food was ready we all sat down around the table for dinner, with the exception of Aselay and her mother, who remained in the kitchen throughout except for the time they spent actually serving the food. The meal started with a round of neat vodka. Not just the usual shot-sized glasses but a good slug in a much larger glass – probably a double or triple shot – downed in one. While the food was being served

Aselay seemed to loiter to try and talk to us, but also seemed to be aware that she shouldn't be with the men while we were eating. The meal was a pasta dish with tomatoes, herbs, scrambled eggs and then meat with bread, salad and watermelon on the side. The daughter had decided by now that it was acceptable, under the circumstances, to stay at the table and I asked her about the food we were eating. It was a local dish with the scrambled egg and rabbit meat on top as an added extra. I paused and thought for a moment but she must have thought I didn't understand what she was saying so kindly clarified what she meant by explaining that the rabbit was in fact the one I had been petting earlier. When I said I had liked that particular rabbit it must have been misinterpreted as being the one I wanted for dinner, not the one I thought was the cutest! I had thought I was complementing her pet, not weighing it up for dinner; but it was absolutely lovely, both in the yard and on the plate, and the eggs had been collected just minutes before dinner too.

At this point the mother, who had been missing for sometime, came into the room and there was an air of excitement. The elder daughter had just given birth at the hospital. To our amazement rather than anyone leaving, the baby's father included, the vodka came out and we became involved in several rounds of toasting the baby! We asked Aselay about this but she assured us that the family would rather spend the time with us; it was that unusual, possibly almost privileged, for them to have foreigners staying. They assured us that they would visit the baby the next day and even seemed keen to take us along too. The mother now joined us for a dessert of chocolate cake and we joined the father with a few more vodkas before being served some green tea. After this I returned to the garden again while Aselay picked apples for us.

The father, who had probably been drinking before we arrived, was now on a mission to show off everything he could, which mostly involved him getting book after book off the shelves to show to us. This really was difficult as he didn't speak a single word of English and was getting impatient when we couldn't work out what he was getting at, even with Aselay trying to help us out.

It was getting late and Foxy had nodded off on the sofa, again. Aselay was trying to convince me to agree to spend the day in the village to meet her friends and the baby, but by now all I wanted to do was get some sleep. It was just before 02:00 when we eventually got to bed. In keeping with our given status in the house, I was given Aselay's bed (I assume she stayed with her brother) but with Foxy now fast asleep and in no mood for moving, he had to make do with a duvet on the sofa. There was no glass in the bedroom window, it wasn't designed to have any, and the noise from the crickets was deafening but for once the air was now cool. I fell asleep trying to imagine what the next day would bring.

7th August – Jalal-Abad, KG to Naryn, KG

I woke just before 08:00 to find the whole family already up and busy about the house. Foxy, sleeping in the lounge, had been woken by people moving around about an hour and a half earlier, but had been told not to wake me as I was sleeping! What a result! We went outside to look around in the daylight as it was already starting to get hot – the whole place resembled a farmyard. We were just considering saying our goodbyes when the father ushered us toward a table on the grass, amongst the animals, and we were joined by the family for breakfast. The mother brought bread and fresh fruit for us and we were joined by the son, son-in-law and a couple of the neighbours we'd met when we'd first arrived the night before. Aselay served us black coffee with sweet honey.

Breakfast – Foxy to the left, me to the right, vodka in the middle

Having had enough to eat, we started to think again about making our exit as we were running out of time. The tourist visas we had got for

Kyrgyzstan had quite a tight time limit and we needed to be sure that we could get over the mountain passes to Kazakhstan. The roads on the maps looked pretty non-existent and the locals were still adamant that our buggy stood no chance of making it over the tops. We didn't need to plan our exit just yet though, as the mother arrived with bowls of steaming food for Foxy and I. Now we're pretty open to eating anything and even more so when it's gifted from the locals, but we both hate, with a passion, rice pudding. Of all the things I'd have expected for breakfast this was certainly not one of them, yet there it was, two bowls of steaming rice pudding. And it was only for the two of us as a special treat. To be fair to them, we were probably the only ones to get any as they had most likely milked the lone goat dry just to make the two huge bowls. Obviously this was another treat for the guests; lucky us. At least one of us was going to have to eat some of the rice pudding to try to appear polite and I lost the battle of the wills, but even before I got a chance to start, the familiar glasses arrived and the vodka was out. It was only 08:30.

The neighbours wanted to toast the arrival of us and the newborn child, and probably in that order. Favouring the vodka over the rice pudding I put my spoon down and joined in the toast. Immediately, the glasses were refilled and we were toasting again. It was at the end of the second oversized glass that I remembered my aversion to downing neat vodka and had visions of having to excuse myself to run to the makeshift toilet, but the glasses were already being refilled. With the prospect of the third glass it also struck me that if this carried on there would be no chance of us driving anywhere today. I explained that I would have to drive later and managed to avoid the third round but the attention now turned to why I was not eating the rice pudding. With everyone watching, reluctantly I spooned some of the sludge into my mouth which didn't settle well on top of the vodka. I continued to poke the rice pudding around and got through about half of it while Foxy made his excuses and got away with less than a couple of spoons but significantly more vodka. They seemed disappointed in us but there was no way I was going to eat all of it so pretended instead to be full.

A local toddler, taken by the boy

Foxy was now well entrenched in the rounds of vodka, having one glass with each of the men in turn, so effectively having three glasses in every round. If we did drive anywhere today it would be me doing all the driving. Aselay was keen for us to head into town to meet her friends, the men wanted to take us to the river to swim, the boy had run off with my camera excitedly taking photos of everything and anything, and the mother wanted us to stay around to go to the hospital and meet the baby. I wanted to get driving again and Foxy was well on his way to getting completely drunk. It was going to be a long day.

The drinking continued at a slower, but steady, pace and Aselay promised us that we'd have no problems with our visas as her father would be able to get the authorities to extend them for us, although I never saw her check this with him so decided it wasn't worth the risk. Having been sitting around for several hours, the men were getting restless that we should go swimming. I went inside with Aselay and she helped me gather our things ready to leave and I drove the buggy out of the yard onto the track. When I got back to the buggy with our bags I found the father and one of the other men in it with Foxy showing them everything inside. I got the impression that they had never been inside a car and they clearly loved it but wanted to take it a step further by taking it for a spin – but neither could drive. With a quick crash course, given by Foxy pointing at pedals and the gear stick, they seemed to have the basics and started the engine. The buggy lurched forward, kangarooed and with the men in hysterics, screamed off down the track in a cloud of dust. In the UK I'd never consider lending my car to a complete stranger, let alone two who had never driven before. Or one who had spent the morning downing vodka. But in western Kyrgyzstan it all seemed fine. As the dust settled I wondered if we'd ever see it in one piece again. Thankfully, after about ten minutes I could hear the distant, tortured sound of the screaming one-litre engine heading our way. They never did figure out the gears, instead just going as fast as it would let them in first gear.

The buggy had caused a stir with the neighbours and Foxy was half-forcibly, half-jokingly, dragged off down the track to meet and drink with some more locals while I stayed behind to chat to the family, all the while becoming more impatient to be on the move again.

Foxy being dragged off to meet more locals

Not long later Foxy and the men returned and at last it was time to leave. At this point the father turned from being joking and friendly to pretty aggressive. He wanted money from us. This would have been fine as we had just had the full use of his house, but the way it was asked for was completely out of tune. Aselay became involved trying to stop him, but on instruction from her father reluctantly claimed that it was for the newborn baby rather than for her father, although she didn't sound very convinced and it was obvious this wasn't the case. We tried to protest but didn't want to appear rude, even though Aselay took up our case and became quite angry with her now very drunk father. In the end we paid him the ten dollars he demanded with some of our Kyrgyz money.

Nothing, given the hospitality, but a tremendous amount in this region, and the manner in which it was taken from us took the edge off the time spent with the family. It also meant that the money we had changed at the bazaar, having bought petrol and food, was now gone and we were once again without local currency. It was 11:30.

Aselay was also looking quite disappointed that we weren't staying to visit her friends, but with the men and Foxy pretty drunk – I had seen over three full bottles of vodka opened and drunk – we had to leave or would be stuck another night and never make it out of the country on time. Aselay moved back to her mother, who had spent most of her time separated from the conversations and the men, almost as if the women were supposed to be in the background, where I imagine Aselay too would have been throughout, had she not had a slight grasp of the English language.

With myself and Foxy in the buggy and about to leave the father staggered over to offer his directions to Kazarman, the next village we were heading for. To our surprise, rather than point out directions, he affectionately hugged all the members of his family and forced his way over Foxy into the gap between the front seats, on top of the gear stick and handbrake. To say it was a tight squeeze in what was an already cramped buggy is an understatement. We waved our goodbyes and with that we were on the road again, off down the dirt track and hopefully towards Kazarman. It was a shame to leave but we'd had a great time and had to get on the move again.

Having made several turns along various tracks I got the feeling that we were heading the in roughly the direction that had been described the night before. The conversation was lacking, due to the language barrier, but the hilarity of the situation was not lost on anyone and the pain of the potholes for the father kept everyone entertained –

especially him – although given how strongly the buggy now smelt of alcohol, it's hardly surprising. It must have been a good ten minutes since we had passed the last house when Foxy and I began to wonder just how far the father would be travelling with us. There were no other possible roads for us to take now, so we had to be on the correct one and we were heading up a one car track into the foothills of the huge mountains ahead. Up the track that no-one thought our buggy would make it over. We had to be on the right route yet the father continued to laugh deeply and point onward whenever we asked it he wanted us to take him back. It was getting to the point where we wouldn't have time to take him back if he came much further with us.

Not far out of the town we came to an armed checkpoint.

Waiting at the checkpoint

We were on what appeared to be an unused track, yet once again the authorities had us. The father tried to do the talking, but was struggling after the vodka, so Foxy had a go which didn't help either and instead, decided to leave it to the father and went to take a seat on a mattress-less, metal bed frame in the corner of the guards' hut. He fell straight off and we were all in fits of laughter, except the guards who were looking very seriously upon the situation. The situation became a lot more serious as they now thought that I was drunk too and I expect their suspicions alone would have been more than enough to land us in trouble, rather than any actual proof. I tried to rectify the situation but the father was busy talking to them. It transpired that we were entering a different region of the country and had to pay a toll. This seemed fair enough, except having given the father our money earlier, we now had virtually none. He argued our corner some more, they seemed happy enough that I hadn't spent the morning drinking vodka, and the father took $3 (£1.60) from us and irritably gave it to the guards. Back in the buggy it was obvious what he thought of them, and it wasn't polite.

As we climbed the switchbacks into the mountains the track deteriorated, not that it had even been good to start with. Still we offered to take the father back yet he insisted we continue. All the while the father was getting thrown everywhere – as were we for that matter – and changing gear was always a gamble as to which I'd get as I struggled to manoeuvre the stick between his legs (second and fourth were to be avoided as they were nestled in his crotch!). The track got steeper and steeper and soon we had to stop to engage four-wheel drive just to have enough grip to keep the buggy moving. The track ahead was starting to worry me. Already it was narrower than the buggy in places, meaning that I had get two of the wheels up onto the mountainside to avoid losing the other two off the crumbling, sheer cliff to the side. In some places where streams, which were now dried-up, had cut across the track they had gouged ditches across so deep that we had to crawl around them or risk getting grounded. And all this with a complete lack of control due to the father being sprawled half across my leg.

Things got worse when I became known as Michael Schumacher by the father, and my two drunken passengers began demanding I go faster. This was good for a while, only for us to come to a shuddering halt in a pothole, the father to cover his eyes, swear in Kyrgyz then demand we go again! Except the buggy wouldn't. It was too steep. After a lot of effort and fiddling around under the father, we managed to engage the low ratio gears and moved on up the mountain. Engaging the low ratio 'box was always a bit hit and miss and would usually take a few attempts but without it I think we would certainly have had to turn back here and possibly even face defeat on the whole journey, given that there was no other route from where we were.

Climbing through the mountains

I really got into the driving and soon learnt just how important it was to keep the momentum up on the hairpin corners, accelerating round them as hard as possible to avoid having to grope around between the father's legs to find a lower gear. This worked well at keeping us moving but caused chaos in the cramped buggy as we crashed into each other and the bodywork with shouts and abuse coming at me from all sides. Added to this, spare parts, clothing and other random bits of kit would continually smash into our heads from the back of the buggy, however much we tried to tie them down and wedge them in the back. We continued like this, climbing higher and higher with the track crumbling over the almost sheer cliffs, descending hundreds of unprotected feet below. The wheels were never more than a few inches from the cliff edge, and at times we would hit a hidden ditch too hard and the buggy would nosedive before lurching forward in a direction of its choice. Miraculously, this was always towards the uphill side and never towards the precipitous drop on the other side. In hindsight, given the way we were racing from point to point and how far into the wilderness we were, it has to be one of the most dangerous things I've ever done in my life (although arguing with Transnistrian guards probably topped it, that didn't seem as immediately daunting as this cliff-edge drive). It doesn't bear thinking about what could have happened, but we loved it – this is what we had come all this way for and we weren't going to waste the moment now we'd got here.

After an eternity we reached the top of the mountain and stopped for some water and a rest. The cramped driving was hard work for everyone, I was streaming with sweat, my arms were throbbing and my passengers were starting to sober up. We hadn't passed a single vehicle all day and we had made it up the road the locals said we couldn't. It was a great feeling and we were literally on top of the world. Again, we wondered why the father was still with us, but he seemed happy enough, though clearly had a hangover, and suggested we continue down the far side of the mountain further away from his home. Not that we would have considered going all the way back the way we had just come, that really would be tempting fate and also take far too long! We were at just over 3,600m (11,810ft) above sea level, there was a glacier in the chasm beneath us and the whole world spread out ahead as if we were in an aeroplane. Winter temperatures on the peaks have been recorded as low as minus -50°C thankfully it was much milder today. Even the enormous mountains ahead looked to be well beneath us and tiny from our elevated position. All we had to do now was get down the other side. We piled back into the buggy, having a minor mishap as we didn't properly secure the rear door, temporarily losing a couple of bags and having to return to collect them.

The track down was no better, worse if anything, as the momentum made slowing down harder and the buggy would soon pick up speed and run away with itself. There were numerous airborne moments and skidded tyres as I tried to compensate for my over exuberance and avoid plummeting over the cliff edge. I blame the fact that I used to race karts when I was younger and there was no way I was going to miss out on a driving opportunity like this. Racing thought the dunes in Kazakhstan had been incredible but the element of risk here was in a different league, which made it that bit more exciting and I'd never get to do this again so was going to enjoy it as much as I could while I could. We had had the conversation somewhere in Russia when we first went off road that we would drive to enjoy the journey rather than to preserve the buggy (we also had similar driving styles and absolute trust in each others driving) and that's certainly what we were doing; looking back it was virtually a miracle that we (I) didn't write the buggy off this day let alone break something.

A flatter section between the peaks

On the way down, we saw our first yurts (traditional, circular, felt-covered nomadic tents) on the distant hillsides that the locals live in wherever the land it at its best. The road started to widen and level out as we got towards the valley floor and soon Foxy and the father were nodding off, posing a new hazard as the father continuously lolled across me before waking up with a start. For the first time all day we were able to regularly get up over 20mph. Eventually, we came onto the beginnings of a crumbling tarmac road, the telltale sign of a village. We were heading into Kazarman, some 100 miles from Jalal-Abad where we had picked up the father, and we hadn't passed a single vehicle or building on the entire route in between. He seemed delighted to be there and directed us to the centre of the village where we were soon surrounded by curious locals. The father seemed to vaguely know a few of them, hugging them like long lost friends, and took us to a small shop selling the bare essentials – vodka, bread and biscuits.

Inside the shop the father started to demand that we buy a large bottle of vodka that he wanted us to go and drink with him at a friend's house and it didn't go down well when we said no. He continued to demand two dollars to buy it. We had no interest in drinking more with him, especially having seen how his mood could swing when we didn't do as he said. We'd been clear all along that we were not returning to Jalal-Abad, and from the look of the father it appeared that we had done him a huge favour bringing him all this way. Looking back at the farewells and the remoteness of the villages we began to wonder if he was ever going back to his family or, if he did, how he would ever get there. It wasn't our problem and with his aggression over the vodka getting worse by the minute – he was now forcibly moving us around – becoming more hostile and starting to threaten us if we didn't do just as he said, we had to leave. We decided to buy the vodka and paid the shopkeeper directly with the loose change we still had – incredibly it only cost £0.15, not the two dollars that had been demanding of us – and casually walked out of the shop. The father was definitely trying to rip us off. With all the people who had been milling about when we had arrived I'd locked the buggy so Foxy loitered while I went back and unlocked the doors, he then rushed across and dived in, locking the door behind him, the father following close after but too late. He tried to pull the door open and shouted after us as we drove off. At least with this village being so small we were

THREE WEEKS INTO THE UNKNOWN

reasonably confident that we had the right road this time and wouldn't have to stop to ask directions.

Oddly, we felt bad about what we had just done. Having said that I'm a hundred percent certain he had no expectation of us taking him back to Jalal-Abad, so it didn't quite make sense to feel bad given the way he was now acting and how volatile he had become, but we did. The others we'd met in Jalal-Abad had seemed genuinely kind and interested yet he had a very different side that was much less predictable and seemed to revolve around us giving him things. Admittedly, he had invited us into his house and provided for us the previous night – for which we were grateful – but to threaten us and demand money or drink was out of order. We soon stopped feeling bad about it and drove on. It had been an incredible experience and his actions had only added to the whole episode. We now had another 125 miles of off-road driving to worry about just to get to the next village, somewhere over the next couple of mountain ranges.

As we continued, we passed one or two vehicles, all much more substantial than ours and they appeared to be struggling more than we were, or perhaps they were just trying to preserve theirs more. We were starting to descend over the second mountain pass when we came across a cyclist. Stopping and taking a break to talk to him it was a relief to find someone who spoke perfect English. He was a Japanese man, from Iran, cycling from his home in Iran to China. He had allowed himself ten months to do this and thought he was on track to do so. We thought what we were doing was mad enough but he was in a completely different league. We wished him luck and continued.

With just the two of us again there was much more room in the buggy and we had a chance to appreciate where we were. The mountains were truly incredible, and the crystal clear air and views extended for miles without a building or man-made object in sight. We were tens, if not a hundred miles or more, away from anywhere, on a road that probably no more than a handful of vehicles used and that virtually no-one except the locals would ever see. It was stunning and I felt privileged to be there. Whatever else happened on the journey, even if it ended this day, I really felt that I had achieved something pretty special and had made it to the kind of places that I had expected this adventure to be all about.

The road we had been on all day was getting no better or worse and I was loving the driving, almost drifting the buggy round some of the wider corners and our progress was improving – especially now that I had full use of the gears! There were some more very sketchy moments and at times it reminded me of mountain biking in the French Alps; when a long straight opens up, you go as fast as you can before braking hard to get rid of the speed, just in time for the corner and hope you don't fall off. Except in the buggy there were more than a few occasions when we'd hit a large rock or ditch and I'd have no control of the situation and I genuinely thought it was irrecoverable as I clung onto the steering wheel. Fortunately, we always came to rest somewhere on the track, though not always pointing in the most convenient direction.

We stopped for a break and to fuel-up from the jerry can. Opening the back of the buggy we found that our kit had been thrown everywhere, and was seriously showing the effects of the constant battering and grinding it was getting from the dust on the roads. There was also an overwhelming smell of white spirit. The remaining three litres of our cooking fuel had burst its container and spilled everywhere, soaking into everything. There wasn't much we could do except hope it didn't catch fire before it evaporated. And as if to make matters worse, and at the most inconvenient time possible, it was also here that we found that our

A quick fuel stop in the mountains

On top of the final set of peaks

Some of the corners ahead

A brief rest at 3,500m (11,500ft) above sea level

fire extinguisher had been battered and shaken so badly that it had discharged its powder into our kit. We hoped a bit more that the white spirit didn't catch fire!

Starting to descend the last set of mountains, the whole road could be seen beneath us like a line of spaghetti snaking all the way down to the wide, flat basin of the river Naryn.

Relentless corners

There was a different type of mountain ahead too. We were leaving the grass and scree covered ones behind, to enter a region of relatively young, yellowy-brown coloured mountains, pyramidical in

263

shape with deep gouges cut down their sides from the flow of streams. They rose out of the dead-flat alluvial plains in a way that a child would draw a mountain range; to me it looked like the mountains you see getting carpet bombed in Afghanistan. They were still over 2,700m (8,850ft) high, yet from up here they looked tiny. The area was also home to many hydroelectric dams. A great idea except, for the widespread seismic activity in the area, which has the potential to reach high numbers on the Richter Scale and would easily destroy the dams and flood the valley below – not that there was anything in the valleys.

Literally on top of the world

Part way down it was noticeable that the back of the buggy was slewing out on right-hand corners more than normal. Foxy leaned out of the window as we descended, only to discover that the left rear tyre was completely flat – going to show just how rubbish the suspension on the buggy was, that we could drive with a flat tyre and scarcely tell the difference!

The straights became longer as we got lower down

We stopped and put on the spare and took another break from the relentless mountain track. Still nothing passed us and nothing resembling any sign of life could be seen. The wall of the tyre was not in the best shape having been run flat for a few miles, and there were a few dents to the rim but nothing too serious. After putting some more petrol in, we drove on down the mountain, negotiating hundreds of corners and dried-up streams cutting across our path, before getting to the dead-flat of the valley bottom which we followed to the east.

Several miles on, we crossed the river and to our relief joined a loosely tarmaced road and were able to finally relax and pickup some speed. The road was still in a poor condition, yet compared to what we had been on, it seemed perfect and was a huge change to the twists and turns and intense concentration required up in the mountains.

Further up the valley we came to the small town of Naryn, pretty much dead in the centre of Kyrgyzstan, although with a population of forty thousand it was huge in comparison to the mountain villages. The area is famous for nothing except its natural beauty and is one of the poorest regions of the country with most people being sheep-, horse- or yak herders. Almost by design the first place we saw on approaching the town was a petrol station. It was fortunate as we only had a few litres left, but as we had used the last of our money in Kazarman, it was going to be awkward as usual. We tried to offer our credit cards and dollars but none were of use. Just as it was starting to look desperate, a couple of men pulled up in a car and started to take an interest in us and the buggy. It was amazing where these people always came from. By now the petrol station owner was poking at our front bumper which, unbeknown to us, had been completely hanging off at one end and was on the verge of dropping off entirely. We lashed it back on with some washing line cord we had brought with us (one of the few random items we had taken with us that actually proved to be of some use!) but our new friend with the car looked disapprovingly at it and seemed to be suggesting that he could help if we let him come with us. We did. There was nothing to be gained from being at a petrol station with no money, even if we were about to run out of fuel, and apparently he knew somewhere we could change dollars. Or at least that's what we understood him to be getting at. Much like the performance only hours earlier, he piled into the middle of the buggy and pointed ahead down the road.

We drove into a small, ramshackle part of town acutely aware that everyone we passed turned to stare – hopefully in curiosity. I had a strange feeling somewhere between the excitement of looking like a famous rally driver that everyone wanted to meet and in trepidation that we were about to be taken to a shady area of the village to be robbed. I've always been quite a sceptical person but my feelings and lack of trust on this trip had been magnified, sometimes with just cause, but it was a shame as I'm sure – and can clearly see in hindsight – that many of the people we met were very genuine, kind and helpful and took great pride in being able to meet and help us. Regretfully, this time my scepticism was certainly the feeling I should have been trusting. We turned off the main road, down a back alley and into a dusty area behind some buildings where a number of men were idly chatting and drinking in the evening sun.

Stopping beside them, we jumped out of the buggy which was immediately surrounded by the men all trying to get a better look inside and around it. We had kit all over the dash and floor and hoped that it would all be there when we got back in as there was not much we could do to stop everyone in their curiosity. Our guide took us inside a shed that doubled as some form of workshop where a man was under a car in the middle of some major repair work. The man crawled out and rather than offer to change our dollars, shook our hands exchanged a few words with our guide and proceeded to fetch some heavy duty cables and a welding torch. This was going to land us with a large problem if he wasn't able to change our money, as we had no way of paying for any repair work. Anyway, while we tried to chat to the guys, the mechanic set about repairing the buggy. He soon had a problem when he found two batteries under the bonnet and didn't know which to earth so that he could safely weld the bumper without frying our electrics – not a problem, he just didn't bother and before we had a chance to explain he had the welding torch fired up and was welding away. Health and safety was great; he did have a welding mask, but soon discarded it as it was hampering his vision and without it he could get a better view of what he was doing. Meanwhile we tried to establish where, or who, could change our dollars. Instead, the conversation seemed to be moving in the direction of whose house we would be staying at. Several drawings in the sand later and it was clear that this was the case. Given the previous couple of days this was the last thing we had time for. We wanted some Kyrgyz money, some petrol and to get on our way – not the trauma of spending the night with the inevitable delays this would cause and our visas were looking tight as it was. It was also quite evident that there was no-one who could change our money. As time went on, the invitation to stay the night became more of a demand and it was obvious that we were irritating the men by declining their offers.

The buggy was pretty much fixed and the guy had done a brilliant job, but now wanted money. From a ridiculous ten dollars we settled at a still over the odds five dollars and I liberated five one dollar bills from under the carpet while no-one was looking. This was pretty much the breaking point. If we hadn't angered the men enough by declining their offer to stay with them, then trying to pay with one dollar bills certainly did. We had learnt that the banks didn't like the smaller bills but couldn't see the problem here, although to make it clear, the man drew a one and a dollar sign in the sand then crossed it out and furiously replaced it with a zero. I wasn't too keen to start looking through the innards of the buggy to find the larger bills with the atmosphere that had developed when, luckily, Foxy found a single five dollar bill in his wallet. Perfect. The problem now was that the man who we'd met first was in the buggy trying to get us to go back to the garage with him even though we still had no money.

When we went near him he physically tried to take the five dollar bill, meant for the mechanic, by grabbing at Foxy's arm and also the other five ones dollars by grabbing at me. This truly was going too far. Demanding money is one thing but this was edging towards theft. It was only five dollars but there was no way he was going to have it given the way they had turned on us and the fact that all he had done was show us a welding shop. Backing away from him through the crowd, we tried to find anyone who may be able to change money for us but it was a hopeless task. Our man reappeared again having got out of the buggy to find his money. Again he started grabbing at us trying to take it all. After some time and lots of shouting, we got away from him and back to the mechanic to whom we handed the five dollar bill. We pushed our way through the men, back into the buggy, thanking the mechanic who had been genuinely polite and helpful, and shut the doors, but the original man forced his way in, climbing into the middle over the gear stick; pointing back down the road to the petrol station. It really was exasperating. We drove back down the road to the petrol station where we all got out, then, as soon as he was far enough out of the way, dived back in and locked the doors as he tried to get back in. He had never had any intention of changing money for us.

It could have been a great experience meeting the guys and even staying the night but the initial kindness was obviously just a rouse to try and get money from us later on. And this time they were much more aggressive than anyone we'd met previously. We had to go.

Given that there was only one road, we had no issues finding the way out of town and didn't even bother to look for petrol. There was a fair chance the guys would soon be back with us and at a place this small there would certainly be nowhere official to get money. There was little point asking if anyone could change money for us – we'd already tried that with no success. Once again, we headed into the hills and drove on into the night now that the sun had set. Stopping to look at the map it was 100 miles to the next village and it was no bigger than the place we had just left, making the chances of getting petrol slim to none. And those 100 miles were all over mountain passes. Realistically, we weren't going to make it, but we couldn't see much alternative.

After about half an hour, we felt that we were far enough out of the village and pulled off the road. It was pitch black and we were absolutely in the middle of nowhere, but we still drove for a good few minutes to park behind a small mound to be sure that we couldn't been seen from the road. Putting up the tents was such a change from the rest of the day. The air was cool and silent, there were millions of stars and the moon was so bright that as it rose, it cast a distinct shadow across the hills in the distance. And for once, even the midges seemed to be leaving us alone. We rustled up a sweet and sour dinner out of a tin over the stoves and got some time to rest and chat, without the hassle of the locals, for the first time since we entered the country. As we chatted about how unnecessarily stressful the days had appeared, we both noticed that in reality neither of us were in the least bit stressed, and were loving every minute and, as with everything, saw the funny side of the events and didn't wish it to be any different. After all, this is what we had come for. Then, as if to spite us for being so endlessly positive, there was the distinct sound of footsteps in the hills behind us. It was genuinely unbelievable. We had to be more than ten miles from any form or civilization yet even here at this time of night someone had found us!

The shepherd and his dog approached, and stopping some distance away and watched us in silence. Once he had taken the situation in, he cautiously came closer to us and began to talk at us without pausing. It was hard to tell if he was warning us off his land or trying to find out who we were and what we were doing. After a while he got the gist that we didn't understand a single word he was saying, paused, and then carried on talking at us, as if by saying more we might finally get what he was saying – a very British technique! Strangely enough it started to work, as a couple of words did actually begin to make sense. He was pointing over his shoulder and inviting us to his 'dome' which must have been his house and the second word we knew all too well; 'woda'. We had used and heard this word many times before, and depending on the very precise emphasis of the pronunciation either meant vodka or water. It was even more confusing in shops as both vodka and water came in very similar glass bottles and tended to cost a similar amount. However, given the time of night it was certain to be vodka that he was offering. After what felt like far too long, and much to his disappointment, he accepted that we were perfectly happy to spend the night in our tents rather than his 'dome' and that we wouldn't be drinking any 'woda'.

Now that he was gone, Foxy went to bed, commenting that it was the best bet in case he came back again and we got stuck trying to talk to him for another hour or so. I foolishly stayed up to try and take some photos of the moonrise. Predictably, no more than ten minutes later, the shepherd was back walking across the hill towards me, only this time he was with a lady, presumably his wife, and a child. They waited some way

271

behind while he approached offering me a large flatbread and some biscuits. It was very touching and I knew that I should accept his invitation to stay at his house, and in hindsight wish I had, but I was so exhausted from the previous couple of days and annoyed with the people we had met, that at the time it was the last thing I wanted. We shared some bread, I gave him some of our water and he went to Foxy's tent – who was kindly leaving me to deal with the shepherd while he pretended to sleep – and left a bread in the doorway for him. We chatted for ages but he wouldn't leave as he was adamant that I go with him. It was all becoming too much hassle so I started to get into my tent and waved goodbye to him. With reluctance, he went back to his family and seemed to be suggesting that he would return in the morning by pointing to the sky and indicating the sunrise.

Moonrise over Kyrgyzstan's mountains

Once we'd waited for him to have got far enough away, we got out of the tents and tidied up the cooking equipment while we laughed at how ridiculously stressful even the most normal and everyday things were becoming. With that we went to bed – fully expecting him to be waiting outside when we awoke.

8th August – Naryn, KG to Shiybut, KZ

We were up quite a bit before 05:00 and had the tents packed away, quietly, within five minutes and left. We could just see the man's house in the distance but there was no sign of him. We had no interest in meeting him again given, that no matter how explicit we were, he wouldn't leave us alone and we had little time to waste if we were to make the border crossings to tie in with our visas. Unless the roads improved and we got out of the mountains it was looking doubtful. Not to mention the fact that we seriously didn't expect to make it beyond the next small town without any fuel or money – and that's if the fuel we had even got us the next 90 miles or so in the first place.

In the night I'd had yet another vivid car crash dream, so vivid that I had to actually get out of the tent for a walk around as I though it was about to crash and I needed to get a better view to manoeuvre the crashing car. It was weird considering that I rarely dream yet I out here I was having the same one time and time again, each time getting more and more realistic. I just hoped it wouldn't become a reality.

Climbing into the mountains again it was looking promising as we found some tarmac, but this soon ended and we were back on the potholed, single-track dirt road winding higher and higher. Occasionally, we would pass camps of yurts. I don't pretend to know much about horses but the ones we passed here were some of the most stunning horses I've ever seen, and looked to be in amazing condition. There were no motor vehicles to be seen anywhere and no forms of power, instead the nomads were relying on the horses and fire to provide all they need. It was wonderful to see the children so happy with such a simple life and none of the trappings of Western society. Everyone was wearing traditional dress rather than the meaninglessly branded t-shirts or football shirts of so many others we had seen so far. Meaningless because almost without exception none of the brands or teams could be seen in the majority of the countries or regions we had visited beyond Europe.

With so much to see and such a constantly changing and dramatic landscape, the distance soon disappeared and we freewheeled whenever we descended in an effort to conserve fuel. Miraculously, we still had some fuel as we hit the tell-tale tarmac that marked the imminent arrival of the next town. Driving into Kochkor (it's strange how easy it was to mispronounce all the place names we saw, and trust me, we did at every possible opportunity) was a relief, in so much as we had got there without running out of fuel. But it also brought with it the agony of having to try and find somewhere to change our money, made even worse by having hardly slept, not just the previous night but the accumulation of many nights. Kochkor was sadly looking like the end of the road for us if there was no money to be found, as we were probably only good for a handful of miles now with the fuel we had. We parked up in the middle of town and looked around for a bank. Even though the Cyrillic for bank looks pretty much the same as the English for bank, we couldn't see anything, so asked and were told very simply and helpfully that it was just down the road behind us. It made a change to get a straight answer and not to be asked for anything in return, and also gave hope that we might not yet be stranded.

We ambled down to the bank in the fresh alpine air, yet it was still starting to get hot even this early in the morning. Kochkor was beautiful, well, its surroundings were, the gigantic snow-capped mountains of the Tein-Shan topped with fluffy, white clouds towered high into the sky on all sides of the town. Animals wandered around the central square and there was a sense that the town was still awakening and coming to life. The bank was quite impressive, given the general state of the town, with its large glass entrance and brass signs. We even had high hopes of being able to use our cards for a change. We shouldn't have been so naïve. Inside, the building looked like it had been derelict for years and had suffered from serious neglect. There were no customers and disappointingly, no staff.

Foxy posed for some comedy photos in the rooms we came to, then we explored some more to see what we could find. Through a small door to the rear we found another glass-fronted counter, again, with the glass white-washed by hand as if it had been shut for years. This time there was a small opening, crudely cut in the glass leaving untidy, razor sharp edges to it, with a face behind it. As soon as she realised that we couldn't speak her language, she must have rightly assumed that we were looking to change money and called someone, and a smartly dressed security guard appeared from nowhere. He led us deeper into the building to another seemingly deserted desk but there were a few locals queuing up. We were taken straight to the front, to an empty cashier point and served straightaway. We tried our credit cards but they were soon dismissed however our dollars were welcomed. The process was, for once, unproblematic and we got enough money to hopefully last us for our remaining time in Kyrgyzstan. The setup looked dodgy but the exchange rate appeared respectable and we left the unlit building into the blinding light of the early morning, armed with money and the prospect of a much less traumatic day ahead.

Back in the centre of the town, the more senior members of the community were milling around wearing tall, pointed, white felt hats as the market came to life around us. In the time it had taken for us to get our money, which for once hadn't actually been that long, the whole market had appeared and been set-up. Our buggy was now pretty much in the centre of the activity and it was apparent that empty space where we had left if had now become the centre of the morning's fruit market.

The morning market, Kochkor

Feeling affluent for once, with cash in our pockets, we were much more relaxed and bought some fruit (the peaches were still huge, easily half as big again as ones in the UK), biscuits and bread to snack on. Walking back to the buggy, there was a shout from the crowd behind us,

"Is that a '92 Suzuki?"

It was a real surprise to hear perfect English being spoken and a man came towards us. It turned out he had studied in London for four years and had correctly guessed the age of the buggy from the registration plate. We talked for some time about what we were doing and life in Kyrgyzstan and London then began the 40 mile drive northeast towards Lake Issyk-Kul. We used most of our money, on the edge of the town where the tarmac again ran out, to get all the petrol we could carry.

One of the locals of Kochkor

Located one mile above sea level, 113 miles in length (running east to west) and over 37 miles wide, Lake Issyk-Kul is one of the largest natural water reservoirs in the world, and is the largest alpine lake, second only to Lake Titicaca. Strangely, the lake has no outflow but over a hundred contributory rivers, several of which are hot springs. It stays at its depth purely by evaporation. Its southern and northern shores are flanked by two monumental mountain ranges, with several peaks rising more than 5,000m (16,400ft) above sea level, the largest of which, just off the south eastern edge of the lake and straddling the Chinese border, is Jengish Chokusu. At 7,439m (24,406ft) it is the highest mountain in the Tien-Shan range (only 1,411m / 4,629ft less than Everest). In the past Lake Issyk-Kul has also been used by the Soviets for submarine and torpedo testing, an activity that is rumoured to be due to resume imminently.

Approaching the lake, we drove for several miles along the south side of a smaller, stunningly deep-blue lake with high, rocky, barren and coarse looking mountains running right down to the water's edge.

A stunningly blue lake

We passed into some kind of national nature reserve, rejoined a tarmaced road and had to pay an entry fee of about three pounds. This seemed very high in relation to the cost of everything else in the country, but at least there was an official notice board outside the gatehouse with a price list – we probably paid the price for a coach or an annual pass! We were now down to our last four pounds having bought the food and fuel; nothing new there then, although it should be enough for the rest of the day.

Getting to the westerly tip of Lake Issyk-Kul, the stark, inhospitable desert mountains gave way to lush alpine mountains with pine forests on the lower slopes and huge toppings of snow and ice, some of which flowed lower down in glacial streams towards the lake. It was strange to be beside the lake with the temperature in the mid to high thirties, yet with the snow so near and clearly visible. Travelling east, along the north shore, we passed a few resort towns which was amazing to see. For days, everything we had seen had been functional and purposeful, but here there were leisure activities and holidaymakers from Kazakhstan, China and Russia. Rather than the focus being on manufacturing, farming or survival, here people were either relaxing or serving those who were visiting. There was even an attempt at architectural styling in the design of the buildings. Nothing unusual back home, but given the places we had been for so long and the work-based, purposeful attitude of everyone we met, it was completely out of character to find a holiday resort.

We drove on a bit further and the lake began to resemble more of a sea; being so wide it was impossible to see the other side. There were yachts, jet-skis, marinas, smart hotels and all the things you'd expect on the Mediterranean, yet it was still relatively peaceful. It felt much more multicultural than anywhere on our journey so far, and we stood out less than we had anywhere else. It was almost midday; we were out of the mountains and with the roads being better than the previous couple of days, we were making good time and could, contrary to our earlier expectations, afford some time off. We still had a day an a half left on our visas and the border wasn't far way. Rather than waste the rest of the day queuing and being hassled at the border, we would wait until late at night. It always seemed much easier to get through late on, when the guards were more lax and we were happier to waste the night at the border rather than the daytime – after all, the only other thing we'd be doing that late would be sleeping.

The backdrop to Lake Issyk-Kul

We left the road and drove down a track, past some roaming cows, through the trees and to the beach. There were perhaps three other people for as far as we could see, so we had no problem finding a spot to sunbathe. It was perfect. The weather was roasting and it must be one of the most picturesque places I've ever been.

The edge of Lake Issyk-Kul

There was the azure lake, a deserted, litter-free, white sand beach, a swathe of grass, willowy, leafy trees with cows and horses lazily pottering about beneath them, then huge alpine mountains covered in snow, and the occasional fluffy cloud high on the peaks, reaching into the pure blue skies. That was it. We'd be going nowhere for rest of the afternoon, we deserved a rest.

Beside Lake Issyk-Kul

Given how high we were and that most of the water in the lake was meltwater, it was surprisingly warm to swim in and a great way to get clean instead of the usual baby-wipe-bath we'd being using whenever we slept in the tents or buggy. It was also nice to be on a beach yet have fresh, rather than salt, water; although apparently it is very slightly saline. As we lay on the beach sunbathing, the cows and horses sauntered around. Well, the horses did. The cows had had their front legs tied tightly together to stop them roaming too far. It was a very crude, but effective, way of preventing them from moving too far from where they were left by their owner, but made progress painfully awkward for them. They had to jump their front legs then shuffle forward with their rears before their front legs crashed back to the ground with their calves following on behind. Cows really weren't designed to jump.

When Foxy nodded off, I went back to the buggy to occupy myself by photographing the horses – I bore of sunbathing all too easily – and successfully broke off the rear door handle on the buggy. Another inconvenience we'd have to deal with as there was no way to repair it. We had always had to clamber over our kit into the rear to lock the back door, as the key had never worked, but now without a handle we would have to do this even to open it.

We woke sometime after 17:30 and went for another swim before deciding that it was time to get moving again. It's said that it's all about the travelling and not the arriving, and as improbable as it may seem, we actually wanted to be back in the buggy and on our way. We managed to rig some string through the remains of the door mechanism such that with the help of some well positioned pliers, the door could be opened with only a small struggle from the outside. We were feeling good after an afternoon off and a swim and continued to the eastern tip of the lake, following the road back into the mountains to the northeast and towards the Kazak border. Immediately after turning away from the lake, the tarmac ended.

I've heard the stories that the only place the ex-Soviet Empire spent its money was where dignitaries and high-ranking officials might have to travel but the way the tarmac ended so abruptly outside of towns, villages and main routes between areas of importance really took me by surprise. It did just literally stop as soon as it was out of the sight of where people of importance may travel. It had been the case in Uzbekistan with the huge four lane tree-lined highway leading from the administrative centre of Bukhara to the nigh-on deserted airport and again on the road to the hydroelectric dam when leaving Uzbekistan. It also appeared that roads leading to borders with neighbouring countries were very low priority to be modernised. The road was extremely rough and we were once again making excruciatingly slow progress. We were also getting covered in the dust that we had only just managed to wash off.

As the sun was setting, we fuelled-up from one of the jerry cans, and without any say in the matter, gave countless midges their food for the day. I knew we were nearing the border from the purposeful feel of the road. I don't know how a road can 'feel purposeful', but they do as they get near to borders. They are the most desolate and neglected roads, leading to nothing but a bureaucratic delay from border guards who would much rather be at a different posting, yet they were the key to the changing phases of our journey and the new things we would experience ahead. Soon there were a couple of lights in the distance and a collection of huts. It seemed ridiculous as a security measure given that, theoretically, all someone would have to do is simply pull off the road and drive through rough ground a few miles to one side of the border post, to enter or exit the country without being stopped. There were no fences or border patrols, making the border post appear somewhat redundant. Or perhaps we just weren't looking hard enough.

Considering how quiet and deserted the road had been (we hadn't seen another vehicle since leaving the lake), we slowed to a crawl as we neared the border compound to remove any impression of being a threat. We weren't too sure what they would make of us arriving at almost 00:45, or even if it was open or not. Fortunately, it was open, although outside the buggy it was freezing cold, and all we had to hand were the shorts and t-shirts we were wearing. We were at quite a high altitude; over 2,000m (6,560ft) which explained the cold night air, and the midges were having a field day. The guards came to begin the process and they were some of the most hospitable people we had met, which was odd given the nature of several of the people we had met in the country. Apparently, it was very rare for them to have vehicles passing through, and even more exceptional for a foreign car, which was almost unheard of. We offered cigarettes around which made them even more welcoming, and when our lighter wouldn't work they gave us a box of matches to take with us – a small gesture, but kind nonetheless. Hitting the borders at night certainly made life easier for us, but this had been a revelation. There had been virtually no questioning, only a couple of forms to fill in and get stamped, and no demands of money or fake taxes to pay; we were there barely an hour and most of that was after we had completed the formalities and we were trying to chat to the guards as best we could by playing the usual games of charades. It was almost as if they weren't prepared for us and were unsure how to interrogate us.

We passed the gate and travelled a good twenty metres before arriving at the Kazak gate where we were duly stopped by a very relaxed, but typically heavily armed guard. He obligingly swung open the barbed wire gate and let us into the compound. Much like with the Kyrgyz guards, we completed the mandatory forms, had a very brief check and were politely waved on down the track to the military stage of the border process with just one locked, barbed wire gate left to cross. But there was no-one there. Beginning to wonder if it was some kind of joke and that the border was shut until the morning, we got out and took a wander around. There was one hut with lights on, so I went up the steps and opened the door to look inside. There was a long table with what looked like a family of about ten people around it. I suddenly felt very rude, as if I'd interrupted an important dinner without knocking and initially they appeared to have nothing to do with the border process. They knew I was there but gave the impression that nothing would happen until they had finished their meal. I was about to leave when a man from the far end of the table stood up, left the table and walked towards me, picking up his rifle loosely in one hand as he did so,

"American?"

He enquired with a seemingly angry look about him as if there was nothing he despised more, yet strangely wanted to have the pleasure of questioning one,

"Nyet. English…Englasi"

I quickly corrected him.

"Bah…!"

Came the half-laughing, half-relieved response as he waved his arm towards Kazakhstan and turned away from me to take his seat back at the dinner table. Evidently the English were of no concern to him and this had saved him from having to do any work. One of the younger men, from the end of the table nearest me, followed me down the steps and unlocked the gate and beckoned us through. It was surreal. Not a single check was made, barely a question asked and we were on our way again.

I couldn't believe how unproblematic it had been as we drove off down the track into the darkness, leaving Kyrgyzstan behind to enter Kazakhstan for the second time. For all the bad experiences with some of the people we had met in Kyrgyzstan it still remains one of, if not the, most marvellously spectacular place I have ever seen and the sheer remoteness and scale of the mountains is something I doubt I'll get to see anywhere else. It had also been blissful not to have the continual police and military stop-checks, thanks to the remoteness of the roads we travelled, which was something we had taken for granted for these two days without even realising, but the days ahead would make this all the more acutely apparent.

I drove on down the track and for the first time on the entire journey we started to head back west. Having travelled down the southern edge of the mountain range, to the north of Lake Issyk-Kul, we had crossed at the first place possible, which was where the mountains lowered at the eastern end of the lake. Now we had to back-track along the northern edge of them. The mountains are quite a thin range that runs east-west at an average height of 4,000m (13,120ft) along most of the northern Kyrgyz-Kazak border and back-tracking was the only way to get back en-route and avoid another huge group of mountains that were now to the north of us; preventing us from taking any form of direct route to Mongolia. It made for a diversion of several hundred miles but it was the only passable route we could see.

The air was icy cold and we even had the heater on, as we both did our best to watch out for major potholes and find new music to listen to, but usually reverted to the Arctic Monkeys, again. Then there was an all mighty thud that pierced through the sound of the music and the constant noise of the gravel hammering the underside of the buggy. We had both seen it coming, much like you see moths in the headlights before they explode across the windscreen – and there had been countless of these – except this had been a huge owl. It was unavoidable and, as it smashed into our near vertical windscreen, the impact was deafening. Given the apparent force of the impact it was amazing that the windscreen remained intact, which is more than can be said of the owl, and very fortunate considering where we were and the remote likelihood of ever getting a replacement. What was ironic was that we had joked several times, and even as recently as that very evening, about how incredible it had been that we had managed to miss so many creatures so far and how hitting a large animal could so easily spell the end of the journey for us. This was just a reminder of how easily it could happen, and how whatever we hit would not need to be very much bigger than an owl to cause a huge problem for us.

We drove until we were too tired to continue, and at about 03:30 pulled up just off the road to sleep in the buggy. The terrain, pitch darkness and fatigue meant that attempting to put the tents up was futile. Foxy had been the last to drive and had to make do with the slightly less comfy driver's seat for the night. Not that either was by any means comfy.

Throughout the night I woke several times to find myself leaning across, grabbing at the steering wheel trying to steer us back onto the road. Each time I would be half-awake, half-dreaming but very much aware that Foxy was at the wheel sleeping. I even tried to get the brake once. Spending so much time in the buggy was not good for me and blurred the difference between dreams and reality to the extent that I constantly thought we were travelling and never sleeping. Thankfully, for my sanity, this was the first night that Foxy started having the same problems and woke me a couple of times 'rescuing' us from an impending crash as the buggy lay motionless, safely parked off the road.

9th August – Shiybut, KZ to Aqtoghay, KZ

After one of the most arduous and useless night's sleep, we gave up trying and set off again at 05:40 having been parked up for just over two hours. It was light, we hadn't been able to sleep in the dark and now the heat of the sun was starting to fill the buggy again. Sleep deprivation is not something I cope well with, but I was surprised how well I was doing and anyway, we had a long way to go. The sun was up, it was yet another perfect day and now that we were getting nearer to Almaty we had recently joined a tarmac road.

Almaty, the largest city in Kazakhstan with over one million inhabitants, was one of the largest cities we actually drove directly though having left Austria, and until 1998, when it was moved to Astana, it had been the capital city. The reasons for the move are uncertain but appear to be down to one of two reasons; either to give the capital a more strategic, central location or to suit the politicians who generally came from the region surrounding Astana and didn't want to have to move. Either way, with only six hundred thousand or so inhabitants Astana has far less impact as a capital.

Almaty was quite a pretty city as far as ex-Soviet cities go and had almost a European, Parisian feel in places. However, its appeal ebbed away as quickly as our sense of direction deteriorated. We knew the road we wanted ran due north from the northern edge of the city, but somehow we couldn't find it. We located what appeared to be the ring-road and followed it until we started to run southwest, clearly having passed the turn we needed, so headed back and tried again. By the time we were going southeast, through some lavish residential suburbs, we knew we had missed it again. The third time we guessed and just took the first big looking road to the north and optimistically followed it. We must have wasted the best part of an hour to get to this point. There were no road signs or people to help us out and our map showed Almaty as about the size of a postage stamp. Miraculously, we had the right road and after several miles on the right heading, saw a sign to Qapshaghay which was a town we expected to be passing.

It was still early morning as we reached the outskirts of a small town, with the usual vulcanisers dotted along the roadside. We pulled over at one to get the tyre repaired from the puncture we'd suffered two days previous. Ever since we had fitted the spare the buggy's handling had been noticeably worse – not that it had ever been good – which was probably due to the spare being a completely different type and width to the others. The buggy had a tendency to hop and skip at the rear whenever we got any speed up and launch itself around the road. This was partly due to the wrecked suspension, broken dampers and further hindered by the ridiculously high pressures we were running the tyres at. We had done this in an attempt to get more speed out of the buggy by reducing the rolling resistance, improve fuel economy and hopefully reduce the risk of damaging the rims when we were off-road, but we had to wonder if the benefits were outweighed by the erratic and hazardous handling we inherited as a trade-off. We opted to blame it on the dampers and carried on with the high pressures for the perceived benefits.

The man and his young son had plugged and patched the tyre for us and by the time we had swapped the odd tyre with the repaired tyre I was dripping in sweat. It had to be one of the hottest days to date and having been laid on my back jacking up the buggy, it was also quite apparent that I had badly sunburnt my back at the beach and would be in for an uncomfortable day or two bouncing about in the buggy. Fortunately, we still had some Kazak money left over from our first crossing and offered to pay for the repair, but our vulcaniser refused with a huge smile. He seemed to like all the sponsor's and rally stickers on the buggy and was happy to help the two Westerners on their way. It was a change to meet someone genuinely helpful and we thanked him and left.

Looking at the map, we had a good 680 miles before we got to the Russian border and set the target of covering five hundred of that before the end of the day so that we could enter Russia the next day. It was a big shout but the roads seemed reasonable, and the map suggested that the tarmac might continue all the way to the border, as there were a few reasonably large towns on our route here and it was pretty much the only road between Almaty and Russia. The most promising feature of the map was that there were no more mountains. As it turned out, it was completely flat and featureless. The downside of a road like this would be its monotony and the inevitable police presence.

We got completely lost at the next town we came to and were stopped to have our documents checked three times. Eventually we found a route out, but our tempers were fraying. It was blisteringly hot, we were hungry, sunburnt, ridiculously tired having only 'slept' for two hours and to be honest, this bit of Kazakhstan was boring the hell out of us; there was absolutely nothing to see of any interest. Admittedly, we had been spoiled by Kyrgyzstan and the tiredness wasn't helping, but today had to be one of the least interesting days of the entire journey so far. I'd have done anything to be anywhere else.

We stopped under the shade of a half-dead tree for some lunch, the only shade we had seen in hours, and to try and reinvigorate our spirits. Delving into our huge plastic box of food in the back of the buggy to find something interesting to eat and raise our morale we were overwhelmed by the stench of rotting fish. Having pummelled through the mountains for the past few days many of our tins of food had either punctured or simply ground themselves to pieces. The dust that had penetrated everything else had even managed to get through the piles of loose clothing, into a covered plastic box and acted like sandpaper to destroy everything – including metal tins. We now had rotting mackerel mixing with broken cereal bars, half a litre of cooking oil, ready to eat curry, a couple of kilos of parboiled rice and a rogue peach that had got lost several days ago. It wasn't pretty and the smell was intensely putrid. A pleasant lunch break turned into a marathon cleaning session to salvage what food we could, clean out the buggy and try to remove the disgusting odour. We ended up removing everything from the rear of the buggy. By the end we had more than three sacks of kit that was either ruined or deemed to be of no use and could be discarded. Fortunately, nearby there was a pile of recently placed skip of rubbish, so we felt it acceptable to leave ours with it as it looked ready for collection. Having finished off some of the salvageable tinned fish for lunch, our supplies were looking limited, but it was a change to be able to have so much more room in the back of the buggy, and with everything lower down and roped in, the kit was less likely to come bouncing into the front while we drove. Although it still managed to do so somehow!

With good access to all the spares, we decided to check the buggy over. For the first time we noticed the coolant had dropped, well not so much dropped but virtually gone in its entirety. We had noted that the engine had been running hot for much of the morning, but had put that down to the exceptionally hot weather we were experiencing, and simply switched on the auxiliary cooling fan to run permanently. After a good search, there was nothing obvious that was cracked or leaking so we added some K-Seal solution, designed to block leaks like this, and filled up the radiator hoping this would fix it.

With a set of matching tyres and significantly less weight the buggy was noticeably more stable and we were making good progress through this inconceivably uninspiring region of Kazakhstan towards Russia. The visual highlight of the day was a brief stop at small, overflowing dam, but even this was ruined by an abrupt and rude local who insisted we leave while he ushered his family towards the water's edge for a private picnic. Not quite appreciating quite how he would need so much space, given there were only us and him at the entire dam, we waited a moment, only for him to come back again and almost forcibly make us leave, waving us towards our buggy. The wilderness just isn't big enough for some people to share.

Perhaps it was our tiredness but nothing seemed interesting on this day, and for the first time the driving was more of a chore than anything else, although for the first time in days we were back cruising at just over 50mph as the bumps weren't too bad. It was too hot to be enjoyable and all we could see was perfectly flat desert and scrub in every direction. We needed to get to something more interesting soon as the tedium, fatigue and boredom were getting too much, and we were both continually on the edge of dozing off. We shouldn't really have complained because, ultimately, we were still somewhere incredible and having an amazing time, we just didn't appreciate it today. We were able to edge the speed up as we got used to the condition of the road and were on target to cover the 500 miles. Then, in the middle of the afternoon on a long, mind-numbingly tedious straight, the buggy seemed to sense our contempt and complacency and took it about itself to liven up the situation, and threw a tantrum.

Completely without warning, the back of the buggy kicked up and the rear wheels pitched sideways across the road. The tyres screamed as they landed, and the buggy shot towards the deep ditch marking the edge of the road before it bounced up again, this time throwing us the other way, across the whole of the road before calming down sufficiently such that we could stop the bucking and regain control. It had been a major scare and it wasn't worth thinking about how different it could have been had there been a truck coming the other way, or if we'd ended up in the ditch. With that we stopped, fuelled the buggy from the jerry can and put the buggy back into four wheel drive. It wasn't good for the gears to travel quickly in four-by-four, or for the fuel economy, but it did seem to make the buggy more stable – and that was becoming the top priority.

As can be seen, little was of interest this day, hence few photos

Driving on, again with no more fuel or money, the buggy did seem more stable and on the horizon there was a huge thunderstorm developing. It was huge and so dark that it looked like night ahead. As we got nearer, the wind picked up dramatically and across the road, from the vast plains on either side, tumbleweed was starting to blow around. It's one of those strange things that everyone knows about and associates with the desert, but somehow it doesn't seem real, but in Kazakhstan tumbleweed really does exist and there was plenty of it kicking around. It may sound like nothing, but in eastern Kazakhstan it was one of the highlights of our day. It really was that bad. Within a few minutes we hit the edge of the storm but to our complete surprise there was no rain, it was a massive dust storm. Sand was literally streaming across the road as it was blown by the winds and the visibility dropped to that of a densely foggy day. The part of the storm we drove through didn't last for long, but all around us we could see vast clouds where similar storms were developing and one gigantic one to the east that had thankfully passed before we got to it.

With the dust gone, we were able to open the windows again to remove some of the stifling heat from the inside of the buggy, only to find that the outside temperature had dropped several degrees. The windows had only been shut for half an hour or so, but the approach of evening and the winds had taken much of the heat away and it was the first time for days that it wasn't burning hot – a dramatic contrast to the morning which had been one of the hottest we'd experienced. There was not much else to see for the rest of the day, no towns, no sights, no hills, nothing but scrub and sand, and more sand with sand beyond that, with the occasional lone bit of tumbleweed to watch, on the sand. There were two graceful eagles, which were pretty impressive as they flew around but our interest in anything was pretty limited today.

We'd managed to cover 435 miles when we finally decided to give up for the day, somewhat short of the 500 miles we'd aimed for. We wanted to stop before dark to cook some food, get the tents up and have a proper night's sleep, but then had to spend about thirty minutes trying to find somewhere suitable to camp. We felt quite vulnerable, isolated and exposed out here, and wanted somewhere out of sight of the road to camp. In a flat, barren landscape, this is easier said than done. We eventually managed to find a copse of trees a bit back from the road and once we had found a way through the huge drainage ditch at the roadside, we hid the buggy behind the copse and got out to pitch the tents. It was freezing and blowing a gale. Stubbornly, I insisted on being able to put my tent up single-handedly and spent the next ten minutes struggling with the thing blowing everywhere as I raced Foxy to try to be the first to finish. Wrapped up in jeans and fleeces, for the first time anywhere on the journey, we gave the buggy the once over.

The cooling fans for the engine had stopped working, as had the spotlights and the hinges for the whole rear door were cracked and it was just about managing to hanging on. Removing some of our kit and looking a little more closely we could see much bigger and more serious cracks propagating across the whole structure of the back of the buggy's body. That's how bad the 'roads' were. We tried the obvious things to fix the electrics, and got the fan working again with a new fuse, but the spots refused to come back to life.

I couldn't care less. It had been a rubbish day; I was cold, tired and sunburnt and wanted some food. We could fix the lights some other time. Although that would probably be when we actually needed the things, it would be dark and I would be in even less of a mood to be working on them. But that didn't matter just now.

We started to cook a chilli. The first problem was that none of our lighters would work – victims of the constant abuse from the dust in the buggy – although somehow, in the growing mess of kit and broken components in the footwell, we found the matches the border guards had given us. The second problem was that neither stove would work. We had two multi-fuel stoves, designed specifically to work in any condition, tested to destruction by their manufacturers on Arctic and Himalaya expeditions; but I somehow doubt they ever tried them in Kazakhstan where it mattered to us. The first wouldn't pump the fuel through – probably due to the days of suffering the dust of the buggy – while the second would burn intermittently with a smoky, orange flame, then flare up with a massive burst of flames and promptly go out, while erratic sprays of fuel continued to stream out. We stood no chance of keeping the thing going long enough to cook the rice, so settled for trying to warm the tinned chilli through. We both huddled around the stove but it was futile, and our efforts helped even less by the raging wind. The one day we had made time to stop early enough to cook food and have a rest, everything that could was conspiring against us. We ate some tinned fish and breakfast bars while trying to convince the stove to warm the chilli. It was evident that we weren't going to succeed so just picked at the mildly-warmed chilli and went to bed, and in all this time, not a single vehicle had passed on the road.

It had been the worst day of the whole trip. The buggy was collapsing around us, there was nothing, absolutely nothing, of any interest to see, we were tired beyond belief and hungry; we checked the maps and estimated we had 370 miles left to get to Russia, fuel for about three quarters of that and no money. We would have to spend ages tomorrow looking for money for the sake of buying fuel to get us 90 miles or so to the border, then have to do it all again as soon as we got to

298

Russia, to get Russian money for the next leg. It didn't seem worth it but there was no other option. My faith in the way that MasterCard and Visa portray the availability of money across the world had been shattered many days before and I wished their marketing teams would come and try this journey, and see if they maintained their inaccurate marketing claims of how available their money is.

Throughout the night the tents held up well in the winds, but the noise of flapping nylon woke me several times and that's when I realised just how cold it was. I had just my face poking out of my sleeping bag but my cheeks were icy cold – it was almost unbelievable given the places we had only just left behind. I drifted off thinking about the route we had picked, and the next couple of days in deepest Siberia.

10th August – Aqtoghay, KZ to Lokot, RU

Even having woken several times in the night with the howling wind, it had still been one of the best sleeps of the trip so far. Undoubtedly this had been helped by the early night and the ThermaRests smoothing out the jagged rocks beneath us.

It was 07:15, cold and windy. We soon had the tents packed away and were ready for off but, as was so often the case, luck was not on our side. The buggy simply refused to start. The engine was turning over but the thing just wouldn't start, even though it lamely coughed a few times. We were completely out of sight of the road and it would take ages to push the buggy to somewhere where a passer-by would be able to see it, let alone do anything to help us. That was also ignoring the fact that there was a six foot high banking to get up, to be back on the road that no-one appeared to use. We persisted, but it was clear that all we would do was flatten the battery, so we stopped to have a think. There were a few options that could be the issue, so we started with the easiest and most likely. We swapped the sparkplugs then the ignition leads. Neither made any difference. We cleaned the distributor contacts with no joy. We had a flick though the Haynes manual and appeared to be trying the right things then one obvious cause caught our eyes. The timing.

We had been so close with the distributor but the manual suggested any problem with the distributor was a 'replacement only fix' whereby we could only fix it with a whole new unit. Clearly this wasn't an option, so we figured out why it wasn't working and set about botching it; we had no alternative and nothing to lose. Remembering back to the advice of the mechanic in Romania we loosened off the unit and turned it until the contacts appeared to mate at the correct points. It seemed like it should work, so we bolted it all back together and tried again. Miraculously, the engine coughed itself into life. Then died almost instantly. We tried again and the exact same thing happened. Hoping that the problem was now to do with the fine setting of the timing, Foxy dived under the bonnet and loosened off the distributor again. While I tried to start the engine, Foxy gradually twisted the body of the distributor in an attempt to keep the engine alive. It was just about working and with one hand twisting the distributor and one pulling the throttle cable, we found a point where the engine was almost able to run without having to constantly rev it, and tightened everything back up. With four-wheel drive and low-ratio selected I tried to move the buggy forward but the engine was seriously struggling, possibly partly flooded from the choke, and almost stalled. I tried again and with loads of revs piled on, slipping the clutch as we went, we dived forward bouncing through the rough and boulder strewn scrub towards the road. The buggy sounded awful and had just enough power to launch itself up the banking, landing on the broken tarmac of the road.

The engine wouldn't run on its own so we ended up back under the bonnet in an effort to fine tune the timing. We managed to find a point where the engine was almost running smoothly throughout the rev range so set off again. It had been well over an hour since we had first tried to start the engine but at last we were off and the heater was starting to warm up, which was a welcome touch this morning.

The landscape remained flat, grey, dull and uninspiring. From time to time we would pass huge, decaying concrete factories surrounded by line after line of equally decaying and deserted concrete apartments, which had once housed the workers who had long since left when the factories had closed. It was strangely eerie that areas which had recently supported so many families were now just ghost towns of crumbling, deserted ruins. I began to wonder just where things are manufactured these days; China seemed like the only place left.

About 300 miles from the border, having adjusted the timing a couple of more times as the engine warmed up, we came upon the town of Ayakoz. It appeared to be a reasonably sized town from the extent of the apartment blocks, though many are now empty and only thirty-five thousand inhabitants remain, and it's also a major stop on the Turkestan-Siberian Railway, so we aimed for the centre. It looked promising for finding a bank. Amazingly, with almost no effort at all – we only drove around the same streets a few times – we parked right outside a bank and walked in. Inside, however, we were soon turned away as they apparently didn't dispense cash or didn't do foreign exchange or didn't like the look of us or didn't do something. Whatever the reasons, we weren't getting any money. Thinking they had completely misunderstood what we were after, we walked to the door, irritated that we would have to start looking all over again not knowing why we had failed here, when one of the employees walked with us and pointed down the road. About 200 metres away we came to a much bigger bank with a huge queue of people pouring out of the door. It was going to take absolutely forever to even get in, let alone get served and try to explain what we wanted. And then there was the risk they might not even accept our cards or like our small denomination dollar bills. We had no choice. We needed the money simply to buy petrol to leave Kazakhstan, and we were uncertain whether or not we'd make the next town, which was over a hundred miles away.

We joined the queue and didn't succeed in being inconspicuous, possibly as we didn't have the Russian-look but more likely that we were unshaven and in pretty grubby clothes. We rapidly got singled out wherever we went. This time it worked massively in our favour. From just down the street a middle-aged lady turned and walked across to us. Speaking English! It transpired that she was an English teacher at the local school and had overheard the two of us chatting away. She briefly complained and apologised about the state of the bank and then walked us around the queuing people, in the main doors passing scores more people, and straight to the counter. It was chaos; there were customers along the whole length of the counter, probably about fifteen or twenty at the counter alone with more behind them, all jostling for position and only five staff. It was more like trying to get served at a packed bar than a bank. Our new friend barged her way to the front, pulling us with her, and reached over the counter waving our dollars to attract the cashier. Within five minutes we had our money changed – we didn't try and complicate things with the cash cards – and had left. I half expected the lady to want something in return as we left, but she was just genuinely helpful and delighted to be using her English on real English people. She didn't get to meet many English in Ayakoz, not that she needed to tell us that given the location of this forsaken town. We thanked her and again, having the affluent feeling and confident that the town was being kind to us, decided to try and find someone to weld the rear door.

The door was literally on its last legs and if it were to fall off, all our kit would follow and be strewn across the Kazakh steppe. While trying to find the bank, we'd passed several places that looked like workshops but now we had the money couldn't for the life of us find them again. The one we eventually found couldn't weld, but helpfully directed us to one that could. After fifteen more minutes searching, we gave up on his directions and headed for the Russian border hoping it would hold together until we could find a workshop.

It was only a further 225 miles to Semey (previously known as Semipalatinsk), at the border, but we had to stop several more times to adjust the timing. It was only when we got out of the buggy into the fresh air that we realised how badly our eyes were burning from the exhaust fumes. Hardly surprising bearing in mind how arbitrarily we had just set up one of the most delicate parts of the ignition system, such that it was probably only burning half the fuel we fed through it. As if the pain of wasting vital fuel wasn't enough for us, it was now doing its best to make us blind too. At one of these stops we thought some more about the mechanic in Romania what he had actually been trying to achieve and took a closer look at the distributor. Turning the engine over gently by hand it was evident that the contacts in the distributor were closed almost all the time thereby not allowing the sparkplugs to work as they should – no wonder we had no power, a dog-rough engine and fumes choking us. The issue was that we had no idea how far to bend open the contacts and nothing to measure them with to get them all equal. Ah well. It didn't really matter and we didn't really care, we just gave them a bit of a bend so they looked similar to each other and were open at some point of the cycle and closed at another. It couldn't be a lot more complex than that surely? To say we're good is an understatement. The engine ran like a dream, not a perfect dream but it was much smoother and had regained much of its missing power. However, as our eyes soon let us know, the issue with the fumes was not going away.

Although we were complaining about the fumes in the buggy, it was nothing compared to what lay in the steppe some 90 miles to the west of us. This was where, in 1949, the Soviets chose to base their atomic bomb programme and the Semipalatinsk Test Site, under the misleading pretence to those who were funding it that the region was uninhabited. It subsequently became one of the most secretive and restricted places in the entire Soviet Union – and worryingly for us was also where the prevailing winds originated from. Over the forty years that the site was operational, 456 nuclear tests were conducted, 116 of these above ground and often with no alerts to, or evacuation of, the local population and with it came uncontrolled exposure to the workers. This now proves to be by far the greatest environmental threat to Kazakhstan, with the high levels of radiation still leading to birth defects, severe anaemia and leukaemia in the area, and specifically Semey, where many of the ex-workers and scientists still live. This again goes to show how little research we'd done prior to leaving that we weren't even aware of this at the time, and probably wouldn't have come this way had we known!

Foxy adjusting the timing, again

The weather was awful and was still taking some acclimatising to. Strange really, considering how much of a shock the intense heat had been earlier in the journey, I hadn't really expected the cold to be such a contrast, even though I had known it would come. For the first time since we bought the buggy – the time in the UK included – we had the windows shut, the heater turned up and our fleeces on. I wanted to be back in the heat and sun of the earlier countries, where there were things to interest us. Instead, we were out here where there was nothing ahead to look forward to except the desolation of Siberia and miles more of this crumbling, potholed road, making it impossible for us to make anything like decent progress.

In fact, to put the road in context it was so bad now, even though it was to an extent tarmaced, that both the driver and passenger had to brace themselves with both hands at all times. This was part of the reason we were getting so fatigued due to the only time it being possible to even consider sleeping was when, or if, we stopped at night. Our days were incredibly long and the hope of sleeping as a passenger had not once been an option since Germany – when we had both been too excited to want or need to. And even at night the sleep was somewhat hit and miss, and at the best uncomfortable.

It was now trying to rain and the sun was a distant memory.

The noxious fumes that were still continuing to burn our eyes were getting worse, my eyes were almost watering, and the noise of the engine getting notably louder. It suddenly all made perfect sense. We pulled off the road and it was no surprise to discover the section of the exhaust under the driver's seat was seriously cracked and the whole length was hanging on precariously by the perished rubber mounts. There wasn't a huge amount we could do here, so we set off again with the windows open in an effort to clear out the fumes. It didn't work. They just came in through the window too.

Arriving at Semey, near the Russian border, we stopped at the first vulcaniser we came across, and made the problem with the exhaust apparent to the mechanic in the hope he would be able to point us in the direction of somewhere that could help repair it. Our luck was in, and rather than turn us away, some more men came out of the building and directed us to drive around the back of the building. At the back was a yard of broken cars, engines and tyres. The metal shutters were open on the building, which must have been almost directly behind where we had just met the men, and inside was a full garage, workshop and a hydraulic lift.

The mechanics wheeled out an engine-less car from the ramps and I drove the buggy in while one of the mechanics directed me. The only problem being the hydraulic ramps wouldn't budge. The mechanics persisted but nothing was happening so they wheeled another car out of the garage to make room over the pit. Again, I was directed as I manoeuvred the buggy over the pit. The steering felt to pull from side to side and the mechanic looked wary as I tentatively moved forward. The reason was obvious when I got out, discovering the inside edges of the buggy's tyres hanging in thin air over the pit. I knew the buggy had a narrow track but this must have been an exceptionally wide pit as it was almost falling in.

By now we had eight men fussing over the buggy – the cars they'd been working on were now outside to make room for us and being ignored – and they had the broken, and still hot, exhaust off ready to repair. It was great to watch as they guessed the correct angles to make their welds such that the exhaust would fit back on the buggy. The other mechanics popped the bonnet to disconnect the battery ready to start welding, only to become confused by the fact that we had two, which took a few minutes to properly explain. With that dealt with, the buggy was earthed and ready for welding – better than the hit and miss approach to welding we'd met in Kyrgyzstan. At this point we were offered some of the Coke the mechanics had been sharing around. It came straight from the 2 litre bottle only to find it to be heavily mixed with vodka! It was a slight worry given the machinery and welding torches the guys were using (and the rate at which they had been drinking) but I wasn't about to tell them how to do their job; or to suggest the use of something as pathetic as welding goggles.

With the exhaust welded back in place, we turned the mechanic's attention to the hinges on the rear door. The lower hinge had now completely sheared off and the top one had ever growing cracks all around it. It was only a matter of time before the door dropped off completely. The mechanics appeared reluctant to do anything and it was frustrating as we explained again what we thought needed doing. It was then that one of the mechanics pointed out the real reason why they didn't want to do the work. The hinge backed onto the piping leading to the fuel tank, effectively meaning they would be welding directly against the petrol-filled fuel tank. The potential consequences were obvious. The mechanics offered to do the work in the morning as it would involve removing the fuel tank and it was already 18:00. We opted to leave the door for now and worry about it later. And given its condition it certainly would need worrying about. The repair had cost less than £4.

As we had spare cash for once we filled the jerry cans with fuel and headed for the border. We hadn't really wanted full jerry cans to take through customs, as there was a risk the guards would try to confiscate it or demand 'import taxes', but we felt it best given that we intended to drive on into the night and were unsure if there would be any to buy late at night in Russia. More importantly, we were back to 93RON petrol instead of the 80RON and, to our knowledge, we had avoided 76RON completely; it was the best we had had in days and at £0.26 a litre it was cheap enough. We also took the time now that we had the room to move the spare wheel off the rear door and put it in the buggy, on top of the other spare, to take some strain off the door hinges.

The road from Semey to the border was quick and smooth and for the first time since leaving Prague we were able to comfortably sit at 65mph. With the exhaust fixed the engine was running sweetly and the ignition timing problems a long way behind us. To have the buggy travelling at this speed was not only a surprise to us but also to our second road-kill of the adventure. Just before Russia we caught a dove full-on and it shot over the bonnet and exploded against the top of the windscreen with a deafening thud. Amazingly, yet again no damage was done, though I doubt the same can be said of the dove, and another potential disaster narrowly missed.

We joined the border queue at 19:15 which wasn't moving in the slightest. Miraculously, we had regained our high spirits. This was probably due to the knowledge we were leaving Kazakhstan and had something new to look forward to, and even though it was Siberia, there had to be more to see than we had experienced in the last two days. While we were waiting we noticed several of the light bulbs had blown and the spots, which were again working, were miles out of line so we repaired these while being eaten alive by the midges. It was worth it to avoid any potentially costly issues at the border. By 21:45 we were out of Kazakhstan and into no-man's land. We were stuck here for a long time, trapped inside the buggy, both to stay warm and out of reach of the majority of the midges. Plenty had found a way in, so we were kept busy killing the ones that had joined us inside, while eating Kazak fish-flavoured crisps. They were rancid. The worst I've ever had and fully summed up the previous couple of days. We continued to eat them more for entertainment's sake than anything else but were glad when they were finished and we didn't have to suffer them anymore.

Getting though the Russian border proved slightly problematic as it transpired that the car insurance we'd bought on our earlier visit was still valid, but due to expire in just three days. It was hard to fully understand the situation but from what we thought we were being told, the extra insurance sounded extremely expensive; well all things are relative, in the UK it would have been a bargain. Rather than do the obvious, sensible thing and just buy the extra insurance we decided we were being conned and instead, set about trying to convince the guards that we would in fact be in and out of Russia within the three days. And trust me, this took some convincing. We made up a route through Russia that bore no resemblance to our planned journey and, looking back, even involved us crossing into Mongolia where there isn't an open border to do so. This route must have been about a third of the distance of the actual route we would be taking and they still doubted our ability even to cover this reduced distance in the three days. Things didn't look good for us making it into and out of Russia. We didn't care. As long as we didn't have to buy the insurance and they bought our story, we could get on our way and worry about it later. Having had various forms stamped, signed, re-stamped and authorised, they finally agreed. Our concern was just how serious they seemed to be about the insurance. It was something that at the time we didn't see as that important, given that we suspected we may have only had valid insurance for about a third of the entire journey so far; technically, I believe even our insurance in the UK was invalid due to us being entered in a 'rally' but no-one out here seemed especially concerned about insurance, except the Russians.

We then had to buy a form for $10 (£5.30). We'd previously bought one of these on our first entry to Russia but had incorrectly given it to the guards when we exited, rather than keeping hold of it; which we were entitled to do because we had a double entry visa so, apparently, should not have surrendered it. It was a fair mistake by us, so we were happy enough to pay this as the Russians did appear to play by the book, and never once made any indication of wanting any form of bribe; though we were still unsure about the cost of the insurance. They just have a ridiculously protracted customs process. At 00:45 we were free and back into Russia after five and a half hours of processing.

11th August – Lokot, RU to Achinsk, RU

The quality of the roads was pretty good and very straight so we were progressing well as I drove us into the night, when literally out of nowhere there was a sharp, ninety-degree bend. The buggy's lights weren't up to much, I was probably starting to doze and it was completely unexpected, so I found myself braking hard, deep into the corner. We just got round, with the tyres slipping, and were straight onto a level-crossing. The buggy launched over the rails, bouncing heavily as it landed on the far side, and we skidded to a halt in a police road block, stopping just inches from the barbed wire blockade. It didn't look good as the guard marched over with his machine gun, his colleagues close behind. To say I was quietly panicking would have been an understatement and the scene was very familiar to that of our first entry into Russia several days previous. After the last couple of days with minimal police stops, I had grown complacent about how prolific they could be in Russia; especially near the borders.

Incredibly, they just inspected our documents, had a few polite words about our travels, shared the few Russian words we now knew and a few smiles and they let us go. No fines, no telling-off, no hassle.

Driving on into the night was not really an option with both of us nodding off, so after half an hour, at 02:45, we pulled in to a truck stop and parked up well out of the way and slept in the buggy. It was the safest place we could find, given that the road was frequented by huge trucks, and there was no road lighting or fields to pull off onto. I wandered around looking for a coffee but disappointingly realised I had nothing to buy one with, so returned to the buggy. I had the joys of the driver's seat for the night and soon awoke with another of the car-crash-nightmares. Except this time I was so confused that I was determined that we had to move the buggy somewhere safer. In my incredible

312

wisdom, I started driving again. I'll never know why I did it, I'll put it down to the effects of severe sleep deprivation, but when I was awoken by the rocking of the buggy later that morning – due to the close proximity of the passing trucks rumbling by – we were several miles from the safety of the truck-stop where we had first gone to sleep. I must have set off again, then decided that I was too tired to drive further, or perhaps thought we were somewhere safer, and stopped with the buggy half on, half off the road. I'm both amazed I didn't crash getting us there, and that no-one hit us while we slept in our vulnerable position on the edge of that dark road, as I still have no recollection of driving at all that night.

At 05:30 we set off again with Foxy driving. He was significantly better at sleeping in the buggy than I was, and we had to get back on the move if we were to have any chance of getting to the next border within three days. We had just over 1,600 miles to cover until the border, which would be about 530 miles a day. On the face of it, it potentially appeared achievable; assuming that we put some very long days in. Considering we could probably only average 40mph (or less) across a day, on good tarmac, we would have to hope for good roads or we would stand no chance, and the long days would be very long! The problem was that it was inevitable that there would be numerous police stops, atrocious roads, towns to negotiate and the potential for breakdowns. Given how seriously the guards had taken the insurance issue, we thought it best to be out of the country before it expired, and the only chance we had of doing so would involve no sleep and a lot of luck. In hindsight we should probably have just stumped up the couple of pounds at the border and taken the extension. Having said that, we had no roubles to buy it with anyway and it was too late now. We were off into Siberia; map in hand. When I say map, what I really mean is a Lonely Planet sketch of Russia.

When we had been planning our route back in the UK, we had hoped to enter Mongolia at the western tip and cross most of Mongolia on the way to the finish at Ulaan Baatar. Unfortunately, there were problems gaining access to Mongolia and the only border they would allow us to enter by was the one due north of Ulaan Baatar. The reason being the Mongolian authorities held little hope of our poor buggy making the trek across the desert and instead would be abandoned, along with other rally cars, littering the desert. It was a fair shout by them and, to be honest, we were amazed the buggy had made it this far. Had we now set off into Mongolia, where there are absolutely no roads in the western section of the country; in fact the only tarmaced roads are in the capital itself, it probably would have finished off the buggy, given its present fragile state. The upshot of all of this meant we had no map. We had looked in the map shop, Stanfords, in the UK, but to cover the sections of Russia we needed we would have had to buy several, huge and expensive maps, so that was that, the matter had never been mentioned again. Until now. Now, when we had a one-page spread in the Lonely Planet showing a 1,500 mile section of Russia sketched on about four inches of paper, the matter was acutely back with us. We had no option but to drive a couple of hundred miles northeast, roughly east for a few hundred miles, then southeast for a few hundred more, all the time aiming for the biggest towns we could and hope we didn't get lost on the way. The idea of taking what looked like a shortcut, by keeping close to the northern Mongolian border, was out of the question because of the hugely inconvenient positioning of the Tannu-Ola, Sayan and, to an extent, the Altay mountain ranges. All of which forced us to take a much longer route to cut around their northern extremities.

By 08:00 we had reached Barnaul, the start of the real Siberia, and the roads seemed promising. The police stopped us on the way into the town and again on the way out to check our papers in minute detail but there was nothing untoward, although it was wasting precious time. Barnaul was pretty big but we hadn't spotted anywhere to get cash, so continued without. This became a problem as soon as we left the town, only to end up on what was virtually a motorway. It was quite a result and gave us the impression that the roads in Russia may in fact be quite good, and would allow us to maintain the speed we desperately needed. We were still impressed with the quality of the road even as we drove up to the toll-booth; we hadn't seen anything this well built since Austria. The pressing problem now was that we had nothing to pay with. Our credit cards were dismissed and so were the dollar bills. We were directed to reverse, causing chaos in the queue, and to pass though a gate at the side. And with that we were off. The lady smiled and simply waved us on with no toll to pay. Awesome. Until the police stopped us about a mile further down the road.

I assumed it was because we hadn't paid, but this was of course Russia and it was simply just another police check. With some more time wasted we headed off towards Novosibirsk, Russia's third largest city which was some 150 miles to the north, with less than 30 litres of fuel to get us there. The two almost added up. Realising that we didn't have the time or the fuel to get lost, we decided to try using the GPS as a compass. We figured that with the GPS we would be able to get the straightest line out of any towns we came to, and then also be sure we were on the right road on the far side; there were so few roads that if we were heading on the right bearing we assumed we must also be on the right road. It had worked a couple of times earlier in the journey when we had used this method for simplicity rather than necessity, but now it was pretty much the latter. The problem being we had now lost the GPS. It was a bright yellow thing and even after we had emptied virtually

315

everything out of the front of the buggy, it was still nowhere to be seen. We gave up searching and resigned ourselves to the fact that the Lonely Planet would have to be our guide.

The buggy was now making an awful, dry-rumbling sound from somewhere in the drive-train that was vibrating up through the seats. It wasn't well and to make things worse it was now pouring down with rain. As a last ditch effort at happiness, we opened the last of the cheesy crouton-like biscuits we had picked up somewhere in the days before. As we drove on, we passed tens of gigantic, disused concrete factories with the customary rows of derelict concrete housing beside them. It was a sorry state. The habited small towns and villages we did pass were all of houses built of wood with a very shanty-town feel. It's best described as something akin to a sprawling allotment plot where the sheds were actually the houses. We were making good time on the relatively smooth and wide roads as we drove though seemingly endless pine forests to Novosibirsk.

At Novosibirsk, typically, the road deteriorated and split into several directions with no obvious through road or signage to help. In a city of almost 1.5 million people, we were soon completely and utterly lost, driving around the huge, indistinguishable estates of concrete flats. A small stroke of luck, however, was that we found an ATM on one of these estates and, miraculously, it accepted our cards and gave us some money. I felt a touch exposed, looking so out of place on this huge housing estate with the cash and was happy to be back in the waiting buggy. We drove on, trying to find the centre in the hope there would be an obvious route out to our next town, but that never happened. Instead we drove past more and more apartments. Getting seriously hacked-off we stopped at a convenience store and bought some crisps, bread and chorizo; it had served us well earlier in the journey as comfort food so thought it was worth trying the Russian version.

After a little over two hours we hit the edge of the city, identifiable by the transition from concrete apartments to wooden shacks, on what we hoped was the right road. We really did need to find the GPS. Fortunately, we were soon stopped by the police. By talking at them as much as possible we'd learnt from experience that they tended to hold us for less time so again we tried this and it seemed to work. They also confirmed that we had indeed found the right road.

With fuel and snack food, things were looking up. We were back up to 65mph but the rear wheel was now vibrating severely from the buckle it had picked up at the last flat tyre incident, and the gearbox was making a terrible whining noise. Opting to keep the jerry cans full rather than using them unless we had to, we stopped for fuel at the first opportunity. With the rain having temporarily abated, we gave the buggy a quick check over, only to find the air-box's mounts had sheared and this was now hanging down in the engine bay. Taking a screwdriver and a hammer we pierced some holes through the body work and using a few tie-wraps soon had that fixed. The next issue was that the whole exhaust was hanging on by just one rubber mount, the rest having perished and given way. It was only a matter of time before the last one broke and we lost the whole thing. With some metal wire we managed to tie it back on such that it was reasonably secure, but it would only be a temporary measure.

Our navigating was now at an all time low. The names in the Lonely Planet were in English and the few signs we did see were in Cyrillic. With Novosibirsk being the last major city we would pass in Russia, it would become even harder to get directions.

By 19:00 we had entered, negotiated and left Kemerovo with only two hours spent lost in the city. That may sound a lot but was actually quite good going for the cities and towns we came to out here. Kemerovo was nothing special but was another of the many Russian cities we travelled through which was notably in decline, having lost over ten percent of its population in the past decade. We were also spotted here by a Russian man, Denis, who emailed our website to offer his help should we need it; sadly we didn't get this until long after we had left, but it was a kind gesture. We were now about 450 miles through Russia but had only covered about 250 miles since 08:00 when we had been in Barnaul – that put us on an average of about 22mph, so even if we drove for the three days solidly we would still be short of our original 1,600 mile estimate to cross Russia. Added to this, our estimate of the distance across Russia had been somewhat out, as we still had 320 miles to cover to get to Krasnoyarsk. Krasnoyarsk was, we guessed from the map we were using, about a third of the way across this part of Russia which would mean that today we would have to drive 860 miles rather than the 530 miles we had initially estimated. You can probably now appreciate just how useless the map we had was that we were that far out on the estimates, and having wasted well over four hours simply negotiating towns, it was irrelevant how good the roads were. We would either have to drive 24 hours a day or be in Russia when the insurance expired, which the more we thought about it, the more serious we decided the consequences would be. The police were stopping us pretty much every half an hour to an hour to check our documents and they always looked at the insurance. We had no alternative and nowhere to buy any now so we ignored it and drove on.

The road was down to a single lane each way again but was straight and quite smooth, I was at the wheel, when, just as it was starting to become dusk at 20:40, there was the most deafening noise as at full speed the whole exhaust collapsed. When we had tied it back up earlier in the day it must have stressed a weak joint and this had now cracked through completely just below the engine. We parked up just off the road and after the exhaust had cooled enough, we removed the wire holding it on and unbolted the sections. We would take it with us in the back of the buggy in the hope there would be somewhere to get it welded in the morning. It had lasted almost 8,000 miles which, given how rusty it had been when we left, didn't seem too bad. With no alternative we started up the engine and carried on. It was absolutely deafening. With the engine at full revs the noise was painfully loud but there was nothing for it as no-one around to fix it in the midst of the Siberian forests. We had to keep moving to make the progress we needed.

The end of the exhaust, Siberia

By 21:05 we were approaching the edge of a village when, out of nowhere, there was a policeman with a speed gun. I assume we were doing about 65mph at the time which will have been well over whatever the unadvertised speed limit in place was. Naturally, we were unceremoniously stopped by several policemen frantically waving their glow-in-the-dark plastic lightsabres. Why was it always me driving when things broke or went wrong? What happened next was a complete shock and revelation. The policeman, whom I was fully expecting to throw the book at us, walked up to the buggy waving his speed gun at us while trying to cover both his ears with his free hand and trying to hide a huge smile in an effort to look serious. He soon accepted that we spoke no Russian except for our favourite line, 'nyet Ruski', which always seemed to help us out, and he resorted to pointing at the speed reading on his radar. Having no interest in dealing with a fine, we simply tried to look confused as if we had no idea what he wanted or what we may have done. He was still trying not to laugh at the noise the buggy was making as its rough engine barked and cackled without its exhaust and he soon gave up. With a wave he let us go and while covering both ears, laughed hysterically as I drove off as gently as I could to try to keep the noise down. Pretty pointless considering I had just driven up to them at 65mph and they would have probably been able to hear us coming through the forest since the moment the exhaust fell off!

It then dawned on us that we had just been stopped by the notoriously uncompromising Russian police for speeding, in a non-roadworthy, foreign vehicle, after dark and had avoided a fine and not even had our papers checked. It was an absolute miracle. Perhaps the exhaust falling off had been a blessing in disguise, even if it did mean the two of us would probably be permanently deaf within a few hours.

We were scarcely back up to speed, well a slow village-crossing-speed to be on the safe side until we were out in the forest again, when we were stopped by yet more police. We were literally half a mile from the first stop. Again, they seemed keener to have this filthy, noisy, foreign vehicle out of their town and they simply waved us on after a few minutes. I purposefully kept the engine running as the noise appeared to be the one thing they didn't have any patience for. Even though the stops were reasonably quick, if they were going to be this frequent we were going to be in for a very, very long night. And we had a long way to go.

By about 22:45 the day was taking its toll on us and we came across a ramshackle café. We pulled in and the whole café looked at us. It was half full with locals whiling away the night over stew and beer. Clearly, they had heard our arrival. There was no chance of trying to remain inconspicuous or do anything with any degree of subtlety anymore and we would have a lot more attention everywhere we went from this point on. A couple of people went outside in search of the huge beast of a race car they thought we were driving, only to be a little miffed by the tiny Suzuki jeep they found. Still, with the sponsors stickers adorning the bodywork, the crazy Englishmen driving it in the middle of the night and the mud splattered everywhere, they found it a whole load more impressive than the reality of it being a £500 purchase from eBay. They were convinced that under the bonnet we'd concealed some kind of rally-spec engine; not the one litre lump that was well onto its last legs. We chose not to spoil the illusion and bought two black coffees and two Twix bars. There was no other food on show and we had no hope of understanding the menu, and anyway, we strangely weren't that hungry.

A couple of the women working in the café were clearly curious. One of the younger ones spoke enough words of English such that we could convey what we were doing to the other people in the café through her. They seemed both impressed and confused that we were travelling so far with but no explicit purpose and then about to give away a perfectly serviceable car for no money. They had a point. They also appeared to have no concept of holidays or leisure time and seemed to think we were millionaires the way we were acting. It was good to be out of the buggy after travelling for so long today, but the coffee and chocolate had done the trick and it was time to be off again. As is often the case, there was a wash basin for cleaning your hands in the main part of the café so we took the opportunity, much to the amusement of the regulars, to have a good wash. They didn't seem to mind and brushed it off now they understood our situation and implied eccentricity. A fair number of the customers came outside to watch us drive off and waved us on our way before covering their ears as the noise became too much for them – at least they only had to bare it for a few moments, we were stuck with it permanently.

At 23:55, not far from the café, the police had us again and this time they didn't seem to be falling for our feigned ignorance or be happy just to wave us on, and instead made us turn the engine off. The policeman was fairly old and didn't speak a single word of English and appeared very irritated that we didn't speak any Russian, preventing him from administering his reprimand with the full effect he had intended. I suspect he had just given us a massive list of offences we were committing and various threats, but our impassive looks made it clear his threats were falling on deaf ears. With his irritation building he barked at one of his juniors who came over carrying possibly the oldest machine gun I had seen to date. Worryingly, he was waving it, with it now pretty much levelled through the door into my stomach. Given his youth, (he looked about sixteen and was wearing a ridiculously oversized military hat), and his apparent lack of experience, he made me feel more than a bit nervous.

He asked us a couple of things and we did the usual of saying where we had come from and were going to, using the Lonely Planet map for added effect. He pointed to where the exhaust should have been and we pointed to the back of the buggy where it actually was. He seemed sympathetic to our cause and waved us on, almost appearing to overrule his senior. Another close escape.

12th August – Achinsk, RU to Arshan, RU

It took almost three hours to cover the next 85 miles to Krasnoyarsk, allowing for numerous more police stops and quick fuel stop from the jerry cans, and we arrived at 02:50. Not a remarkable town by any means, and also with a declining population. This is not surprising considering that it has recorded temperatures as low as -56°C in the winters; a good enough reason not to live there and in my book, pretty much justifies Siberia's reputation. In keeping with all the Russian towns, and Kazakh towns for that matter, the road signs we wanted to be following were quite clear at the beginning of the town, only for the road to virtually disappear as we entered the town and split into several indistinguishable options; none of which had any signage. On the verge of giving up all hope, we were stopped by the police. Having dealt with the formalities we asked the way and he pointed, gestured and waved for several minutes and we were none the wiser. His colleague came across and drew a much more helpful map for us, but it still looked very ambiguous. The one good thing was that he put the Cyrillic name of the town we were aiming for, so once we got to the far side of the town we could at least check the mile-markers to see if we had actually found the right road.

We now found ourselves in some form of industrial area and again hopelessly lost, driving up and down the same roads time and time again, both losing patience with the town and each other. It was here that an actual police car stopped us, rather than the usual static roadside stops, sirens blazing and lights flashing; not that we ever heard the sirens until we stopped and I have no idea how long they'd been following us for before we realised. The policeman seemed somewhat bemused and after he had warned us about speed (thankfully, with Foxy driving this time) and checked all our documents he pointed roughly in the direction

324

he thought we needed to be heading. Finally, at 03:30 we escaped the maze of a town that had been much bigger than we had expected, and considering it had a population of just fewer than one million; forty minutes hadn't really been all that bad.

Me, looking thoroughly unimpressed, trying to sleep in Siberia

Just after 04:00 we came across a collection of cafés in the middle of the dense and seemingly endless pine forest, all with wood-burning stoves and all still open. It was quite strange; there must have been about seven or eight cafés, all sharing the same roof with a large, covered seating area along the front of them – and they all had practically identical menus but different owners. Even stranger was that they were all staffed and open at this time with seating for probably a couple of hundred and only about five customers. There were a couple of truckers eating at one so we took a seat there and picked some kind of huge pork kebab, which the lady cooked for us on the open wood burning fire. Deciding that we should rest for a while today, we got a couple of bottles of local beer and ate the food before getting into the buggy for some sleep at 04:45. It was freezing but we could hardly run the engine to get the heater working due to the horrific noise and ended up talking until sometime after 05:30. We had been on the move today for pretty much twenty-four hours and with it now fully light again we both nodded off.

By 07:00 we were too cold and uncomfortable to attempt sleeping any more and went back to the cafés for some strong, black coffee. With that dealt with, we were feeling surprisingly awake and I optimistically went in search of the toilets for a touch of luxury, having been living rough for a few days. They were nowhere to be seen so I went for a look outside but still without any luck. I tried to ask a couple of guys who were walking around with their coffees while admiring our buggy but, obviously, they didn't understand a word. Taking a tried and tested method, I used the buggy's windows as a blank canvas and drew a picture of a toilet and wrote 'WC' next to it in the caked-on grime. It worked perfectly, except, once the guys had pointed to a promising-looking wooden shed up the hillside in the forest, they then grimaced and pointed indiscriminately into the trees, suggesting I should go there instead. Naïvely, I still walked up to the shed but even within ten metres or more I knew it was going to be a challenge from the stench and the gathering flies. Braving the remaining steps, more out of a perverse curiosity than anything else, I looked into the shed to see two half-rotten planks traversing a deep pit alive with flies. The 'toilet' must have been in this state for some time considering the condition of the surrounding forest floor. I left. Siberia was not looking too promising. Five minutes up the road we found a much more pleasant section of forest devoid of the stench and swarms of flies and smelling much more pleasant in the fresh, damp morning air.

Having crossed another huge swathe of forest we came across a large town. Again, the signs began by directing us around the edge of the town before directing us into the centre of a monstrous, high-rise housing estate where the road became a track and the signs ended. Almost as if they had part-created a bypass then given up. It was a disappointingly familiar situation and soon we were lost.

It struck us here just how much of a time warp we felt to be in. Everyone was dressed in shell-suits and track-suits, often with luminous colours, the cars dated from a bygone era in the 1980s and everything looked to be on its last legs, including the tram network that every town appeared to have. It was strange to notice this here, given this had been the case pretty much everywhere from far-eastern Europe – with the exception, perhaps, of Uzbekistan, Kyrgyzstan and a tiny handful of the more affluent cities in Russia and Kazakhstan – but it just seemed that much more prominent here.

Back on the open, or rather forest encased, road we were stuck again. This time at a level crossing. The trains just went on forever, but with such enormous distances for them to cover, it made sense for them to have fifty or more trucks at a time and several giant locomotives to pull them.

It was somewhere around here that things once again took a turn for the worse. The M53, the only road running west to east across southern Russia, and the only road on our map, went without warning from a four lane tarmaced highway to a single lane, or less. And with it, the tarmac vanished and the surface became rutted hardcore, thick with mud. This was a joke. It was like jumping on the motorway on the outskirts of London and travelling as far as Glasgow on nothing more than a mud-covered farm track. And looking at the map that's about how far we had to go to get to the next big town. From experience we knew full well that the authorities didn't build or maintain roads unless they formed very major routes and, sadly, there was no reason to link the towns on the route we were talking. There was simply nothing out here; nothing except forests, midges, rain and an abundance of very ominous looking prisons.

The prisons were generally a mix of concrete and wooden buildings with machine gun posts periodically dotted along the rusting barbed wire perimeter fences. It was like something from World War II but still very much in use. Since my return to the UK I've heard several people speak of a wish to visit Siberia as if it's some mystical and exciting, even romantic, place. I think it's more to do with them wanting to sound as if they're being more ingenious with exciting sounding 'holiday' destinations in an effort to impress people who know nothing of the place, while evidently knowing nothing of it themselves. All I have to say on the matter is that there's a very good reason for Siberia's notoriety as being where some of the harshest, most inhospitable prisons in the world are to be found, and none of those reasons tend to give rise to anywhere worth visiting – Genghis Khan even gave prisoners the option of execution or exile to Siberia – you do the maths. Siberia's not even dramatically harsh; it's more a dull, depressing and monotonous harshness. We were simply passing through and the sooner we passed the better; I'll certainly never return.

Now we were really in trouble, with the M53 having completely let us down by lulling us into a false sense of security that it may have been tarmaced all the way to Mongolia. We had the same huge distance to cover and it was going to be in thick, dangerously slippery mud, rather than the rough tarmac we had just about got used to. We were often forced to use the whole width of the road just to recover the sliding buggy on the hilly and undulating road; miraculously there was never any traffic around us at the time. On the flatter sections we had to contend with huge potholes that could easily have rolled or irreparably damaged the buggy, and in other parts the mud was simply too deep to drive though.

The true quality of the M53, Siberia

There was little traffic on the M53 but what there was tended to consist of monstrous trucks designed for the job with numerous spare wheels and enormous ground clearance. And we were being held up by them. In our wholly unsuitable buggy we somehow focused our driving and while concentrating as much as possible, we managed to dart around the potholes and catch the slides before they became too severe. There were some serious heart-in-mouth moments. It was ok though; were determined to make it out of Russia on time and this was working. The problem our relative speed threw up was having to overtake. Given the condition of the road and stretches of deep mud, which could last for several miles, we had to chance our overtaking like we had back in the desert at night, although now in starkly different conditions. There was only one usable line on the road which tended to weave all over its full width such that should you meet anything coming the opposite way someone had to yield to allow the other to pass; it was so bad that two vehicles couldn't possibly drive in opposite directions at once. There were two main risks to overtaking. The first was coming off the usable line and into the potential minefield of potholes that were no doubt lurking on the part that was not being used. These were deep enough, with sharp enough edges to break a car or worse. The second was much more dangerous. Out of control articulated lorries. As the huge trucks struggled for grip, often at up to 40mph, they would slew right across the road as their wheels dipped into a rut or just caught the thick mud. The last thing the drivers would expect is to be overtaken out here and even if they did see us, there'd be nothing they could do to stop forty tonnes or more of truck from swiping us off the road. And if they weren't sliding they would still be weaving everywhere in an attempt to find the most passable part of road.

A drier section of the M53, Siberia

The best method we found for overtaking was to sit off the rear of the truck and weigh up the road ahead until it looked at its best, then go as fast as possible with the lights on and a few blasts on the horn. Incredibly, it worked most times and there were only a few occasions when we had to abort as it all looked a bit too hairy when the driver changed direction across our path. Then there were the times when we would get past, only to have too much speed to avoid the upcoming dangers on the road and almost shoot off into the trees as we hit potholes or engulfed the wheels in the thick, greasy mud. We were airborne far more times than we were happy with and, ignoring our own mortality, it wasn't good for the longevity of the buggy. The rear door was now truly hanging on by hardly anything more than the latch itself, cracks were appearing in most of the bodywork and the suspension had given up days ago.

A typical Siberian town

We continued on the road toward Irkutsk, passing ramshackle, timber villages consisting of huts-for-houses with little sign of life, shops or industry, all the while the mud on the road got more and more swamp-like and the forests thicker.

The familiar sight of another disused factory

The exhaust was still completely deafening us and to make matters worse had developed a backfire, like gunfire, every time we came off the accelerator. Stopping for fuel, we met a Serbian guy filling up his motorbike who chatted to us in English for a while. It turned out he was riding on his own from Belgrade to Vladivostok in eastern Russia on a 7,500 mile route. It seemed odd that he was going all that way on his own, but it emerged that his friend had been in an accident earlier in the journey, breaking his arm, and had had to abandon the trip, leaving this guy to carry on alone. It seemed unbelievably risky to be travelling on this remote and neglected road alone but oddly, he seemed more impressed by what we were doing than his own insane journey. We swapped details, wished each other luck and continued.

We drove on through much of the same; endless forest, merciless prisons and a railroad with occasional trains that stretched on further than the eye could see. There was nothing else to see, although it still had the edge in terms of interest than the plains of eastern Kazakhstan. We stopped again in the relentless, pouring rain for fuel and, now it was dark, to try and figure out why the headlights had become so dim and intermittent. Fortunately, we spotted the problem quite soon – the metal wire we had used to fix the air-box the day before had snagged the wiring to the headlights, worn it through and earthed it to the chassis. Another huge improvement to the lights was the use of a couple of baby wipes to clean the lenses from the days of caked-on mud and grime and in an instant we could see again. Back in the buggy we were cold and awfully wet. Hardly surprising given the average annual temperature here is just 0°C.

By 21:00 it was time for some food and a break. There wasn't much hope of anything too exciting, but we found what looked like a bar or café on the side of the road about half a mile out of a village, so pulled in. Our arrival had hardly been subtle with no exhaust and we certainly didn't look like the norm for this part of Siberia as we walked in the door. Like something from a gun-swinging Western movie, the whole room fell silent as everyone turned to look at what had just arrived. It really was a local bar for local people. There was a group of about ten student-aged people drinking in the far corner and a few older couples in small groups around the rest of the room. It was incredibly local and we were inconceivably foreign; dressed in our shorts, fleeces and flip-flops.

Disappointingly, there was no food on display for us to easily pick from, no indication as to what we might expect and no menu – not that

that would have been any help. This was going to be awkward. We took a seat and waited for the lady who appeared to be a waitress to come across. We had only waited a couple of minutes but in this time our novelty had certainly caught the interest of two thirty-something ladies sitting nearby who, from the empty bottles on their table, had been there for some time. They spoke to us and asked us several questions, clearly in good humour from their laughs and smiles, but we still spoke no Russian and they equally didn't understand our English. The banter had regained the attention of most in the bar and the students-types in the corner became involved, but all we could make out was 'American'. Realising their error, we corrected them with a shout of 'An-glee-skee' and this, and probably our accent, seemed to delight them. We knew that Americans weren't flavour of the month from some of the guards we had met in the previous week. This prompted even more intense questioning from the two women, interspersed with laughter around the bar when no doubt we should have been responding, instead just looking confused. Some of the younger people spoke bits of broken English and soon a three way conversation developed with the younger people acting as translators between us and the women. Everyone wanted to know what we were doing, where we were from, where we were going and the recurring and impossible question of why we were doing it. So far, in all the countries we had travelled no-one had grasped why we were making this journey.

Making it known we wanted some food the women asked the lady in the kitchen something which had her laughing too and soon she returned with examples of several dishes of food to show us. It all looked pretty non-descript and all looked like the same thing just in different hues. We ordered two soupy-stews which when they came looked slightly different to what we had been shown, but not knowing what either was, we didn't care much. It consisted of a watery soup with chunks of meat and vegetable in the bottom and almost a whole half-inch thick layer of oil floating on the top. I assume this was to help the locals through the bitter winters. It tasted remarkably good if, unsurprisingly, a little oily.

The conversation continued and to make things easier I went back to the buggy to fetch the maps to show around. There was a real sense of excitement in the bar and everyone seemed to be hanging on our every word. Asking if we spoke any Russian, we recited the few word we had picked up with 'spaa-see-ba' proving to be a favourite and generating so many laughs we had to wonder if our pronunciation actually meant something else. They loved the maps and were fascinated by the places we'd been and were almost flattered that we had come to their remote village on our travels. Apparently, they never had foreign visitors. By now they knew pretty much our entire life story, future plans, that we were only students, yet on this massive trip with a car of our own that we were going to give away (the thought of this implied that we were rich beyond belief!) - and our relationship status. With this the conversation turned to their future plans. Obviously having decided that we were pretty eligible, they started trying to match-make in an attempt to make us stay in the village or whisk two of the local girls back to the UK to live with the two 'millionaire' Englishmen.

We had an amazing time but eventually had to leave. Pretty much the whole bar followed us out into the cold and rain to pose for photos and look at the buggy. They loved the noise of the 'race car' and all clapped and waved as we drove off, thankfully without having become married to any of them.

Not a great deal more happened that night and the going was slow in the dark, the poor visibility making it almost impossible to see the deeper mud and potholes, many of which were filled with water so couldn't been seen anyway. I wished we had fitted more than the two extra spotlights we had.

At 01:00 we physically couldn't go any further and had to stop for a power-nap.

13th August – Arshan, RU to Kyakhta, RU

01:45 and we were off again. The road was a nightmare and deeply flooded in many places, making for hellish driving conditions. The darkness and our tiredness severely hampered our progress and on several occasions we hit water so deep that it came right over the bonnet engulfing the windscreen, leaving us blinded for several seconds until the feeble wipers could clear the sticky, muddy water. At these times the only choice was to feel where the buggy was being pulled by the ruts and mud and allow it to slide until we could see the road again. It was an uncomfortable situation, as the sections of deep water coincided with the sections of road that needed the most concentration and skill to avoid hitting things – yet we were always blinded for the first few seconds, hoping not to hit anything. An added inconvenience to all of this was that the footwells were now also full of water so we had constantly wet feet.

By 03:00 we couldn't stay awake any longer and had to stop for another forty-five minute power nap. If we carried on like this we would have serious problems staying awake through the day ahead, but neither of us was that concerned that we actually stopped for any longer, and at least for the moment we continued to make progress. After all, we only had to sustain this for the rest of the day and by then we would have done all we could to exit Russia on time. We hoped the daylight would help us both with the driving and staying alert.

An hour later, at what we thought was 04:45, we arrived on the outskirts of Irkutsk, some 30 miles to the north of Lake Baikal. Oddly enough, we spotted a clock on a building that read 06:45. Soon enough the police had us at a roadblock and having checked our papers and looked very disapprovingly at the (lack of) exhaust, confirmed it was in fact two hours ahead of what we thought. Checking the Lonely Planet we realised that while in Russia we had in fact crossed two time zones. That put us another two hours behind and we were already desperately short of time. We chose not to stop in Irkutsk and thankfully found our way in and out without getting too lost. We had just got back on the open road when we hit another flooded section, this time the water coming right over the roof as we went in, leaving the engine spluttering and barely running for the next few miles. There was just no way to know if it was a puddle or a deep pool and given how much flooding there was we simply couldn't slow down to check the depth of all of them. It was several more miles before the engine fully cleared up and got back to its normal, somewhat less than healthy, sound. The footwells of the buggy had been wet for a couple of days now, but with this most recent flooding they were a full couple of inches deep with standing water, and with us both wearing flip-flops, the driver would end up with cold and wrinkled feet from using the pedals. I wanted to be back in the sun.

We were now, a very roughly estimated, 370 miles from the border and amazingly it looked like there was an outside chance that we could make the crossing on time – and it was probably that outside chance that kept us going. We had seventeen hours to work with. Although this assumed that the border was open until late and there was a fair chance that considering how remote the crossing was, it wouldn't be a twenty-four hour crossing. It was going to be one last big push and there wouldn't be any sleep involved, which we hoped we could sustain for this last leg of the journey. We were convinced now that the repercussions of being caught without insurance weren't worth the risk and that there would be a reasonable chance of being arrested for it, or at the very least being landed with a huge fine which, with our money issues, we undoubtedly wouldn't be able to pay. We were no more than 100 miles due north of the Mongol border, but were having to track alongside it before turning away to the northeast, to Ulaan-Ude, where we could then eventually head south to the border crossing at Kyakhta. There were simply no other points where the border was open to traffic; the only other vehicular entry point to Mongolia being the one we had passed days before on the western tip of Mongolia bordering with Russia near Kazakhstan. This was more than 800 miles away as the crow files and we had been disallowed from using that one. Mongolia is certainly not an easy country to drive into.

For a short while the road seemed to improve, before rising and snaking into the mountains on the southern edge of Lake Baikal. This was another hugely impressive feature on our travels and at 1,637m (5,370ft) deep, the deepest lake in the world, 395 miles long and 50 miles wide giving it the largest volume in the world. It also holds one fifth of the total fresh water on the Earth. The surface is also some 5.5 miles directly above the continental rift which has formed the region, making it the deepest rift on Earth, and it's still very young and seismically active. Oh, and it was yet another World Heritage site on our travels – we passed so many they became a common occurrence!

Driving along the road in Ulaan-Ude we came across a pair of Scots in a Volkswagen Polo, also on the Mongol Rally. The first ralliers we had seen in days. They had taken a more direct route than us, sticking to the better roads through Kazakhstan, rather than dropping into the central Asian countries of Uzbekistan and Kyrgyzstan, but their car had suffered and they had lost time on repairs. We stopped for a chat but the weather was hardly conducive for chilling out at the roadside, so we soon moved on agreeing to meet for a beer in Ulaan Baatar where we were hopeful it wouldn't be raining; the Scots, having no time pressure, headed into town for lunch while we raced for the border.

Our engine was playing up with the ingress of water and everything mechanical was making tortured and pitiful noises. Knowing we needed cash we opted to head for the airport. It was roughly on the road to Mongolia and would avoid the risk of getting lost in the centre of Ulaan-Ude, which was quite likely, and would waste precious hours. The airport was reasonably easy to find, especially after the police stopped us, again, and helpfully pointed us in the right direction. We then just followed the biggest, widest, most impressive, tree-lined road we could find. It was deserted, but certain to lead to the airport as in all the ex-Soviet states we had seen. We were right and fortunately, although with some difficulty, we found the ATM in the airport foyer (singular, as even at the airport there was only one) and got some cash for our last fuel and food of the entire adventure. It was almost an emotional moment. Shocked that it had been so easy, we took a few moments to give the buggy the once over in the vast expanse of the empty car park to the front of the airport building, with its ever-present and hugely imposing, communist signage on top of the building. It was almost like they had built this massive airport but forgotten to tell anyone it was there, so it remained virtually unused. It is said to have the capacity to serve four hundred passengers an hour, though generally it only sees only half of that across an entire day.

Thankfully it wasn't raining here, and the only new issue with the buggy was the final eighteen inch long section of exhaust had sheared. We had to undo the one bolt that was loosely holding it on to remove it. Not an easy task given its location and extreme heat, nestled deep under the engine and gearbox. Severely scraped and burnt knuckles later, we popped it in the back of the buggy to join the rest of the exhaust.

We set off again and headed south to the border. The buggy sounding sicker than ever, and backfiring with ear-splitting volume any time we eased off the power. The rest of the time it was just unbearably and painfully loud. A further problem was that we now had an engine venting its exhaust directly into the engine bay, which gave us significant issues with heat on the electrics under the bonnet. We stopped at the roadside to check things out and grabbed some chicken in a café. We were the only people in the café so decided for once to resort to the Russian phrase book. We spotted chicken on the menu and by judging the prices assumed it to be a main course. Well, it cost more than the items at the front and less than those at the back, which we assumed to be the starters and desserts respectively. We'd proven it to work before; genius. What we actually got were a couple of legs of chicken, some bread and Coke. Not the best lunch but good enough to keep us going and we once it arrived we didn't really have time to order anything extra.

With the buggy now cooled off, we noticed that all the secondary electrics we'd fitted had stopped working and the additional battery had flattened itself and couldn't be recharged. The combination of being repeatedly flooded then subjected to extreme heat wasn't good for electronics – obviously! Driving on through the lashing rain, the flooding continued to periodically come up over the windscreen and roof, leaving the buggy coughing until the water had passed though the system and we could get going again. You just never could tell if the water was an inch deep, two feet deep or if there was a wheel-sized pothole in the flood, and we experienced them all.

As time went by the road improved slightly, a sure sign that we had to be nearing the border, and the rained eased off allowing the brief moments of sunshine to break through. Coming down out of the mountains we crossed a very dilapidated bridge with a seemingly solid iron frame but a rotten and rickety wooden floor, with significant chunks missing. Further on we passed numerous military installations and more military hardware than I have ever seen. There had to be hundreds, probably thousands, of Russian tanks and artillery guns lined up with troops bustling around on exercises. It seemed extraordinary given that the Mongols have no significant army, no defences and, to my knowledge, little interest in invading Russia. The only explanation could be that it's seen as an easy and unexpected route for the Chinese to take to get to Russia, should the mood take them. Who knows?! I'd have loved to take some photos but given how sensitive they are out here I thought better of it.

A bridge near the Russia-Mongolia border

We arrived at Kyakhta, which was a typical, rundown, end-of-the-road border town and home to fewer than eighteen thousand people, and to us a welcome sight. Assuming, rightly, that there would be nowhere to buy fuel between here and the capital of Mongolia, Ulaan Baatar, we spent every Rouble we had on fuel and went in search of the border. Oddly, though not really a surprise anymore, there was no sign indicating the way to Mongolia but, reliable as always, the police stopped us. Obviously realising that we would soon be out of their country they didn't seem too bothered with the deteriorating condition of our now considerable un-roadworthy buggy. With a quick scan of our papers they pointed us down the road and, finally, out of Russia.

This was it. After twenty-three days on the road (well, technically twenty-two as one was spent stuck in the Ukrainian garage) and against all the odds, we, and our £500 buggy had made Mongolia. I really can't describe how much of an achievement this was to me and we started to talk about what we had actually accomplished with so little prior knowledge and planning. Looking back, we really had had no idea what we were going to come across, and I expect most of it hasn't translated with anything like the true reality and gravity with my descriptions in this text. We agreed there must have been a huge amount of luck (which was confirmed in the next few days) but the majority of it we put down to general common sense, being completely calm in some pretty hairy situations and most importantly, never arguing or doubting each others ability. I can't think of anyone else I could say that about.

Almost on cue, the rain stopped and the evening sun started to shine though. Everything was looking perfect. We had made the border in time and had just less than 200 miles to the finish in Ulaan Baatar; we even joked that for that distance, if the buggy did break, we would dump the thing, buy a horse and ride to the finish. I really was feeling quite elated, excited, relieved and to an extent, amazed and proud. The anticipation of being so close to the goal that we had been chasing and building up to for over nine months was like the feeling of being six again on Christmas Eve.

We joined the queue at the border at 18:00 – and even this was quite short with only a couple of trucks waiting to the side, a couple of cars and a few minibuses. It was all quite low-key with a single barbed wire fence, a guard post and, set back in the compound, a disproportionately large and fairly modern looking four storey customs house; as if they were expecting more traffic than they were ever likely to receive.

Nothing was moving. We must have only been three or four cars back from the gates but nothing left, nothing entered and there were no signs of life. Walking around the cars we established from a Mongolian that the border had actually shut at 18:00, just as we'd arrived. Asking when it reopened, by pointing to the gates and our watches, he shrugged as if to say 'whenever they feel like it'. Asking other people, the consensus seemed to be that they were only shut for dinner and would reopen at 19:30. We hoped they were right. There appeared to be no order to the queue with the cars jostling for position by the gates as the odd person gave up and headed back to town. With nothing to occupy us, we decided to play them at their own game and somehow ended up with our buggy right at the front, almost against the locked gates. At least now when they did open we'd be the first through. We undertook some repairs to the buggy, hardwiring the inverter to the remaining working battery so we could charge the iPod and camera batteries and looked at the seats. They had been loose for a while and the cause looked quite serious. The box-section of the chassis that we had mounted them to had begun to collapse and the holes for the now-loose-bolts had ovalised and would no longer tighten. We'd just have to make do with rocking seats for the rest of the journey.

While doing this, with the buggy immobile, we had somehow lost our spot at the front and amazingly two Russian minibuses had taken advantage of our predicament and had us in a pincer movement, forcing us into a disappointing third at the gates; although it was still up on where we had started, which I suppose was the important thing.

It was now after 19:30 and there was no sign of any military or customs officials beyond the gates. With dusk approaching, the midges had returned in force so we were pretty much trapped in the buggy and it was staring to get cold. I expect we must have severely irritated and deafened everyone around us when we started the buggy to get the heater going, and probably also the residents of Kyakhta. Just after 20:00 there were signs of life from the customs house and a group of uniformed soldiers came toward our gate. At last we would be beginning the agonizingly tedious customs process for the final time. Except the soldiers diverted slightly, collected several sturdy wooden crosses joined by coils of razor wire and positioned them across the road inside the compound, before locking them to two concrete pillars. The soldiers walked though the gate, past the queuing cars and off in the direction of Kyakhta. It began to dawn on us why the queue was so short. The border was shut for the night, it was Sunday after all. Popular opinion, as we understood it, suggested that it would reopen at, give or take a couple of hours, 09:30. We could practically see Mongolia (ok, technically we couldn't due to a small hill in no-man's land) and were unable to reach it for at least the next thirteen and a half hours. That's an awfully long time to sit in a non-moving traffic jam with nowhere to go and nothing to do.

With the border now well and truly shut for the night a semi – very semi – official man started walking around the queuing cars with a clipboard. He was writing down names and taking bank notes. We had no idea how much but it was obvious that the more notes given the higher on his list you went. It was the most blatant and unashamed bribery we'd seen anywhere. And we had no money to join in; just a few spare coins worth a couple of pence. Our spot at the front was in serious jeopardy.

We had spotted a couple of Westerners in a minibus earlier and they had now returned with some food and beers, having found a small shop over some rough land towards a small collection of houses. They were using the minibus simply as a shuttle to get them to the other side of the border where it would drop them off before returning to Russia with a different set of people. Apparently this was common place at many borders and is a much speedier way get through the customs process than on foot; especially here as only vehicular access is currently allowed. I expect that the passengers pay an amount to the driver who then pays a proportion of this to the customs officials such that fewer questions are asked, everything takes less time and everyone profits.

The remains of a once beautiful church

With nothing else to do, I set off on my own to see just what I could afford with 92 roubles (£1.84). Foxy stayed behind to keep an eye on the buggy and make sure we didn't get pushed back any further in the queue. Some twenty minutes later I'd passed numerous deserted blocks of flats, a huge dilapidated church that would once have been stunning but now lay crumbling and a vast, ornately decorated hall in a similar state. It was quite sad, but by now no surprise. It was like being in a ghost town or some war torn town and with darkness setting in, quite eerie. A couple of stray dogs ran past and barely noticed me. I felt quite vulnerable in such a place, alone, with no money or phone and my passport and ID back at the buggy. I was less than comfortable walking the rubble strewn streets between the towering concrete apartments, which had the unmistakable signs of being inhabited, yet somehow still appeared deserted. Many parts of the concrete structure were turning to dust and simply powdering away. I could hear my every step in my flip-flops, and was sure everyone else could too, so tried to walk more quietly – it seems ridiculous now, but it's strange how the mind plays tricks. Spotting a light and some people in an unmarked building, I wandered over to find a small convenience store with a few locals inside. I got the impression not many people from the border ventured here and I felt very out of place, unshaven and in my shorts and flip-flops; not looking in the least bit Siberian or local. Fortunately, all the items on the shelves behind the counter had prices written on them so I would be able to make the most of our money without having to hold the queue up too long while I tried to spend the remaining 92 roubles. First up were two bottles of beer, I thought these to be critical to getting through the night, two packets of crisps and a loaf of bread. Anything more exciting would have blown the budget. This still left me with some money so I showed her how much I had and opted for a mix of biscuits from the assortment the lady had in large open boxes on the front of the counter. Biscuits seemed popular through all the regions we had crossed and were always on display in large, square cardboard boxes. Having got them on the scales she proceeded to swap larger biscuits for smaller, lighter ones to get the price just right even going as far as breaking one in half to get the exact weight. This seemed very weird, but I'd seen her do the same with others ahead of me; actually, no, having said that it was still weird, to spend all this time for the sake of fractions of a Rouble either way with the queue building behind me, but that's how they did things here. I left, having spent the whole 92 roubles, with the last items we would be able to buy in Russia now in my possession. I just hoped we wouldn't need any to get through customs; blatantly, 92 roubles wouldn't have helped, but we hadn't even considered that we may need money at customs when it finally did open.

Foxy dining in style at the Russia-Mongolia border

Having traced my route back through the buildings, negotiated several metres of broken glass and clambered over some old, rusting barbed wire, I got back to the buggy to find nothing had changed. With it now almost dark it had become quite cold and hot food would have been good, but with the stoves playing up we had to settle for some cold, tinned pasta in sauce, baked beans and the nibbles and beer from the shop. The other drivers still seemed pretty irate by our prime position in the queue and the fact that we hadn't paid to be there. Several times we were told to move but chose to stand our ground and wait for the morning and see what happened. The problem was we didn't want to leave the buggy in case someone towed it out of the way while we were gone. So again, we'd be sleeping in the buggy.

We were ill prepared for a Siberian border crossing, even if it was the middle of the summer. It was freezing. We woke several times due to the cold and the sound of people starting their engines to get their heaters going and it wasn't even late yet. This was going to prove to be one of our longest nights and there was nothing we could do; given our lack of exhaust this we could hardly run the engine to keep warm. It was going to be a very long and uncomfortable night. We wrapped up in as much dry clothing as we could find – which wasn't much as we hadn't really brought anything with us. There was no chance of using the sleeping bags as the interior of the buggy was sodden from the rain in the previous days and nowhere to pitch the tents. We did however discover two fleece blankets in the back which we could wrap around our legs in an effort to stave off the cold; although we did now look like a pair of OAP's. We chatted and listened to music, hoping not to flatten the buggy's battery, until we dozed off. Having woken up and fallen back into a doze countless more times, it was starting to get ridiculously cold but there wasn't anything we could do about it.

14th August – Kyakhta, RU to Ulaan Baatar, MN

It was still dark at 07:15 when I woke to the sound of a couple of car engines being gently revved, having decided there was no point trying to doze anymore. Agreeing that everyone in the vicinity had slept for plenty long enough, and no doubt in more comfort that us, we decided it was fair game to start our engine and get the heater going. To the unimaginable annoyance of those around us, our engine fired into life and stayed there cackling and exploding for several minutes. There were now people milling about all along the queue and we were getting some very cutting stares from virtually everyone. We did our best to ignore them and persisted until the buggy was warm again. Everyone in the queue, and all of Kyakhta, was now certain to be awake but we felt much more positive about the day ahead with the sun nudging its way over the horizon and providing some warmth around us. We'd thought we had had no friends in the queue last night and this was now a certainty.

We categorically weren't the flavour of the month, and with less than two hours to the expected opening time, the dirty tricks started. All the minibuses and cars behind us were edging forward towards the gate and, in some cases, working together to block others while their friends gained some critical inches nearer to the gate; even the two ahead of us were trying to slide nearer to the gate to get more vehicles in behind them and ahead of us. Being right at the front, we were the focus of this whole affair. People were coming up to us and, in Mongolian or Russian, telling us and pointing and shouting at us to move back out of the queue. Right, good one. As if we were going to give up our prime location now. I think their reasoning was that we were in the minibus queue. Odd, given that there was only room for one queue, so I have no idea how they thought we'd fall for this one.

Deciding to go on the offensive rather than the defensive, Foxy got out and stood directly in front of the most aggressive minibus, which appeared to have the best chance of nudging us out, while I started the buggy. The driver was shouting a whole load of abuse at Foxy but he wasn't listening to her and neither had it seemed were the passengers, who found the whole situation pretty entertaining. I slipped the buggy into reverse which fooled everyone into thinking we were actually submitting and leaving the queue. Naïvely, a couple of minibuses edged back to give me room, which I gladly took, then moved forward again at such an angle to block the whole gate, sealing our spot in third place with no chance of being edged out.

Securing our position at the Russia-Mongolia border

Everyone had been watching, partly due to the noise but mainly to see if the inexperienced Englishmen would actually give up their space, and were now laughing at the move we'd just pulled and seemed quite impressed. Foxy came back to get in the warmth while the driver behind used some universal hand gestures to express herself. With that episode over we'd passed some time, entertained the crowds and could all get on with queuing again.

At 08:30 the gates opened. It could be that our watches were wrong but it didn't matter. The first minibus was waved in, then the second, and about half an hour later we were the third vehicle in. We were directed past the first barricade into the compound while the driver of the minibus jokingly waved her fists at us and laughed; Foxy blew her a kiss and all was forgiven. We'd be in Ulaan Baatar for lunch if all went well.

Keeping the revs low, in a futile effort to make as little noise as possible and make the buggy appear slightly legal, we edged towards the customs officials who looked far from pleased to see us. Having drawn the short straw, I was driving and so had the majority of the paperwork to deal with. I visited several offices, some repeatedly, but it all seemed above board and was progressing well. I was even surprised by how civilised everyone was being and how smart the place was. There were proper concrete offices for the processing of paperwork and a five storey building where the passengers from the minibuses went for processing; quite a change to the ramshackle wooden huts that had been the norm at the past few crossings. Further down the hill, but still in the compound, was a military base with various tanks and guns and troops marching about. It all appeared quite efficient; this of course all being in the context of the borders of the previous days.

With everything finalised, I was directed to an office for what had to be the final time and our passports were laid out on the desk next to the rubber stamp, ready for the all important final check. It never came. Instead he asked for the buggy's insurance. This had been checked already but immediately I knew this was going to be a major headache.

Technically, it had expired at midnight while we had been at the gate and experience told me that a technicality was enough of a reason for, at the very least, a bribe to be demanded. Experience also told me that the Russians tended to be less bribe-happy than I had expected and this could turn into an official matter very quickly.

The official was being extremely unhelpful and wouldn't accept that we'd been at his border before it shut and before our insurance expired; all that mattered was that he was checking it now and it was invalid. Had we known this would happen there would have been no reason to put in so much effort to rush through Siberia to get to the border. It was clear there was a fine to pay, this had been made quite explicit, but there was no mention of how much. It was looking more and more like a bribe, which could be a good thing as far as speed was concerned, but we were determined not to have to pay one, having made it through so many countries without. Our reluctance was evident and we were returned to the buggy to think about what we had done and directed to park at the far side of the compound. We were left alone and given no further information.

With nothing happening, we returned to the office on foot only to be sharply told to come back at 12:00 because the chief customs official had been called and that's when he'd be arriving. Well, this was translated to us from the head guy by his younger junior, who spoke some broken English. We were stuck and it all sounded pretty serious. We couldn't go back to Russia as we had no insurance and couldn't buy any. We couldn't go forward to Mongolia as the Russians wouldn't allow us to leave because we didn't have insurance. Not having insurance meant we were stuck in no-man's land with the Russians neither wanting to keep us nor let us go. It was ridiculous. Furthermore, even if we did agree on a fine or bribe we had no roubles with which to pay it, and being in no-man's land there was nowhere to get any.

Out of the office we tried to establish what was going on by speaking to the more junior guards. It seemed the problem was two-fold. Firstly, the guards who had allowed us to enter Russia three days earlier should not have allowed us in on such a short period of insurance; the only reason they had was that we had bent the truth, saying we were exiting Russia at Tassaannur, hundreds of miles sooner than we actually had. This wasn't a major issue to us and something they could slog out themselves to determine if it was our fault or that of the guards. The second issue, however, was more concerning. No-one could fathom how we had come so far, from the border crossing near Semey, in such a short amount of time. To do so we must have altered our paperwork or been speeding, which seemed unlikely in the buggy. I didn't want to tell them that we hadn't stopped once to sleep as I'm sure that wouldn't have gone down too well. To be honest, I was quite pleased that they were so bewildered, and hoped we might be remembered for years to come in some kind of border-patrol-folklaw as the Englishmen who travelled the forsaken M53 in record time.

Anyway, this wasn't helping us get to Mongolia and it was unclear what was happening, other than that we had to wait for the arrival of the chief customs official. It was always about waiting at borders but this was in the extreme. We went back to the buggy and did some more checks on the mechanics to try and pass some time. The buggy didn't look healthy and the more we looked, the worse it looked, so we sunbathed and dozed in the sun instead. It didn't have far to go now anyway.

We returned again to the office just after 12:00 to see it the chief had arrived but there was no progress. It was baking hot now and we had no food and little water. Boredom was killing us. We'd been here all the evening and night before and were now stuck in this concrete compound with nowhere to go, nothing to do and nothing to see. We'd done all the time wasting jobs and games already. I sunbathed on the concrete ground, on the ThermaRest and on the roof of the buggy. I took to throwing stones at other stones. They got bigger and harder the more bored I got. They got quite big.

Foxy decided to go and explore the main building in search of water and a toilet, as there were no bushes to hide behind in this barren, concrete compound. A while later he returned looking far from happy having found the toilet. It was the first sit-down toilet we'd come across for days which should have been a good thing, yet this one had clearly never been cleaned since its installation. The entire toilet, and most of the room it was in, was covered in excrement.

A helicopter came and went and again, we went back to the office to see if we could get any further. Something must have happened as I was marched to the main building while Foxy was kept behind to fill in some more forms. I met someone in quite an important looking uniform and hat who took my passport and filled some forms, asked a few questions and dictated to a typist. I moved to another floor with him and did the same again, then to another room to sign some more forms. I have no idea what they were and he didn't seem too interested in telling me. I should have cared, but it seemed to be helping and the abject tiredness I was suffering from meant I really *didn't* care. Looking back, I'm not too sure I fully realised what I was doing. I could have been agreeing to anything, which is something I'd never do in any normal situation. I could have been signing away all my rights way and incarcerating myself. We returned to each of the rooms again and collected the finished paperwork then, after what seemed like an age, went back outside to the office where Foxy was.

Foxy had been signing various forms, all different to the ones I had, and had had to write a letter to the head of immigration and customs expressing his apologies for our misdemeanour. Outside there were now two other rally cars queuing up who seemed to be having less issues – they had insurance – and it was good to see some of the attention being turned to them. We had a quick chat but they seemed keen to distance themselves from us which was understandable given our seeming criminality. Foxy finished signing his forms, of which we had each signed about twenty, and we were now apparently good to go. With all the paperwork together they now had a ring-bound paper file of probably over sixty pages. Except there was a new issue.

The officer now realised that Foxy had written the apology yet I was the lead name on the insurance. I was instructed to copy out the whole letter verbatim. I loved the touch at the end where Foxy had signed-off; expressing his most sincere apologies and that he was really, really sorry however, in all actuality it hadn't been our fault and we weren't that sorry after all, especially given all the hassle and grief, but we'd say sorry just to make them happy and get out of Russia! I copied this too and handed it over. It's a good job they couldn't read English, although the letter probably remains in a Russian archive to this day, should they ever desire to check it.

We jumped in the buggy, drove back to the checking bay over a deep pit and purposefully kept the engine running with the choke partially out to maintain a high tick-over, to make as much noise as possible, in an effort to make the guards keener to move us on. Soon they waved us off and to the military check. They didn't appear very interested and with that, at 17:45, we moved across to the Mongolian border. This was it. Russia wouldn't have us back as I'm sure we must have signed away our future entry rights on one of those forms, so we would have to make it to

Mongolia. Or live in no-man's land for the rest of our lives. This may sound like a ridiculous notion but I would later hear a story of one rallier who, for various reasons, got to this part of no-man's land only for there to then be an irregularity with his passport, leaving him stuck. The Mongolians wouldn't admit him and the Russians had become aware of the problem after he had cleared their section so wouldn't take him back. He managed to get word to the British embassy in Mongolia, get a new passport issued and have an embassy worker come to no-man's land with the passport and new visas to collect him!

Immediately, a lady tried to stop us to pay for a 'disinfectant tax' on the buggy. We were expected to pay for the privilege of driving through an almost dried-up sheep dip. We opted not to do so, given there was no disinfectant and no receipts being issued. We could tell that the lady knew that we knew we were right, but it didn't stop her feigning anger as we drove on to the customs building.

Inside, the whole process was very quick and painless. We even managed to get some dollars exchanged for Mongolian Tugriks at an official office and buy a couple of days worth of car insurance. It was here that we also got a dispensation form for the buggy to allow us to donate it to the children's hospital in Ulaan Baatar, without having to pay the exorbitant importation taxes which would have cost many times more than the intrinsic value of the buggy. We also bumped into the guys from the cars we'd just seen and had a chat about the journey they'd had. They'd taken a much more direct route, missing most of central Asia in an effort to get to Mongolia as quickly as possible. They had also paid numerous fines and taxes en-route; they even asked us how much we'd just paid for the 'disinfectant tax'. They'd apparently bartered this down from the twenty dollars they'd initially been asked for. We tried not to laugh too much but never did find out just how much they'd been ripped-off in the preceding three weeks and left them to sort out their customs papers.

Back outside we met some very chilled-out guards who didn't seem to have a care in the world, choosing to read porn and smoke cheap cigarettes rather than harass us. With everything in order we went back to the buggy only to be pounced on by the lady with her sheep dip. She virtually dragged Foxy back to her office demanding money, our cause clearly not being helped by the other cars, which had paid. Oddly, the other Mongolians at the office were all laughing at this and it was clear that it was more of a game to see who could get the most money out of the people crossing the border; this lady was obviously not prepared to let us pass free of charge and be seen to lose. She hadn't however banked on meeting Foxy. After a few minutes of good humoured banter Foxy came running back to the buggy with the lady comically chasing him and the others laughing as she did. With both of us now in the buggy, still with all our money, it was acknowledged that we had clearly won and there were smiles all round as we drove off to the customs check hoping our documents were in order.

There were no issues and all the Mongolian officials seemed much more relaxed than the Russians and soon we had passed the customs and military checks. At 19:17, after over twenty-five hours at the border, we entered Mongolia, the last frontier of overlanding.

The village of Altanbulag at the border was full of children playing on the street and every one of them covered their ears and watched as we drove past. I'm sure they'd have waved had the noise not been so bad and in such a remote area, it was probably the loudest thing they'd ever heard. We stopped off at a store and bought some much needed food. Leaving the village, an expanse of nothing was laid out ahead of us; Mongolia. We could see for miles in every direction but, with the exception of the tiny village at the border, there was nothing. No roads, no buildings, no fences, no boundaries, no trees, no power cables, absolutely nothing. All there was to see was the single road we were on, heading south to the capital through the crystal clear air.

The road to Ulaan Baatar – which was surprisingly good

While parked at the Russian border, the buggy had picked up a new sound, and this one truly sounded terminal. It was a loud clanging sound, even audible over the non-existent exhaust, and was connected to whatever was generating vibrations through the whole buggy. It sounded like a length of wire cable was caught around the axle. We took it in turns to lean out of the windows to listen but couldn't pin-point it. Foxy jumped out and ran alongside so he could look and listen, while I drove slowly along the road. Then it became obvious. It was either the transfer box or possibly the main gearbox. The two notoriously weak points on Suzuki SJ's and one or both of ours were about to give up after all this time. And if they did we'd be walking. In hindsight we probably shouldn't have been driving for prolonged periods at speed in four-wheel drive but we had had to for stability on the roads. I suppose we could have driven more slowly. Whatever. We had 200 miles to go and if it was going to break it would have done so by now. As a compromise, we promised to be gentler while accelerating and changing gear but decided there was no real point in travelling any slower. There was a bar in Ulaan Baatar, not far away, which was awaiting our arrival.

The final push through northern Mongolia

The road was pretty good and one of the only tarmaced roads outside of Ulaan Baatar, but we continued to get thrown about with the buggy doing its usual trick of launching across the road or towards a ditch without warning, landing with a squeal of the tyres then darting off in another direction until we regained control. The noises coming from all parts of the buggy were awful and I fully expected something to terminally break at any moment. The most significant noises (well, those audible over the exhaust) were coming specifically from the gearbox, transfer box, suspension (lack off), rear door, cracked bodywork, engine (very rough again), and wheel bearings. Ignoring all that, and the layers of dirt, the buggy was as good as new.

The landscape was stunning, just mile after mile of unspoilt hills with nothing man-made to be seen. The Mongols have little infrastructure and the concept of a fence or boundary appears foreign in this stunning part of the world, where the majority of the population is still nomadic.

Even so, I just wanted to get to the finish. There'd be a bed, a beer, a whole load of relief and an immense sense of achievement.

We talked a lot on this road and whichever way we looked at it and whatever happened next we'd actually made it to Mongolia. Mongolia, via a load of countries I never knew existed until I picked up a map to find out where Mongolia itself was. We hadn't been prepared for what we had seen and come across, not by a long shot, and that was what was so great about it. We never knew what was coming next, so never had unfulfilled expectations or fear – something I think we may have had more of had we known more about the adventure beforehand. Our naïveté had helped us out so many times it was amazing, so had our general common sense, carefree attitude and implicit trust in one another. I don't think we argued once; though Foxy may disagree. And all this stemmed from some idle chat in a bar in Covent Garden, London and a few emails between me in Bristol and Foxy skiing in the French Alps.

If, somehow, you've got a copy of this, have read this far and are considering doing the rally; don't. You know too much. Go somewhere else. You won't have the experiences as you know what's out there. You'll have expectations that will be, or will not be met. And also, it's probably far too commercial now – I know the 2007 rally was on TV. You'll over prepare. And the guards will be expecting you…much more than they were expecting us.

We were stopped again at the entrance to a National Park and had to pay just over two dollars for entry which, judging by the large tariff list on a wooden board and pre-printed receipt, appeared pretty legitimate. We carried on until I drove us though a police checkpoint that I simply didn't see – I really did need a sleep by now – but the policeman didn't seem too bothered, took a look at the buggy, seemed quite impressed and appeared not to want to hold us up and happily waved us on.

I would later learn that a day or so previously, the rally had been front page news on all the national newspapers informing the country of the imminent arrival of the first drivers in this epic, international rally. It was a major event, and we were being touted as being much more important and professional than I was ever aware we actually were. It had never specifically been a race but we were sure that we were somewhere near the front of the field, and to me the end had very much become a finishing line to cross. It was going to be like Uzbekistan all over again where we were treated like full-on racing drivers, only with the added effect of the exhaust noise we'd surely do better at pulling it off here.

Our welcome was short lived and totally wiped out when we came across the next policeman. It was dusk now but we had seen him in good time and slowed to a more reasonable speed as we approached, stopping in good time, but this hadn't helped. Foxy was driving so it was his turn to take the brunt. The passports were checked and then Foxy was beckoned out of the buggy to be shown some defects. The exhaust was the prime concern but Foxy pointed to this in the back of the buggy to clear up that point; though not excusing the violation. Then there was the broken headlight bulb, the apparent (but unproven) speeding and numerous other lesser issues. It was quite a list and bound to be costly given they were all genuine offences as far as I could see. It was a fair cop. Foxy leaned in to grab his licence to show to the policeman; fortunately it didn't really matter if we lost this now and it was duly inspected. What happened next was pretty remarkable. The policeman pulled his notebook out of his pocket and a laminated card as he read the charges to us. The card had each offence in a number of languages so he could say it in Mongolian while pointing to it so we could see the offence and the fine next to each one in English. There were several and it was all adding up. By the end the buggy sounded like a write-off and we had a fine of over 5,000 Mongolian Tugrik which, not being too hot on the exchange rate sounded like a small fortune (actually, it's just less than £2.50). As we momentarily wondered how much this was and if we could reduce it, he pointed to another part of his card,

"Sorry to have troubled you."

We couldn't believe it. We'd been caught fair and square, were completely in the wrong with an official charge sheet laid out in front of us yet he was completely letting us off. And with that he looked up with a smile, gleefully shook our hands and waved us on our way! Perhaps the rally, and charity work associated with it, was much more prestigious out here than we had imagined.

After that nothing more happened and we could soon make out Ulaan Baatar on the horizon, officially the coldest capital city in the world. It was huge. A massive industrial sprawl. I don't know what I had expected, I knew it was the capital, but for some reason had assumed it would be somewhere between a village and a small town and all pretty and countrified. In reality it's home to more than a third of the Mongol population. As per everywhere else, we had no map but knew we had to meet at 'Dave's Place', a bar in the main square, Sukhbaatar Square, somewhere in the centre. Not an easy task given the now apparent size of Ulaan Baatar.

For simplicity, we stuck to the road we were on and drove along until we felt to be about halfway through the capital and looked for the largest buildings. The hope was that we would recognise one of the buildings on the Lonely Planet's guidebook map of the very centre of town – made for walkers. Just before we did, a car pulled alongside us at some traffic lights and started chatting to us through the open windows. They knew of the rally, spoke a tiny amount of English and were desperate to be able to help and get involved by bringing one of the cars to the finish. They also seemed to know where we were meant to be heading. We followed them through the manic traffic, cutting lanes and pulling all kinds of moves that I'm sure we shouldn't have been. All the while Foxy was checking the map and spotted one of the buildings, yet the car ahead didn't seem to be going the right way. I think they genuinely wanted to help but didn't actually know where we were supposed to be going and didn't want to admit that now. We pulled alongside and got them to follow us.

The buggy sounded to be in a desperate state as we pulled into the car park in front the palatial buildings that form part of Dave's Place, in one of the most enormous and impressive squares I've ever seen.

It was 00:35. We had covered 9,592 miles (15,437kms), been on the road for 23.5 days and had made it. And the bar was shut.

We looked in the guide book, found a couple of hotels nearby and set off in search of a proper bed for the night. Irritatingly, the car which had tried to show us the way was still loitering about and insisted on trying to show us the way to a hotel and soon we were lost again. Deciding that they had no more idea where they were going than we did, we took a sneaky turn at a junction and managed to lose them and find the hotel we had been aiming for only minutes later. The hotel was ok, had secure parking and seemed a bit pricey at $55 (£30) for the night, but all we wanted was a bed and this was the easiest option.

As the sign says, 'The end of the road', Ulaan Baatar, Mongolia

15th August – Ulaan Baatar, MN

We were woken just before 07:30 by persistent knocking on our room door, and however much we ignored it they wouldn't go away, I had to open the door and anyhow, we were awake now. To my amazement it was the lady and her husband who had been directing us the night before. Somehow they had found us again after we had managed to lose them and now wanted us to go with them. I had no idea where. They really were starting to stalk us and it was actually a bit concerning. All we wanted was some sleep. Having now left behind the hassles of police and border guards we thought we would have been able to get some peace. We told them we would be leaving the hotel at midday and they seemed happy with this and wandered off. With them out of the way we showered, checked the couple weren't waiting outside our door and went downstairs for breakfast. A breakfast which consisted mostly of bread and spam. Great, what a treat, it was just like eating in the buggy. Talk about living the highlife. We sneaked out of the hotel and walked back to Dave's Place, well before midday, and without our stalkers anywhere to be seen.

On the terrace outside Dave's there were a couple of other ralliers who were staying at the Nassan's Hostel on the opposite side of Sukhbaatar Square for just 3,500 Tugrik (£1.60) a night. We stayed at Dave's long enough to have a quick chat to the others before heading off to Nassan's to look for a bed and then the street beyond for flights home.

Nassan, an elderly lady, was helpful enough, although the tone she took when asking if we were part of the rally made us lie immediately and deny everything about it. She seemed much more helpful and showed us to the dorm that we were to share with a couple of travellers who were already there. It was much more convenient to get to than the hotel we were in and more importantly, it was the place the ralliers were all heading for.

Deciding to get all the chores sorted at once, we went to the next street where there was a plethora of travel shops, and headed to the one that the ralliers at Dave's said they'd used. Inside it was quite smart, pleasantly air-conditioned, very efficient and the staff spoke English. There were loads of choices for flights over the next couple of days but after the 18th (the official finish of the rally) there were virtually none. They had apparently been pre-booked by ralliers who had assumed they'd be there in time to use them. I wondered how many would actually make their flights, as there didn't seem to be very many having made if to Dave's as yet. My options were a costly direct flight to the UK, ones via Moscow or a hop to Beijing and a direct flight back from there. I opted just for a hop to Beijing, for the sake of visiting Beijing, and would research the Beijing to London leg myself on the internet. The agency didn't seem very cheap for that part. Ulaan Baatar to Beijing would cost me £85 which, given it was due to leave in two days time, didn't seem too bad and due to other commitments I didn't have much alternative as I had to be back in the UK soon anyway.

We went back to our hotel, collected our bags, paid and left. Having managed to get caught up and lost in the one-way system most of the city knew we had arrived and by the time we pulled into Dave's a few people had gathered to see what monster was making so much noise – admittedly we were using the choke to pump fuel through the engine. A couple of days earlier we had discovered that by doing this, the excess fuel had a habit of exploding as it ignited in the remnants of the manifold when we eased off the power. Such a pair of kids! There were a couple of cars outside Dave's including the Scottish guys we'd seen the other day. Dave, an ex-pat living in Ulaan Bataan, had also arrived and was happily dishing out free, ice cold beers to all those who had driven in that day. We sat on the terrace in the hot sun, which, with Siberia now some way behind us, was back into the thirties, and compared stories until Tom arrived.

Tom was the guy behind the rally. He'd had the idea for the adventure some years earlier, when he and a friend decided to see just how far they could drive. Foxy and I had been only the 15th car to make it in so far, the first Suzuki this year and the first Suzuki Santana ever to make the finish; this, given their popularity among the current and previous entrants, was quite surprising. It turned out that the transfer boxes and gearboxes had tended to fail on previous attempts which, given the noises coming from ours, would be the same fate ours would probably befall in a just a few miles time. To say we had been lucky would be a huge understatement.

Talking to the other guys it also turned out that we were the only people so far to have come through all the central Asian countries and, more amazingly, to have made it over the mountains of Kyrgyzstan. This, we were told, had not been successfully attempted before. The others had taken more direct routes with fewer countries – and hence fewer timely borders to cross – and, in our opinion, missed some of the most interesting and exciting places and experiences. None had been to Transnistria and even Tom seemed impressed by our naïveté at adding this militia-controlled republic into our route, even if it was by mistake. Overall, we had covered the best part of a thousand miles more than any of the fourteen teams who had arrived in the couple of days ahead of us. We were impressed with our achievements and we appeared to have had the most varied and best experiences of anyone to have arrived so far.

With no more driving to do, nowhere to get to and no police or guards to harass us, we were at a bit of a loose end so decided to have one of Dave's legendary full English breakfasts with some more beers – luckily he was willing to start a tab as we had virtually no Mongolian money having paid for the hotel and Nassan's. As part of the rally a charity sale had been organised so that as the cars arrived any spare kit could be sold off in aid of the local children's hospital. Conveniently, this was based at Dave's so we set about sorting our kit and repacking it so that we could get as much of the useful stuff back home. Within moments people were milling around asking to buy things from us, mostly the things we actually wanted to keep, so we managed to dissuade them for long enough to give us a chance to decide just what we wanted before letting them have a free reign on our battered belongings. Most of the people appeared to be quite smart, dressed in shirts and trousers, and were probably local business people who could afford buy the mass of kit that was arriving at Dave's to sell on later. A few spoke English and again we were made offers on the buggy for between $6,000-7,000 (£3,200-3,750). It was very tempting but we had all along intended to donate the buggy to the children's hospital so decided to stick with the original plan. While all this was going on, an Englishman, also a resident of Ulaan Baatar, was milling around taking photos. He introduced himself as a professional photographer, but in reality looked quite amateur.

A couple of people walked past with portfolios of watercolour paintings of varying sizes and quality trying to sell them to us. We ignored most of these, but one boy had some that were exceptionally good and now that we were at the end of our travels, they would probably survive the journey home. We leafed through, selected a few, haggled and came away with four or five for just a couple of pounds.

Unfortunately, they never made it home, getting lost somewhere between Mongolia and London.

With the buggy emptied, the Scottish guys joined us on the trip to the children's hospital on the other side of the city where we would part with the buggy for good. Getting rid of the buggy now meant that we'd be free of it and would be able to join the others for a few beers.

The road to the children's hospital

The Scots had a map, so led the way in their Volkswagen Polo with us following through the dense traffic, the exhaust drawing the attention of everyone. The buggy sounded truly dreadful and I was slightly apprehensive of it even making this final journey without terminally breaking down. The gearbox literally sounded like a bag of bolts topped with broken glass. Some twenty miles out of Ulaan Baatar we came to the hospital and, with very little sense of occasion, signed away our beloved buggy. Oddly, we had become quite attached to it over the brief amount of time it had been in our lives, we knew its habits inside out and had escaped some tricky situations together. And with that, after a short wait, we boarded a bus and headed back to town. It was so slow and stiflingly hot; it was over 30°C outside and many more in the un-air-conditioned bus.

Finally parted from the buggy

In the middle of a huge, non-descript, concrete housing estate miles from where we needed to be, the bus stopped yet again and the odd person got on and off. A couple of men boarded and ushered myself, Foxy and the two Scots off the bus. We were far from happy with this, having no idea where we were, no money and even less idea of who these men were. As the bus pulled away I began to wonder what kind of situation we were entering into, given that the estate had the look of somewhere in the UK you wouldn't even drive through, let alone walk though, and how we could get out of it. The answer was quite simple and had even been laid on especially for us. The men who had ushered us off the bus simply pointed to a waiting taxi on the other side of the road

371

that had been sent to take us the quick route back to Dave's. The bus would have taken forever but the taxi would just be a few minutes drive. Clearly, I still had a complete mistrust of everyone I met.

Back at Dave's we entered into an afternoon and evening of drinking with the Scots and a few other ralliers in the sun on the terrace with a full view over the expansive Sukhbaatar Square.

Sukhbaatar Square, Ulaan Baatar

It was strange to have nowhere to get to and no buggy to look after anymore. I almost wanted to carry on travelling but I knew it had to stop and also knew the buggy simply wasn't up to it anymore. We all chatted about the adventures we had had and a couple more cars arrived as the day drew on.

The evening of drinking became a night of drinking and we all moved into the basement, which was where Dave's bar was actually situated, to keep the authorities happy. I think the terrace was essentially part of some government building he just used in the daytime. Inside the bar a random street-kid joined us for the night who loved posing for photos and everyone found it great fun to get him high by giving him cans of Coke which he clutched with both hands and drank as he ran around. We headed across the square in search of a cash machine so we could pay off our tab but failed, although in the end it didn't matter as Dave was happy enough with dollars.

The random street-kid, Dave's Place, Ulaan Baatar

It was icy cold back in the square, probably due to the city being at an altitude of 1,310m (4,300ft), and we made it back to the hostel sometime after 03:00 where we met and chatted to an American in the kitchen who was sharing our room.

16th August – Ulaan Baatar, MN

We managed a small lie-in and headed to the internet café at 09:00 to catch up on the past few weeks. Nothing much had happened and for the first time I felt like I was slipping back into the world I had left behind 26 days ago in London. I did a quick search and found a cheap flight out of Beijing on the morning of the 19th. This would give me a day and a half in Beijing and get me home just in time. There were also huge, lengthy security warnings on all the booking pages about baggage issues which, on checking the BBC website, turned out to be to do with terrorism and various issues that had kicked-off while we had been away. I had no choice, hoped it wouldn't affect me and booked anyway.

Beers at Dave's, me on the far right

Just down the road we tried a bank, failed to get money, tried the next and successfully got some without too much hassle and headed to Dave's for another of his breakfasts. The Mongolian's aren't famous for their breakfast and I felt no shame in eating English food given what I had been living on for so long. While lazing at Dave's a guy from the Associated Press Agency arrived and did a quick interview for some news programme or other.

A few more beers were had and a couple more cars arrived. Around lunchtime, an Indian guy (whose name I cannot remember) arrived, rounding up people to play cricket. He was a friend of Dave's, a restaurateur, and had heard that lots of Englishmen were arriving in town who he could play cricket with. We were happy to oblige and agreed to meet in a hotel car park across the square at 15:00, even though in this heat all we should have been doing was nothing.

Foxy and I went for a quick sightseeing walk around the city which was worthwhile but, not surprisingly, there wasn't much to see apart from a market and a dated-department store so we headed back in time for the cricket. Mongolia's all about the countryside and certainly not the city.

There must have been about fifteen of us assembled in the car park when the guy arrived with some of his friends, a box full of cricket pads and bats and a plastic crate of ice packed with Tiger beers! He was one of the most well-spoken people I have ever met, almost as if from the bygone era of Imperial India, and had knowledge of everything and an amazingly quick wit that he could apply to every situation. It was going to be an interesting afternoon. He and his friends managed to rustle up a few passing taxis and random cars that were willing to take us, and we headed out of town to the steppe for the match.

It transpired that he was a member of the national cricket team and his brother, also playing this afternoon, was the best man on that team; I hadn't swung a cricket bat in over ten years. A mile or so out of town we stopped and walked across the steppe for some way to a relatively flat area and moved the larger stones from what was to be the pitch before the Indian and his brother selected two teams. We had just taken up our positions to field when we were all apologetically called back in – to have a beer – then the game was allowed to commence.

The backdrop to the cricket match

It was comical, watching the ball bouncing all over the steppe, but was also taken very seriously and became quite competitive. Foxy and I were on the same team and fielded first, with Foxy catching the first guy out on the first ball. Good skills. And I managed, somehow, to bowl someone out. With the opponents dispatched we broke for a chat and beers – with these running low, a couple of ralliers who still had their car were dispatched to find some more.

The Indian had moved to Ulaan Baatar some years ago and had set up a restaurant above one of the hotels off the square which he claimed, and we later confirmed, was the best in Ulaan Baatar. Obviously, we took this with a pinch of salt at the time and he could see this, so he immediately invited everyone back for a meal that evening.

Cricket on the Mongolian steppe

We accepted without hesitation, well, it would be rude not to. His tales and spontaneous jokes continued with a mix of history and Mongolian culture. He was also mildly irritated with the ineptitude of the Mongolians who tired to modernise but often seemed to get it so wrong; for example, Ulaan Baatar had three power stations but only one was operational. Two had suffered minor electrical fires which had been extinguished with, of all things, water, thereby destroying the entire plant, leaving, at the moment, just one functioning. And the list went on. However, he was too chilled out for any of this to really bother him.

Sitting on the steppe it was disappointing just how ugly Ulaan Baatar was, given how beautiful the surrounding countryside was. It was the usual concrete mess with no architecture of note, shanty slums on the outskirts, with too much litter and no system to properly dispose of it, leading to sprawling, overfilled landfill sites. Beyond that were the gers (or yurts; circular, felt tents) where the nomads who wanted the benefits of the city without the full lifestyle change lived. These were densely packed around the city and further beyond these were the gers of the traditional Mongolians who still live a nomadic lifestyle. These became more sparsely dotted on the hillside until they were miles apart. The rest of the population lived in the hundreds of miles of Mongolia devoid of roads, buildings, power cables or anything man-made. The true Mongolia.

Mongols watching the cricket

The fresh beers arrived and with that the game resumed. In the distance a Mongol on horseback was with his son moving his herd of horses across the steppe and, bemused, stopped to watch us for a while.

The image was a stark contrast to the cityscape in the opposite direction. After the game and the beers were over, we all wandered back to the road, to see how many people we could cram into the rally car that had been driven out to the game; seventeen people.

A Mongol watching on

Packing people into a Polo

Herds of cattle on the steppe

We waited on the roadside trying to flag down taxis but ended up with a mix of taxis and normal cars which were all more than happy to help and ferried us back to the Indian restaurant.

The restaurant was on the top floor of a hotel in central Ulaan Baatar, it was incredibly smart and was probably the best Indian I've ever had. The owner dined with us and took great pride in ensuring that everyone ordered the best thing for them, asking each of us in turn what we felt like, and then getting his staff to cook it to perfection with any changes made to his specific detail. He practically devoted his entire night to making sure we had the best service, the best food and plenty to drink. It was brilliant. News was drifting back that more teams had arrived and were waiting at Dave's, so after the dinner we headed back across the square.

Three more teams had made it in and oddly enough we had met them all already. One was the car from beside us in Hyde Park (lovely couple; the girl lives in Clapham, London, just down the road from where my new house would be on my return to the UK), the next was the yacht broker from the afternoon in Prague, who was now with his girlfriend. Talking to him, it was evident they made it to Ulaan Baatar by paying a load of money to get through borders, staying in hotels and getting repairs done. The others were the guys form Astrakhan (who were great guys and loved their beer). All had been driving Suzuki SJ's and we spent most of the night chatting about our adventures and drinking the time away – fuelled by large rounds and some freebies from Dave. It was well after midnight and getting worryingly close to my flight to Beijing.

17th August – Ulaan Baatar, MN to Beijing, CN

By 02:45 I'd left Foxy, who was staying on to travel around Mongolia and China, and made it back to Nassan's with four other ralliers who were due on the same flight as me to Beijing. With just enough time for a quick wash I packed my bags and we all met outside for the taxi. I was sharing with Lloyd who had never flown before, his friend who had passed her driving test just the Thursday before the start of the rally and another guy and a girl. We finally left Ulaan Baatar, late, at 03:35 after delays with the taxi and headed off for our 04:55 flight. Fortunately, the airport was close by and the check-in procedure smooth – a surprising change to the customs to which we had become acquainted in the previous few weeks.

Boarding the plane, all of us in our respective team t-shirts, we were soon stopped by a curious lady who couldn't ask enough questions and had a business-like efficiency about her. We chatted for a while then swapped email addresses so that we could continue in more detail when we got home – she was a director of programming for the ITV television channel in the UK and was fascinated by what we had all done; it's amazing who you bump into.

It was a strange feeling to be back to using such civilised methods of transport, being efficiently dealt with and to be running to other people's timescales and having fixed times to have to be places. It was also an odd feeling to be travelling without the buggy. It seemed wrong and I almost wanted to stay behind and carry on driving but sadly I had to get back. At the same time I was excited by the prospect of visiting China, albeit briefly, as it was yet another country that had captivated me since my childhood.

We landed at about 06:00 and I went straight for the taxi rank, saying my goodbyes to the others who were flying straight back to the

UK. I was short of time and had no intention of messing around with trains. I grabbed some money at the cash machine, opting for the middle value of the eight offered. Through experience we had found this to be generally a sensible and useable amount to go for when we had no idea of the exchange rate. We had had a Lonely Planet guide to China but I'd left it with Foxy as he would have more use for it over the coming weeks. I knew it wasn't far into Beijing city centre so assumed a taxi wouldn't cost much. The problem was I had no idea where in the centre to head for or how to ask for it. Without the buggy I was now relying on other people for once rather than just making it up as I went along and this meant I'd have to tell the taxi driver something useful. I thought back to school and my knowledge of China. It was limited. All I could think of was the 1989 student massacre in Tiananmen Square. Possibly not the best thing to bring up in conversation, but I knew it was pretty much in the centre of Beijing so I asked for it.

My Chinese accent was evidently miles off the mark as the driver had no idea where I was hoping to get to. I went over the name in several ways and he repeated it back to me in a manner that sounded just like the place I was looking for, yet he still looked puzzled. He drove on anyway. At least I'd get to somewhere.

The humidity was almost unbearable; we'd had exceptionally high temperatures on this adventure but not really any humidity. The temperature here must have been about 30°C even at this time in the morning but the humidity was remarkable and coupled with no sleep, was making life difficult. The highway into Beijing cut through mile after mile of high-rise residential accommodation, mixed with literally hundreds of semi-constructed, high rise tower blocks, all being worked on and filling the skyline in every direction. I wondered where all the people would be coming from to fill them in a city already of seventeen million residents. It's a well known and well publicised fact that China is undergoing massive expansion and development, but to see it first hand made the scale of work seem even greater than anything I could ever have imagined. What was also obvious was the thick, exceptionally thick, smog. Even at the airport, tens of miles out of the city centre, the smog was thick and oppressive and hung in the air throughout my stay.

As we got closer to the city centre, every small park I passed had large groups of people performing their morning stretches standing in long, neat, uniform grid patterns. It was all very organised but I couldn't tell if it was for motivational or health reasons, or just a legacy of a history of conformity. I was still unsure if the driver knew where I was heading to but at least we appeared to be driving in just one general direction and sticking to the main roads. We dropped down off the raised highway into the streets below and pulled onto the concourse of a very plush looking hotel and immediately I suspected that I was about to be dropped off as part of a commission making scam by the taxi driver. Instead he waved the concierge over, who asked me where I was heading to. I said the name of the square just once and he relayed it to the driver. In an instant the driver's eyes lit up with a new found understanding as he repeated 'Tiananmen Square' back to me. In my mind, just as I had said it the first time and just how he had been repeating it to me at the airport, but there must have been some subtlety on the pronunciation. Whatever the reason, we were off again in the right direction. We joined a huge eight lane road between some impressive and imposing buildings when, for the first time, I recognised something. There was a huge painting of Emperor Mao on a perimeter wall; the wall around the Forbidden City on the edge of Tiananmen Square. Perfect. I got the driver to do a quick lap of the square, which, given its size was far from quick but it gave me a chance to look for hotels. There were none but I had noticed some on the road we had used to get to the square so I directed the taxi back there and just a moment from the square we stopped and I got out just in front of Raffles. The hour in the taxi came to 50 Yuan (£3.20) and I hoped this would be a sign of how cheap the hotels might be. I opted not to try Raffles, assuming that even in China this might be a touch out of my league, instead walking two buildings further down to the huge, white, curved building that was the home of the Beijing International. The heat and humidity hit me as soon as I got out of the air-conditioned taxi and having come from the cold night of Mongolia I was hardly dressed for it. I was carrying a huge rucksack weighed down with heavy, metal tools from the buggy, was hung-over, hadn't slept for even a minute all night and desperately needed a soft drink. Having crossed the well kept lawns and passed the ornamental fountains lining the path to the hotel entrance, I was already dripping in sweat as I entered the lobby and it was only 08:15. I really hoped the hotel would be affordable as I had no interest in shopping around and with the buildings on this road being so colossal it was a fairly long walk to the next.

The lobby was pretty amazing. Smart, uniformed doormen, massive glass and wood doors, polished white marble floors and pillars, huge gold ornamental chandeliers, massive vases of fresh flowers, a grand piano in the corner and smart, very smart, gents walking around with ladies in long dresses heading to breakfast. And me. In dirty jeans and a t-shirt, unshaven with a filthy, dust-streaked rucksack slung over my back looking like death-after-the-night-before with no sleep. I must have hidden it well as the receptionist was perfectly polite and hadn't yet decided that I was a homeless stray when I asked for a room. Perhaps being English had helped making me, by default, rich and eccentric. Fortunately, she had a room on the fourteenth floor which would be ready by 09:30. Until this point I hadn't quite realised what the time of the morning it was and had just assumed I'd be able to check-in there and then for a quick sleep and a shower. Not to worry, it was one of the best hotels I'd ever seen and was only going to be 450 Yuan (£30) for the night! I dumped my bags with the bellboy who obligingly fetched me an ice-cold bottle of Coke and I headed back outside, camera in hand, into the intense heat to do some sightseeing until my room was ready.

I'd spotted the railway station from the taxi and as it was just over the road from the hotel, I wandered over in search of a guide book so I could decide what to do for the next day or so. I already had some ideas from reading the Lonely Planet in Ulaan Baatar but after the affair in the taxi I wanted to have words to point at in future. The station was a crazy place. I suppose it was rush hour, but there were simply thousands of people rushing everywhere and after spending so long in the middle of nowhere it was quite a change. I passed loads of tourist stalls all trying to sell organised tours to The Great Wall and various other tourist destinations, but they all seemed to involve spending an entire day of travelling on a coach to spend about an hour at the wall and then visit various shops and markets en-route. It sounded like my idea of hell, given that The Great Wall was only about forty miles out of town and so could only take an hour to get to, meaning the tours must have involved about four hours of shopping in special 'tourist trap' markets. I walked on. Inside the station it was very evident that I was in China as, unsurprisingly, everything was in Chinese. In the countries I'd been to so far it was often possible to make out the odd word or two but not here. I found a bookshop and found a guide to The Great Wall which, conveniently, had one page in Chinese and then the same page translated into English. I also picked up a tourist's city map in Chinese as this showed pictures of the key sights with their names in Chinese and so would be perfect for asking directions by me pointing and them reading. I got another Coke and wandered back along a smart shopping street towards the hotel and dived into a department store. It was much like Selfridges and just as smart. I clearly didn't fit in but no-one seemed to mind, but most importantly to me was that the back entrance was near the station and the front was near my hotel, with air-conditioning throughout. I picked up a clean t-shirt for next to nothing and went to investigate my hotel room.

I arrived back at the hotel in a pool of sweat but that was soon forgotten when I got to my room. The bed was gigantic, the bathroom impressive, the vase of orchids attractive but best of all was the full height, full width, curved window making up one entire wall of the room with views overlooking Tiananmen Square. And this was the room they'd allocated to the tramp who had arrived an hour or so earlier for just £30 a night! It was a good thing I didn't suffer from vertigo. I wondered what the other rooms and suites were like and as I leafed through the hotel literature, noticed that I had just checked into my first 5-star hotel. I took a shower and decided that as I had so little time in Beijing there was no point going to sleep and headed back out onto the streets with yet another Coke – hoping the caffeine and sugar would keep me going.

With my map I was a lot happier and went straight for a walk around Tiananmen Square. What I did find amazing that there wasn't a scrap of litter anywhere, not even gum on the pavements; it was impeccably clean – if you ignored the fact that the whole city was shrouded in thick, dense smog. On the way, and all over the square, students kept walking with me and asking continual questions about me. After a while the questions started to repeat themselves but one girl seemed a bit more interesting and genuine, so I decided to chat to her for a bit – even though I had wanted to explore on my own. She told me they were all simply university students, not after anything in particular, just wanting to practice their English on a real English person and now they had found one, they all wanted to speak to me. Her English was unexpectedly good and she pointed out a few things of interest before suggesting I go to look at her college a few streets away. Having no fixed plans I went and met a few of her friends who all seemed happy to see me and I looked at some art they had painted. There was an element of soft-sell going on but I actually quite liked some of it, and as they only wanted a few pence for them, I took some. It was as cheap as buying postcards but much better. With that I left them to it and ventured back to the square. More students came to me and I politely got rid of them but their persistence was starting to annoy me slightly, although their commitment was admirable. I couldn't talk to them all and they were all asking the same set of questions. Repeatedly.

The expanse of Tiananmen Square, Beijing

I got some respite when I got into the main part of the square and walked across its great expanse, thinking back to the images on TV all those years ago of the tanks rumbling through. The square, the largest in the world at 440,000 square metres and with a capacity for over a million people, seemed to go on forever. There were lots of very stern looking, smartly uniformed, armed police walking around in pairs but at only five-foot-something tall, it almost seemed hard to take them seriously. Although I suspected that China was still somewhere where the police are still probably feared.

The Forbidden City, Beijing

I headed back to the Forbidden City, on the edge of the square, and passed under another iconic symbol, the huge painting of Emperor Mao. The Forbidden City was OK and had the architectural style and artworks I'd hoped to see, but much of it was either closed off or under hoardings being restored ready for the 2008 Beijing Olympic Games. I also discovered that much of the restoration is being done hastily, to meet unrealistic deadlines and so is losing much of its originality. I also heard that whole swathes of the old town on the other side of the square were being demolished to make way for the Olympics. I decided to head over there next to have a look while it still remained.

The entrance to the Forbidden City

Fending off the students, I crossed the square, passing some huge, imposing statues; Mau's Mausoleum, the Zhengyangmen Gate and the Monument to the People's Heroes, before stopping to get yet another Coke. Everything seemed to have been designed to be enormous and to show the might and power of the authorities in an effort to keep order with the people back in the days when China was much more strictly communist than in more recent times.

The Monument to the People's Heroes

The old town was an area of traditional buildings used as homes, shops and businesses with intense and busy markets packed along the streets. Above the streets were hung ribbons, lanterns and various brightly coloured decorations. There seemed to be no tourists here and most of the people appeared to be going about their everyday business. I wandered among the buildings where I met two more students who wanted to chat. I'd had a while to myself so decided to walk with them which turned out to be quite useful as they explained the history of the city, the area I was in, the effects of the Olympics (positive and negative), life in modern China and asked about how I'd got to be in Beijing. As usual this took some explaining.

As we got deeper into the old town there were fewer shops and more houses in the maze of alleys we went along. They explained how the homes each had a pair of dragons to either side of the door to ward off evil spirits and prevent them entering the house and how the door had to be in the centre of the wall and how the poor people had doors to the side of the building as they couldn't afford dragons. It all sounded interesting and plausible but I've never checked it out for authenticity; although I like the idea and have no reason to doubt them.

Looping back to the centre of the old town, we decided to go for a drink and went to a teahouse. Apparently, as was keenly explained by the owner, it was one of the oldest in Beijing, dating back hundreds of years. I also noticed it was pretty much in the middle of the area earmarked for demolition for the Olympics. China's good at progress with its 'can do' attitude but I think there should be some restraint on just how they plan things. Inside, the teahouse was full of ornaments, lanterns and decorations and we were shown to a table upstairs in a private room where an attentive lady in colourful, traditional dress tended to us and prepared the teas; which was quite a long and complex process. We stayed for an hour or two having various teas, each elaborately prepared and served with different flavoured pumpkin seeds to nibble on. I learnt the customs and etiquette associated with drinking tea, more about China and a few Chinese words before we parted and I headed back towards the station, picking up a couple of peaches that were almost the size of a small melon to eat on the way.

I tried the tour stalls again but no-one could do a quick, simple tour to The Wall without having to also go on a shopping spree, so I gave up and went for a coffee. With it getting late and my enthusiasm running out, I returned to the hotel and enquired about their tours to The Great Wall. They were as bad as the ones at the station and didn't even go to the area I wanted to; I'd decided what I wanted to see from the pictures in the guide book and it was to be the section at Badaling. I took a look at the revolving restaurant on the twenty-eighth floor of the hotel, it looked amazing and was even quite cheap, but I was too tired to have enjoyed it so went back down the lift to a different restaurant and had an amazing steak for next to no money. Not very Chinese but it's what I wanted and got into my huge bed just before midnight, absolutely shattered.

18th August – Beijing, CN

Having woken later than I'd hoped, I steered myself away from the amazing panoramic view of the city at the end of my bed and enjoyed the luxury of being able to have a shower for the second consecutive day. During the night I figured out that The Great Wall was only a little further than the airport so it would be quite feasible to take a taxi out there, have a walk around, and then get one back. I'd considered the train but decided there was little point given how short of time I was. The taxi would give me the freedom to spend as long as I wanted there, avoid the tourist markets and actually cost less than the official tours.

Wanting to be independent about this, I wandered out of the front of the hotel to look for a taxi, guide book in hand, but couldn't see any and didn't really want to have to walk back to the station again, so gave up and had a word with the ever-helpful bellboy. He pointed to the row of immaculate taxis, ready to serve the hotel, which was basically a line of executive-sized silver Mercedes and Buicks. Not quite what I had had in mind so I asked if there was somewhere I could get something more appropriate for my trip, he smiled, shouted over the line of waiting cars and soon enough out popped a suitably dilapidated yellow and green taxi. Perfect. I pointed to the bit of wall I wanted to visit, about forty miles to the north of the city. The taxi driver didn't speak any English, so the bellboy did some explaining and off we went at 09:00.

He was hilarious and very keen to show off his city, almost stopping from time to time right in the middle of the highway to point things out from palaces to parks and statues. Anything I said to him was met with a cheery 'yes' – seemingly the only word he knew in English and sadly I'd managed to forget the Chinese I'd been taught only the day before. With fewer things for him to point out he focused his attention on making progress though the traffic and began to drive like an absolute

394

loon. He created a new lane all to himself by straddling the dotted line to squeeze between slower cars or just taking to the opposite side when the traffic came to a standstill, but continued to smile throughout with liberal use of the horn. Ultimately, it did get us there sooner than queuing like everyone else.

Arriving at Badaling I got some money ready to pay the driver but he wouldn't take it. Instead, he pointed to his watch, still with his huge, comical smile and indicated he that he'd wait by the café with some other drivers until 15:00. Awesome! I had no idea how much this was going to cost me but assumed it wouldn't be much and anyway, it was the last day of my adventure and this would save me hunting around for someone to take me back to Beijing. He strolled off to join the other drivers who were all wearing similarly non-descript clothes and I wondered how I'd ever find him again.

I had the option of taking a cable car up to the wall or simply walking and given I'd been in a car for the past few weeks, decided I should walk. Badaling, no more than a tiny village, is high up in the densely forested, ridiculously steep, sheer and jumbled mountains and this section of wall was completed during the Ming Dynasty. It's utterly amazing that anyone would build anything out there, let alone a huge wall stretching for over 4,000 miles, perched precariously on the tops of these mountains. Never does the wall come around the side of a mountain, where it would have been much easier to build, but always sticks tightly to the highest ridgeline for the best vantage. It's thought some two to three million people died in its construction, and at its peak was guarded by over a million soldiers to keep the Mongol hordes at bay. The result of this is that from any part of the wall it's possible to see much more of it as it snakes its way over the mountains, at times doubling back on itself for miles to maintain its height, taking a very indirect route. I have no idea how they managed to get the materials to build it, make the foundations solid enough or had the patience to build it, but the wall has survived incredibly well and would easily have stopped armies from invading China. It would have been virtually impossible to cross the mountains without the added inconvenience of a great big wall on the tops, patrolled by armed Chinese.

The Great Wall of China, Badaling

I walked along the wall for almost three hours in the thirty-five degree, humid heat. It was a pity that the city smog extended as far as Badaling as it restricted the views to a couple of miles but did give the mountains a certain mystical feel. The wall itself is the best part of eight feet wide and is implausibly steep in places. At times it became so steep that I was practically walking on my toes to get up the rises. In the steepest places it was possible to touch the steps ahead with my hands as I walked up, as if being on a giant stone ladder. While the wall here has been fully restored, it was quite easy to get further on to the unrestored parts where I had the wall all to myself. Having seen all there was to see, after all there's only so much a wall has to offer, I took the cable car back down to look for my taxi. I shared the gondola with a small girl and her parents and they seemed to be talking about me although I couldn't be sure. It wouldn't be surprising as I had only seen a handful of Westerners in all the time I'd been in China so will have been something of curiosity. Then the girl spoke to me in English, she said she was only six but was asking me things in English and relaying it back to her parents! It was incredible how good her English was and on the way back to the car park we had a quick, if basic, chat about life in England and theirs in China. With no real optimism of finding him, I set off to find my taxi driver. I needn't have worried as he'd spotted me a mile off and came rushing out of the café, tea in hand, waving goodbye to the other drivers. He briefly showed me off to the other drivers as he quickly finished his tea and with that we headed back to Beijing.

Taking a look at my map I realised the Summer Palace – a huge palace, lake and grounds with other assorted buildings – was only a few miles off our route so asked if we could go there. The smile and manic nodding said it all. Again, we were passing tens and tens of giant tower blocks all undergoing frenetic construction, apparently all in preparation for the Olympics. They were each bigger than anything in London and they were everywhere as far as the eye could see – not that that was very far in the smog! I began to wonder if it was a stunt to create employment and give an impression of development to visitors and officials. At a rough estimate they appeared to be doubling the accommodation available in Beijing and that would take some filling.

At the Summer Palace the taxi driver again indicated he'd wait at a café and I went for an explore. The smog was horrendous, the crowds from the coach tours huge, the humidity oppressive and the famous views across the Kunming Lake of the Seventeen Arch Bridge virtually non-existent. I had a quick walk along the lake's edge to some ornately carved and decorated buildings, past many bronze Qilins statues and through the Long Corridor with over 14,000 paintings along its 728m (2,400ft) length.

A Qilins statue, Summer Palace, Beijing

The corridor was worth the visit but everything else just looked like silhouettes in the smog so I gave it up as a bad job. There was no point being here today and I was back at the taxi in just over an hour. My driver laughed when I returned, so soon after I'd left and sodden in sweat, and it was obvious he was thinking the same as me so took me straight to the café where he'd been waiting and bought me a freshly squeezed orange juice (why don't you get this kind of service in the UK?). We sat for a while as he pointed at things and carried on talking to me as if I could understand. I couldn't but it didn't matter.

We joined the traffic but with this chap driving progress was good. There was an abundance of restaurants along the roadside serving full dinners for about twelve pence and it looked amazing but I'd already decided to try the hotel's restaurant. We were back at the hotel by 19:00 and I had a moment of worry as I realised I'd had the services of my taxi and driver-cum-tour-guide for the best part of ten hours and was about to be billed. The staggering cost for this was 150 Yuan (£10)! I was amazed that this could possibly be so cheap so gave him 180 Yuan (£12) which was still only £1.20 an hour. Simply amazing.

Realising I had nothing clean to wear I called reception and for about thirty pence sent a couple of t-shirts, socks and boxer-shorts for cleaning while I went for a shower. They were all cleaned, pressed and delivered back to me before half past eight that evening. The Chinese really do have service that puts the rest of the world to shame. I went to the restaurant on the 28th floor and was shown to a table beside the floor to ceiling windows that encircled the entire restaurant, looking down onto the city 106m (350ft) below. I ordered a Chinese beer, out of curiosity, while I looked at the menu. It was easy to choose. The whole of the raised centre area of the restaurant was a huge and perfectly prepared buffet with a seemingly endless array of sushi, oysters on beds of ice, lobster, mussels, red snapper, gigantic prawns, eels, raw tuna, salmon, about eight types of snail, octopus, squid, types fish I'd never seen before, caviar (possibly fish roe but I'd like to think it was caviar), a multitude of cold meats, duck and a whole load of Chinese dishes. There was no way I was missing out on this. The wine was slightly harder. They had Italian, Chilean, South African, French and the like and also a reasonable amount of Chinese. I opted for a bottle of middle of the range Chinese red, taking into consideration it was something you don't see too often on UK menus and I'd never tried it before.

I spent the best part of the next four hours trying my hardest to get through as many different types of food, but probably focused on the sushi a little too much. It was all gorgeous and faultlessly prepared. The service was equally perfect with impeccable attention to detail; the empty plates were swiftly removed, and my glass always half full. I didn't do too badly with the food, got to see all of Beijing several times as the restaurant revolved and ended up chatting to an American couple on the table next to mine who insisted on buying me several cognacs as the night wore on into the early morning to celebrate my making it to Mongolia. The whole night had cost less than fifteen pounds. No doubt a huge amount in China but, considering it included drinks, was no more than the cost of a dinner in any chain restaurant in the UK – and there is no way you could even begin to compare the food, location or service in any way to that.

I briefly checked my emails and thought back to home and a few friends who'd emailed me before calling it a day. The trip was pretty much over.

19th August – Beijing, CN to London, GB

After a lot of black coffee to shake off the effects of last night, I checked out of the hotel at 06:45 and took a taxi, much more sedately than yesterday's, back to the airport. This time they allowed me one of the luxury Mercedes, yet it cost no more than the taxi that had brought me in two days earlier.

I got to the check-in desk and immediately my bag was rejected. It was odd to be having hassle at customs, again, but also strange after the border crossings of the previous few weeks that I should have been surprised – I was already slipping back into UK ways but I was still nowhere near being back home. At first I thought it could be to do with the tightened security I had half-read about when I booked the tickets in Ulaan Baatar, but it proved to be much simpler than that. In my bag I had as many of the tools as I had been able to carry and various odd metal and electronic items. I unloaded a few suspicious looking bits and tried again. No luck. A few more. Still rejected. The customs officer showed me the scan and the offending item. It looked remarkably like the barrel of a shotgun and I wondered what I may have unknowingly picked up and how many years in jail it would cost me. He stood, tentatively on edge with more guards now looking on, as I dug into the bag to remove it and all became clear as I sheepishly presented him with an extendable wrench. Fortunately, I was wearing my nicely cleaned team t-shirt and so had some kind of explanation for all the tools, syringes, medical supplies and oddities in my bags, but it wasn't easy. As usual, I was quickly bored of duty-free, so as I waited for my flight at 11:25 had another coffee to fend off the onset of the American-induced hangover from last night.

After a twenty minute delay it was time to board, so I waited for the unnecessary rush of people to clear – why rush for a pre-numbered seat when you're going to spend the next twelve hours in it? – then joined the queue and presented my passport to the boarding clerk.

"Ahhh, Mr. Irving. Someone on the plane knows you are coming, they are expecting you!"

And with that he waved me past. No smile, no more information and I had no idea as to who was expecting me. I thought back to the various issues at borders, the numerous police who'd stopped us, the issues with my bags, the copious indiscretions we'd committed and the stalker-woman in Ulaan Baatar. However I looked at it I couldn't find a positive angle and expected the flight to be a nightmare, stuck with someone who would be badgering me all the way home. I also, quite seriously, considered that I would be removed from the flight before we even left and taken somewhere to be interrogated over one of the many, many misdemeanours committed along the journey. I boarded without resistance and was shown to my seat, somewhere down the back of the British Airways 777. A terribly polite, and somewhat attractive, blonde stewardess asked me by name, which I should have found odd given that she hadn't seen my ticket at this point, if I wouldn't mind sitting by the emergency exit for a while. With the extra leg room, it was the perfect place for me and I was more than happy, but I didn't even pick up on the 'for a while' in my tired state. She smiled and commented on how lucky I was; again I didn't read anything into this at the time but thanked her and agreed. I was just happy that no-one seemed to have been waiting for me and suspected that the boarding clerk had got it wrong. Within moments I had just about nodded off but I was awoken by the same stewardess.

"Mr. Irving. Could you please come with me?"

This wasn't good. The stewardess already had my hand baggage from the locker as she directed me to the front of the plane and to the kitchen area where she asked me to wait for a moment. Here, I fully expected to met by the police and be unceremoniously disembarked as I noted that the lady was, according to her name badge, the head of the cabin crew. It was also strange that most of the cabin crew around the galley seemed to know who I was and congratulated me on my expedition. I put this down to the t-shirt I was wearing which pretty much stated what I had just done but then it dawned on me, just as the stewardess returned to talk to me,

"We have a new seat for you if you would like to come with me?"

Now, I had been happy with the emergency exit seat with the extra leg room, but suspected that this could be something better, so agreed. By now I had also factored my brother into this, who happens to be a pilot for British Airways, and guessed he'd been doing some meddling. At some point I must have texted my flight details home. I had become so conditioned to thinking the worst and being so sceptical over the past few weeks that I just wasn't looking for the good in anything if there was a possibility of a worse ending, even when the good was staring me right in the face. And with that I was shown to my nice first class, full length, fully flat bed. With its fully adjustable lumbar support, headrest, footrest, table, lighting, DVD player – fully adjustable everything in fact. It was massive and one of the best beds I'd had anywhere since the UK. I tried not to play with the toys too blatantly. The stewardess popped by for a chat and to ask if everything was OK; I was tempted to say no but it was perfect! A few minutes later the First Officer popped down from the flight deck to see me. He happened to know my brother, though I'm not sure if they had flown together; the Captain had. We had a chat about the expedition and he asked if there was anything he could get me and he soon returned, through the half-empty cabin, with a fresh copy of the Financial Times for me; closely followed by the stewardess who decided to take it upon herself to look after me and spoil me all the way home. I was more than happy to oblige.

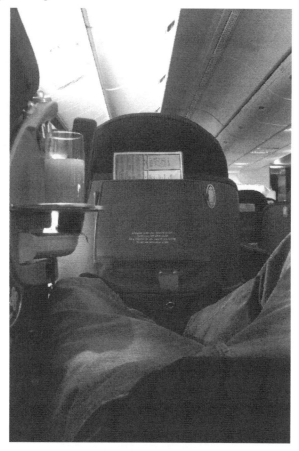

Relaxing on the flight back home

The flight was slightly delayed but, to be honest, I couldn't care less. Delays were nothing new after the border crossings we'd been through. Especially as this one was measured in minutes rather than hours and in my bed I was perfectly happy. The stewardess came to offer me a drink, so not wanting to push my luck asked for an orange juice to which she asked if I'd like a glass of champagne with it, playing on the occasion and realising that I was the only non-frequent-firstclasser in the cabin and would genuinely appreciate it. The twinge of hangover was forgotten and soon enough I'd got through various biscuits, nibbles, fruit and a couple of glasses of champagne. I was presented with a leather-bound menu and opted for the salmon gravlax, roast pork and cheese board. By the end of lunch I had got though the best part of a bottle of Heidsieck, thanks to the stewardess continually topping me up, and various bits of extra food. She seemed intent on getting me drunk and went as far as possible without actually saying so, although it was obvious. Good game! The service was awesome and the food equally good, although I'm not sure if it would be worth paying full price. My flight had cost me £230 whereas to have bought the first class equivalent would have set me back around £6,500, but with the upgrade being free I was going to make the most of it and couldn't fault it.

I watched a film, had a little sleep then was kindly awoken with a coffee and biscuits to choose my dinner. A dinner of chicken salad, paprika beef on gnocchi and fruit salad with some very good white wine. Spot on. Port and cheese, more coffee, another film, another sleep and I was home, feeling as fresh and awake as if I hadn't travelled anywhere, let alone all the way from Beijing to London. I thanked the crew who were all still cheery, polite and attentive and stepped into to the UK.

Walking though the mêlée at Heathrow airport I was disappointed just how normal and simple everything seemed and I realised that I was back to my reality, whichever the better world was, this was mine and, through conformity, where I'd be staying. It was strange to have become anonymous again and no longer a novelty. I was slipping back into it without even thinking about it. It was like I had never left but I would never, ever forget the experiences, the sights, cultures, kindness and the people we saw. I had seen so many simple, cheap and beautiful things, experienced how happy people can be with so little, yet I have now, somewhat predictably, fallen into the trap of so many graduates to start a career in London working in a world obsessed by money within investment management and chasing all the things that a capitalist society brings with it – as I much as I long for my next adventure I will never forget this one.

Prevailing Foreign Exchange Rates

Rates are tourist rates, shown as of August 2006, based against pounds Stirling.

Chinese Yuan	-	15.48
Czech Koruna	-	43.40
Euro	-	1.520
Hungarian Forint	-	414.3
Kazak Tengy	-	239.5
Kyrgyz Som	-	80.40
Moldovan Leu	-	26.95
Mongolian Tugrik	-	2,173
Romanian Leu	-	0.542
Russian Rouble	-	50.01
Ukrainian Hryvnia	-	10.20
US Dollar	-	1.867
Uzbek Som	-	1,814

Sponsors

All Vehicle Repair

Aztec Outdoor

Bourne & Coningsby Dentist

Bourne & Galletley Medical Practice

CG Motorsport Clutches

Fast Films

Fiat Coupe Club UK

Force Ten Tents

The Gasket Shop

Haig Transport

Kalimex Repair Solutions

Lifeytems

Lowe Alpine

MJICCS Computer Services

Mountain Equipment

Nomad Travel

Opie Oils

Ormerods Solicitors

Polysigns

Primus Stoves

Rekri8 Ltd

ThermaRest

Vango

WestPoint Mortgage Management

Printed in Great Britain
by Amazon.co.uk, Ltd.,
Marston Gate.